SELECTED READINGS AND PROJECTS IN *Social Psychology*

SELECTED READINGS AND

RANDOM HOUSE

NEW YORK

PROJECTS IN *Social Psychology*

Edited by

Richard R. MacDonald

&

James A. Schellenberg

WESTERN MICHIGAN UNIVERSITY

Introduction

Writing more than a century ago, the French scholar Auguste Comte pointed to a most interesting fact concerning the evolution of knowledge. An examination of the history of science indicates that the progression of human knowledge began first with those phenomena most remote from man himself, namely, astronomy and celestial mechanics, and then advanced through physics, chemistry, and biology. Only within the last century has man systematically attempted to understand his own behavior.

We live in an age when it has become increasingly apparent that man cannot escape the necessity of understanding himself. Unfortunately, the marked triumphs in space technology, physics, chemistry, biology, and medicine often obscure the more recent developments in the study of man. These *Selected Readings and Projects in Social Psychology* are offered to enhance the dissemination of already existing knowledge about human behavior.

An effort has been made to include reading materials not only from professional journals but also from novels or any other source that might make a viable contribution to enriching the student's understanding of behavior. The readings are organized under six broad headings: (1) Social Role, (2) Socialization, (3) Identity in Interaction, (4) Attitude Formation and Change, (5) Group Processes, and (6) Social Structure and Personality. The sections selected are not intended to be exhaustive, and obviously they are not. Similarly, the readings included in a section are not seen as "covering" the literature but are meant only to be illustrative of some of the conceptual orientations that may be organized under a particular heading. Although both authors share responsibility for the entire book, MacDonald did most of the work on Parts I, III, and IV, while Schellenberg's efforts were concentrated primarily on Parts II, V, and VI.

Most projects are related to specific readings and are intended first and foremost as exercises to familiarize students with basic concepts introduced in the readings. This means that these projects will allow the student to deal with operationalized concepts that should increase his understanding of the often abstract presentations in the readings. Accordingly, not all projects deal with hypotheses, since occasionally all that is entailed is the measurement of a particular phenomenon. However, the authors have set up many of the projects in such a manner that more sophisticated exercises in research methodology can be experienced.

Since many of the exercises are designed so that students may perform as respondents, the specific purpose is usually not stated. Only the necessary instruments for gathering data are included in this book. An accompanying instructor's manual provides a more complete orientation to each project, including the statistical procedures required for analysis. For students who will participate in the statistical analysis, a special appendix has been prepared indicating how certain techniques may be employed.

The book has been designed so that both the students and the instructor may exercise a great deal of flexibility in its use. It is hoped that teachers and students will be alert to insights and applications beyond those specified here.

Readers who find a particular selection of interest are reminded that many of the selections are excerpts and that consulting with the primary sources will often be valuable. Also, footnotes and references have generally been omitted. The reader should refer to the comprehensive bibliography at the end of the book if he desires to pursue the references mentioned in any particular selection.

We deeply appreciate the willingness of authors and publishers to allow use of their articles in the present form. Also special acknowledgment is made to Elaine Rosenberg of Random House, whose supervision of the editing process has greatly improved the final product.

Kalamazoo, Michigan
January 1971

RICHARD R. MACDONALD
JAMES A. SCHELLENBERG

Contents

SELECTED READINGS AND PROJECTS IN *Social Psychology*

Social Role

The concept of social role provides the means for understanding the relationship between an individual and the behavioral expectations shared by members in a society. This is accomplished by understanding a social role as a cluster of norms (behavioral expectations) associated with a given social position. A social position is considered as a location in social space, such as the social position of employer, father, friend, and so forth.

As Daniel Levinson indicates in his article "Role, Personality, and Social Structure," it is useful to say that a person "occupies" a social position, but it is inappropriate to say that one occupies a role. The role represents the privileges and obligations accruing to an individual by virtue of his occupying a social position at some specified time. In this sense, role reflects the range of behaviors considered socially acceptable for the occupant of a particular social position. The group attempts to ensure congruity between its expectations for behavior and the individual's actual role performance through sanctions. Generally the group sanctions most strongly those behaviors associated with a social position that are most important for the group's functioning.

The excerpt from *As You Like It* by William Shakespeare reminds us that the metaphor of a social role is not new. It is useful to understand the basic dramaturgical model that served as an impetus for perspectives which view behavior analogously to an actor's role.

Since the early borrowing of the metaphor from the theater, social psychology has been virtually inundated with different definitions of role and role-related concepts. Raymond Hunt provides an excellent introduction to the various distinctions that have become associated with the concept of social role. The reader is reminded, however, that these distinctions may be referred to elsewhere by terms other than those employed by Hunt. This variation continues to plague the literature on social role.

For a long time it was generally held that social expectations were shared by all occupants of a social position and that their behavior simply reflected these expectations. Levinson emphatically argues that such a version is myopic. One cannot assume the congruity between socially defined expectations, the individual's own role conception, and actual behavior. Project 1 is designed to provide the reader with experience in researching the relationship between students' perceptions of universities' definitions of appropriate student behavior and the students' own personal definitions. Here again, as in the Levinson article, the congruity between an organizational definition of role as perceived by occupants of a social position and their own personal role definitions cannot be assumed. The congruity or lack of it is an empirical question to be answered through research.

When we focus our interest on a specific category of social positions, those that are a part of the division of labor, certain questions are raised. Before a social role is relevant for any individual, he must have access to the associated social position. As Hughes suggests, to gain access to any given occupational social position, certain "qualifying" characteristics must be possessed by the individual. While some of these characteristics obviously relate to the ability of an individual to perform necessary tasks, others that do not reflect task ability tend to become associated with a social position. These are referred to as auxiliary characteristics. For instance, in our society a person with task ability may be barred from occupying a social position for other reasons. For example, a tremendous reaction among male jockeys was noticed when a female tried to break down the barriers and become the first woman jockey. The question was not so much a matter of her ability but instead focused on the auxiliary characteristic of being a woman.

Project 2 deals with auxiliary characteristics. It is constructed to measure the degree of association between specific characteristics of respondents, such as whether they are male or female, Catholic or Protestant, and their perceptions of job discrimination based on these characteristics.

As Hunt suggests, in Selection 2, to understand social role, we must consider it in the context of interrelated social positions and their respective social roles. Merton's article "The Role-Set" elaborates on this distinction and introduces the notion of role conflict. Role conflict occurs when incompatible normative demands are exerted on an individual occupying a particular social position. The person must make a decision as to how he will resolve these discrepant demands. Merton outlines certain factors that are related to the severity of role conflict and its resolution.

I. *The World as a Stage*

WILLIAM SHAKESPEARE

William Shakespeare was a literary genius with a keen understanding of human interaction. His great sense of perspective in conjunction with an extraordinary ability to empathize provides his works with an enduring quality.

It is instructive to remember that many concepts useful in contemporary social psychology are not sui generis. Such is the case with the perspective that views human behavior as performances by individual actors carrying out their social roles. This metaphor is probably as old as the theater itself. Certainly, the following material written by Shakespeare several centuries ago suggests the relative timelessness of this idea.

JAQUES: All the world's a stage,
And all the men and women merely players.
They have their exits and their entrances;
And one man in his time plays many parts,

From *As You Like It*, by William Shakespeare.

His acts being seven ages. At first the infant,
Mewling and puking in the nurse's arms.
Then the whining schoolboy, with his satchel
And shining morning face, creeping like snail
Unwillingly to school. And then the lover,
Sighing like furnace, with a woeful ballad

Made to his mistress' eyebrow. Then a
   soldier,
Full of strange oaths, and bearded like the
   pard,
Jealous in honour, sudden and quick in
   quarrel,
Seeking the bubble reputation
Even in the cannon's mouth. And then the
   justice,
In fair round belly with good capon lined,
With eyes severe and beard of formal cut,
Full of wise saws and modern instances;
And so he plays his part. The sixth age

shifts
Into the lean and slippered Pantaloon,
With spectacles on nose and pouch on side,
His youthful hose, well saved, a world too
   wide
For his shrunk shank; and his big manly
   voice,
Turning again toward childish treble, pipes
And whistles in his sound. Last scene of all,
That ends this strange eventful history,
Is second childishness and mere oblivion,
Sans teeth, sans eyes, sans taste, sans
   everything.

2. *Role and Role Conflict*

RAYMOND G. HUNT

*While the concept of social role emerged from the dramaturgical metaphor, it has
been greatly elaborated through the efforts of many different social scientists.
In fact, this proliferation of distinctions has become so great that the neophyte
very rapidly finds himself confused. Only too often, authors use different
terminology to refer to essentially similar phenomena. Hunt's article has the virtue
of including the most fundamental distinctions within the framework of a logically
consistent vocabulary.*

*In addition, some of the important studies he cites dealing with aspects of
social role can be useful to students who wish to pursue their understanding of
the concept further.*

Conceptual Framework

Any social system, and especially a formal
organization, may be viewed structurally as
an at least partially interlocking complex of
positions. These positions represent the functional divisions of labor deemed useful to
achievement of the system's goals and are
populated by a collection of particular individuals each of whom occupies at least one,

From Edwin Hollander and Raymond Hunt
(Eds.), *Current Perspectives in Social Psychology*,
New York: Oxford University Press, 1967, pp.
259–265, with the permission of the author.
Hunt's article is an abridgement from Chapter
4 of H. J. Hartley and G. E. Holloway (Eds.),
Focus on Change and the School Administrator,
Buffalo, N. Y.: State University of New York,
School of Education, 1965, pp. 37–46.

but commonly more than one, of them (cf.
Gross, *et al.*, 1958, and in connection with
much of what follows).

Organizationally the positional structure
of social systems follows a general "principle"
of complementarity. Positions tend to be
grouped as dyadic units around a set of complementary rights and duties—complementary in that the "rights" of a given or *focal-
position* are the "duties" of some other or
counter-position and the "rights" of the latter are the "duties" for the former. Thus the
focal-position "child" may be analyzed in
relation to complementary counter-positions
"mother" and/or "father." Each position in
a system, therefore, is differentiated with
reference to one or more other positions in
relation to which it stands in complementary
contrast.

This complementary contrast is, of course, a function basically of the complex patterns of behavior organized around these positions and embodying the relevant mutual expectations (the rights and duties) *vis a vis* one another held by occupants of positions. It is possible, therefore, to regard social process as an interaction of positions patterned in terms of these complementary expectations which are themselves called *roles*.

It will be seen that a role represents the content of a position or the behavioral implications of positional occupancy and that, for a given social system, the shape of social interaction will depend heavily upon the position-role differentiations and definitions current within it. Moreover, because roles entail expectations for attributes (i.e., personal characteristics) as well as for behavior, they also contribute to definitions of personal identity (self) and thereby further influence interaction indirectly (see Goffmann, 1959, 1961).

It is important to remember that a role can be comprehensively described only with reference to other roles associated with positions complementary to that occupied by the "role player." In most instances a given focal-position or role (e.g., teacher) will stand in organizational relation to more than a single counter-position (e.g., pupil, colleague, principal, etc.). The totality of counter-positions that can be set in meaningful complementary contrast with a given focal-position is therefore said to describe that focal-position's *role-set* (cf. Kahn, *et al.*, 1964). Thus, the role-set of a "teacher" includes, among others, the counter-positions "pupil," "colleague," "principal," etc. Taking these counter-positions one at a time, the particular array of expectations associated with the relationship between a given focal-position (teacher) and a single counter-position (principal) is termed a *role-sector* (cf. Gross, *et al.*, 1958). The idea of the role-sector makes plain the fact that roles vary somewhat depending upon the particular counter-position comprising the other half of the dyad at a given time. In other words, the "teacher" role is different in relation to "principal" from what it is in relation to "pupil."

We might observe that some theorists (e.g., Sarbin, 1954) regard positions as the units of *society* (structure) and roles as the units of *culture* (content or function). It is also useful to point out that the term position is here used as some earlier theorists (Linton, 1954) used the term *status*. We shall see later, however, that it is useful to reserve the term *status* for another purpose and so avoid much confusion.

The Differentiation of Roles

We may assume that through the complex processes of socialization individuals develop modes for representing the panoply of positional differentiations and role patternings defining the social system in which they operate. Some of these representations they will acquire as a result of direct experience and others will develop as a consequence of indirect influences. At all events these representations will be *individualized* matters and so will entail some variation between persons even within the same social system. Therefore, our conceptualization of roles must be sufficiently discriminated to accommodate the fact and ramifications of variation.

Hence it is helpful to consider the following role varieties:

1. ROLE PRESCRIPTIONS These may be thought of as the "cultural requirements" within a social system. A description of a role prescription is an *abstraction* drawn from aggregating the behaviors of a number of occupants of comparable positions. Thus it represents some sort of behavioral central tendency among the several positional occupants distributed through space and time. Consequently, a role prescription, once stated, is extremely unlikely to be exemplified by any specific single individual. This is why the anthropologist commonly employs a number of informants before constructing a "model" of a society's role patterns.

2. ROLE STEREOTYPES While we can take role prescriptions to be abstractly defined cultural givens, we must recognize that individuals encounter concrete representations of them in a manifold of ways and contexts. These we can call variant manifestations. From these, we postulate, the individual synthesizes personalized representations of the cultural requirements which may exhibit considerable variation as between persons.

These personal role constructions we call *role stereotypes*. It is important to bear in mind that the word stereotypes here implies no judgment of the adequacy of the construction. A given person's stereotype *may* be highly idiosyncratic or it may be largely shared. The point is that it is necessarily stereotypic psychologically for there is no determinate evidential base for its evaluation. It is a cognitive or meditational process built up from a "sample" from the universe of possible exposures.

3. ROLE EXPECTATIONS We have already observed that any construction of a role includes specifications concerning the behavior both of the person himself and also of the behavior of the occupants of positions complementary to his own. It is common practice to refer to that aspect of a total role construction that refers to the behavior of another as a "role expectation." While we have talked of this matter in terms of complementarities of positions it would be perfectly legitimate to use the term "role expectation" to refer to any anticipation of particular behavior patterns contingent upon another's occupancy of any given position regardless of any relationship to one's own.

Persons holding expectations concerning the role performances of others commonly strive to communicate their expectations to the focal-person in hopes of influencing the latter to conform to them. Each of the counter-persons communicating such expectations can be thought of as a *role-sender* and his communicated expectations can be called a *sent-role* (cf. Kahn, *et al.*, 1964). A focal-person's perceptions of the totality of sent-roles respecting his position will weigh heavily in shaping his role stereotype—indeed, if we define any source of information (including mass media, films, etc.) concerning a role as a role-sender, then we could define role stereotypes as synthesized perceptions of sent-roles.

With these statements in mind, it can be seen that any social system, constitutes a more or less complex mutual influence network. Organizationally, the system is describable and definable in terms of the temporally-relative functional relations or influence patterns among the positions into which the system has been structurally differentiated.

4. ROLE ENACTMENTS The constructs we have stated thus far have been cognitive or mediational in form. We may posit that they will operate among the determinants of the actual behavior manifested by a given positional occupant. However, as these cognitive aspects of roles are abstract and/or stereotypic they function as schemas or behavior models and not as exclusive causal agents. In short, the actual role *behavior* exhibited by a person will be associated with a variety of antecedent conditions and variables among which the cognitive components of roles will be only one (though highly important ones). Thus we shall refer to a person's actual role behavior as a "role enactment." Now from what we have already said it is plain that role enactment can vary between individuals occupying similar positions either as a result of variations in their cognitive role constructions, or because of variations in the "stimulus" field in which they behave, or, of course, both. Furthermore, the role enactments of a single person can vary through time as a function of the same factors.

5. COUNTER-ROLE EXPECTATIONS While this label is unfortunately cumbersome, it refers to another highly important aspect of role phenomena that requires mention; from his perceptions of sent-roles, and also from more subtle sources (see Goffman, 1959), each person not only develops constructions pertaining to his own behavior and expectations of others' behavior, he likewise forms constructions of what others expect of him. Indeed, in practice these several conceptualizations mutually reinforce and modify one another, and some theorists have even held that the later one is a prime determiner of the former two (Mead, 1925). In any event, a person's conceptualization of others' expectations will be an important influence upon his behavior.

Salience and Definiteness of Role Constructions

The *salience* of a role refers to its prominence and/or importance in a person's life situation. By implication, the more salient a role the greater will be a person's "investment" in it and its components, the more will he tend to organize his "view of things" around it, the more will he strive to augment its clarity, the more will he tend to resist change in it once cognitively organized, and, hence, the more will it tend to dominate his behavior. For present purposes we can view salience as a dimension of role that refers to the quantitative emotional involvement in it of the person. Anticipating subsequent discussion a bit, conflict among elements of salient roles will be more intense than any involving less salient roles.

Definiteness of a role refers to the clarity and/or articulation of elements in a differentiated role construction. The clearer and more articulated a role construction the more significant will it be as a behavior determinant. And the more a definite construction is articulated with other role constructions the more flexible will be the person's behavior. Finally, the more indefinite and inarticulate a role construction the greater will be the possibility for conflict involving it and the greater will be the person's anxiety in performing it.

Many factors influence the definiteness of a role construction, but we have need to mention only two: positional awareness and experience. Obviously the most basic requirement for a definite role construction is awareness of the positional differentiation defining the distal social system in which the person functions. As a corollary we may observe that it is also necessary that the person allocate position occupants with some precision. It should be clear that awareness of the positional structure of a system is, by itself, insufficient to effective social behavior without accompanying awareness of the distribution of particular others among these positions. Hence, without adequate and comprehensive positional awareness, a person's social behavior is likely to be less than apt—even inept.

The second factor of interest to us as a contributor to role definition is experience. It is highly credible that, in general, the more "practice" a person has in role playing the clearer and more differentiated will these roles become. Furthermore, their reciprocal features are likely to be sharpened with the result that greater consensus among role constructions is likely to be achieved. No less important is a growth in "sophistication" entailing a relaxation in the rigidity of role construction and enactment. This proceeds from greater awareness of and sensitivity to the variations in role construction and enactment common in the community and the functional interrelationships between these variations and other system components. Sophistication also implies a continued awareness of the fundamental invariance of the role as a positional attribute with observed variations being represented as variant forms of the same role structure.

Role Conflict

In any complex social system involving a large number of interrelated positional differentiations and with individuals simultaneously occupying a variety of positions, some related and some not, there is obviously wide latitude for confusion and conflict. This will be especially true in any setting where normative guides are uncertain or inconsistent—a condition akin to what Durkheim and Merton have called *anomie*.

Actually there are a variety of conditions that can produce role conflict. None of these will be discussed in exhaustive detail, but we shall inventory certain prominent circumstances. Before doing so, however, we must be clear about the usage of the term "conflict" in this discussion. We shall use the term to denote one or both of two conditions, the second of which is not typical of psychological discussions of conflict.

In the first, and usual, sense conflict refers to a condition where an individual *experiences* the simultaneous arousal of two or more incompatible behavioral tendencies. In this case the person is likely to be "aware" of the conflict, though not necessarily able to resolve it or even to identify clearly its sources. In the second, atypical, sense "conflict" may refer to a situation in which the objective social *requirements* would be such as to demand simultaneous, incompatible responses from the person. In this case, the person himself might not be aware of the "conflict" owing to an inadequate definition of the situation or because of indefinite, inarticulate position-role differentiation. Thus the term conflict is used here to denote any condition wherein the person functions in a field the requirements of which are in conflict whether he perceives it so or not. The reason for this broad usage rather than the more usual "intrapersonal" formulation is that the focus of our interest in dealing with role concepts is *interpersonal* and conflict may exist if not, strictly speaking, within either of the participants, then *in the relationship* where the resulting "tension" may be expected to have behavioral consequences of great disruptive potential because its sources are unrecognized and therefore difficult to cope with adaptively.

With this preface we can turn to a survey of some prominent circumstances productive of conflict.

1. The most obvious of these is represented by a situation in which the person perceives himself to, or does in fact, occupy two or more positions, both of which are relevant to the situation and the role constructions of which are incompatible. An illustration of this variety of role conflict can be seen in the well-worn Hollywood plot theme in which a dedicated policeman is called upon to arrest his miscreant brother.

2. A second condition is one wherein an individual's role expectations are incompatible. In this case the conflict involves the projected performances of the occupants of counter-positions. Exemplification frequently can be found in the demands of parents that their adolescent offspring behave at once independently and subordinately.

3. A third condition is one wherein an individual's role stereotype is incompatible with his construction of the other's role expectations. This form of role conflict, involving perceptions of sent-roles, is authentically interpersonal whether the person's constructions are accurate or not for it refers explicitly to the matter of one's behavior in relation to others. In some ways this species of conflict is similar to the first type and, indeed, either or both kinds could be aroused by the same circumstances. What differentiates them is that in the first type the person perceives himself as occupying *multiple* and conflicting positions whereas in this third form he perceives himself as occupying a *single* position the counter-role expectations of which are inconsistent with his role stereotype. For instance, the policeman in our first example might regard the conflict as entirely one of his "duty" and his brother's expectations that he will subordinate duty

to familial sentiment.

4. Another condition would be represented by a circumstance wherein an individual's role expectations are incompatible with the role enactments of the other or vice versa. This form of conflict hardly needs further elaboration; it simply refers to those frequent circumstances when another person's behavior is not what we think it should be.

5. A final circumstance, not typically included in these discussions, is one wherein some constraining element of a role is behaviorally inconsistent with some other non-role-related feature of the stimulus field. For example, a conscientious teacher concerned over his economic circumstances might be cast into conflict by perceiving his role-linked "professionalism" to be inconsistent with a seeming necessity to strike and picket as a means to produce change in an unsympathetic school board. This condition does not represent a role conflict *per se* perhaps, but one entailing conflict among behavior determinants. It is of great import, however, because of its relevance to problems of status to which we shall come presently.

Although we shall not discuss the matter, it is to be expected that different kinds of conflict will entail different implications for social process, and it should be evident now that the varieties of role conflict and of role-linked conflict are many. What is important to keep in mind is that the role-conflict can arise from actual requirements of the behavioral field whether veridically perceived or not, or from perceptual error, or from failure to achieve an adequately definite and articulated construction of position-role.

Status

Status in this discussion is not synonymous with position but is conceived as an attribute of positions. Without laboring the point, status can be thought of as referring to the "rank order" of a position within a system of positions. These rankings are a result of a number of factors a consideration of which would take us too far afield. Suffice it to say that any position may rank high or low relative to others and that this status connotes variations in the power and/or prestige-respect accruing to a position.

Now, there are a few complicating matters. In the first place, since status accrues to a position, any occupant of the position acquires or is *ascribed* that status. However, even within a given position, an individual's *achieved* status may vary upward or downward from this base, depending upon features of his performance in the position. To be brief, a person's role enactments serve to "validate" his status and so may modify it. Consequently, ineptness in role enactment will lead to a loss in status.

The second complicating factor is perhaps of even greater significance: There is a frequent tendency to think of status as a sort of unitary monolith. However, while it is true that we can grossly characterize a *person* as having a certain status, strictly speaking status is associated with positions, not persons. Since each person will occupy multiple positions, each of which accords him a status, we can with justice think of persons as being characterized by *statuses*. And Homans (1961), for one, has reasoned, there is an interpersonal tendency to maintain congru-

ence among these statuses and any interaction involving incongruencies among statuses will be strained and conflictful, independently of any *specifics* of role behavior.

Conclusion

From the preceding remarks it can be seen that a large part of the variance in interpersonal relations and organizational functioning can be understood in terms of interactions among persons as occupants of positions and players of roles. In fact, many phenomena appearing in such relations and regularly ordered to personality traits and peculiarities of the individual parties involved are probably more properly viewed in terms of aspects and relations of positions and their correlative status. In other words, it must of needs be recognized that large parts of individual social behavior are formally determined and have little to do with the specific intrapsychic aspects of the behaver.

3. *Role, Personality, and Social Structure in the Organizational Setting*

DANIEL J. LEVINSON

Focusing on the analysis of formal organizations, Levinson delineates three specific ways in which the term "role" has been used in the literature. Accordingly, role can be seen as the structurally given demands associated with a particular social position, as the person's own conception of his role within the organization, and finally, the actual behavior performed by members of a social position.

Levinson argues that to consider these three interpretations of role as highly congruent is unacceptable. It is more advisable to consider the matter of the congruence between behavior, social prescriptions, and individual role definitions as an empirical question to be answered through research.

My purpose here is to examine role theory primarily as it is used in the analysis of

Excerpted from Daniel J. Levinson, "Role, Personality, and Social Structure in the Organizational Setting," *Journal of Abnormal and Social Psychology*, March 1959, **58**, No. 2, 170–180, by permission of the author and publisher.

organizations (such as the hospital, business firm, prison, school). The organization provides a singularly useful arena for the development and application of role theory. It is small enough to be amenable to empirical study. Its structure is complex enough to provide a wide variety of social positions and role-standardizing forces. It offers an almost limitless opportunity to observe the individual personality *in vivo* (rather than in the psychologist's usual *vitro* of laboratory, survey questionnaire, or clinical office), selectively utilizing and modifying the demands and opportunities given in the social environment. The study of personality can, I submit, find no setting in which the reciprocal impact of psyche and situation is more clearly or more dramatically evidenced.

"Social Role" as a Unitary Concept

The concept of role is related to, and must be distinguished from, the concept of social position. A position is an element of organizational autonomy, a location in social space, a category of organizational membership. A role is, so to say, an aspect of organizational physiology; it involves function, adaptation, process. It is meaningful to say that a person "occupies" a social position; but it is inappropriate to say, as many do, that one occupies a role.

There are at least three specific senses in which the term "role" has been used, explicitly or implicitly, by different writers or by the same writer on different occasions.

(a.) Role may be defined as the *structurally given demands* (norms, expectations, taboos, responsibilities, and the like) associated with a given social position. Role is, in this sense, something outside the given individual, a set of pressures and facilitations that channel, guide, impede, support his functioning in the organization.

(b.) Role may be defined as the member's *orientation* or *conception* of the part he is to play in the organization. It is, so to say, his inner definition of what someone in his social position is supposed to think and do about it. Mead (1934) is probably the main source of this view of social role as an aspect of the person, and it is commonly used in analyses of occupational roles.

(c.) Role is commonly defined as the *actions* of the individual members—actions seen in terms of their relevance for the social structure (that is, seen in relation to the prevailing norms). In this sense, role refers to the ways in which members of a position act (with or without conscious intention) *in accord with or in violation of a given set of organization norms*. Here, as in b, role is defined as a characteristic of the actor rather than of his normative environment.

More often, the term is used in a way that includes all three meanings at once. In this *unitary*, all-embracing conception of role, there is, by assumption, a close fit between behavior and disposition (attitude, value), between societal prescription and individual adaptation. This point of view has its primary source in the writings of Linton, whose formulations of culture, status, and role have had enormous influence. According to Linton (1945), a role "includes the attitudes, values and behavior ascribed by the society to any and all persons occupying this status." In other words, society provides for each status or position a single mold that shapes the beliefs and actions of all its occupants.

In short, the "unitary" conception of role assumes that there is a 1:1 relationship, or at least a *high degree of congruence*, among the three role aspects noted above. In the theory of bureaucratic organization, the rationale for this assumption is somewhat as follows. The organizationally given requirements will be internalized by the members and will thus be mirrored in their role-conceptions. People will know, and will want to do, what is expected of them. The agencies of role socialization will succeed except with a deviant minority—who constitute a separate problem for study. Individual action will in turn reflect the structural norms, since the appropriate role-conceptions will have been internalized and since the sanctions system rewards normative behavior and punishes deviant behavior. Thus, it is assumed that structural norms, individual role-conceptions and individual role-performance are three isomorphic reflections of a single entity: "the" role appropriate to a given organizational position.

It is, no doubt, reasonable to expect some degree of congruence among these aspects of a social role. Certainly, every organization contains numerous mechanisms designed to further such congruence. At the same time, it is a matter of common observation that organizations vary in the degree of their integration; structural demands are often contradictory, lines of authority may be defective, disagreements occur and reverberate at and below the surface of daily operations.

To assume that what the organization requires, and what its members actually think and do, comprise a single, unified whole is severely to restrict our comprehension of organizational dynamics and change.

It is my thesis, then, that the unitary conception of social role is unrealistic and theoretically constricting. We should, I believe, eliminate the single term "role" except in the most general sense, i.e., of "role theory" as an over-all frame of analysis. Let us, rather, give independent conceptual and empirical status to the above three concepts and others. Let us investigate the relationships of each concept with the others, making no assumptions about the degree of congruence among them. Further, let us investigate their relationships with various other characteristics of the organization and of its individual members. I would suggest that the role concepts be named and defined as follows.

Organizationally Given Role-Demands

The role-demands are external to the individual whose role is being examined. They are the situational pressures that confront him as the occupant of a given structural position. They have manifold sources: in the official charter and policies of the organization; in the traditions and ideology, explicit as well as implicit, that help to define the organization's purposes and modes of operation; in the views about this position which are held by members of the position (who influence any single member) and by members of the various positions impinging upon this one; and so on.

It is a common assumption that the structural requirements for any position are as a rule defined with a *high degree of explicitness, clarity, and consensus* among all the parties involved. To take the position of hospital nurse as an example: it is assumed that her role-requirements will be understood and agreed upon by the hospital administration, the nursing authorities, the physicians, etc. Yet one of the striking research findings in all manner of hospitals is the failure of consensus regarding the proper role of nurse.

In attempting to characterize the role-requirements for a given position, one must therefore guard against the assumption that

they are unified and logically coherent. There may be major differences and even contradictions between official norms, as defined by charter or by administrative authority, and the "informal" norms held by various groupings within the organization. Moreover, within a given-status group, such as the top administrators, there may be several conflicting viewpoints concerning long range goals, current policies, and specific role-requirements. In short, the structural demands themselves are often multiple and disunified. Few are the attempts to investigate the sources of such disunity, to acknowledge its frequency, or to take it into conceptual account in general structural theory.

It is important also to consider the specificity or *narrowness* with which the normative requirements are defined. Norms have an "ought" quality; they confer legitimacy and reward-value upon certain modes of action, thought and emotion, while condemning others. But there are degrees here. Normative evaluations cover a spectrum from "strongly required," through various degrees of qualitative kinds of "acceptable," to more or less stringently tabooed. Organizations differ in the width of the intermediate range on this spectrum. That is, they differ in the number and kinds of adaptation that are normatively acceptable. The wider this range —the less specific the norms—the greater is the area of personal choice for the individual. While the existence of such an intermediate range is generally acknowledged, structural analyses often proceed as though practically all norms were absolute prescriptions or proscriptions allowing few alternatives for individual action.

There are various other normative complexities to be reckoned with. A single set of role-norms may be internally contradictory. In the case of the mental hospital nurse, for example, the norm of maintaining an "orderly ward" often conflicts with the norm of encouraging self-expression in patients. The individual nurse then has a range of choice, which may be narrow or wide, in balancing these conflicting requirements. There are also ambiguities in norms, and discrepancies between those held explicitly and those that are less verbalized and perhaps less conscious. These normative complexities permit, and may even induce, sig-

nificant variations in individual role-performance.

The degree of *coherence* among the structurally defined role-requirements, the degree
of *consensus* with which they are held, and
the degree of *individual choice* they allow
(the range of acceptable alternatives) are
among the most significant properties of any
organization. In some organizations, there is
very great coherence of role-requirements and
a minimum of individual choice. In most
cases, however, the degree of integration
within roles and among sets of roles appears
to be more moderate. This structural pattern
is of especial interest from a sociopsychologi-
cal point of view. To the extent that the
requirements for a given positon are am-
biguous, contradictory, or otherwise "open,"
the individual members have greater opportunity for selection among existing norms
and for creation of new norms. In this process, personality plays an important part.

Personal Role-Definition

In the foregoing we have considered the
patterning of the environment for an organizational position—the kind of sociopsycho-
logical world with which members of the
position must deal. Let us turn now to the
individual members themselves. Confronted
with a complex system of requirements,
facilities, and conditions of work, the individual effects his modes of adaptation. I
shall use the term "personal role-definition"
to encompass the individual's adaptation
within the organization. This may involve
passive "adjustment," active furthering of
current role-demands, apparent conformity
combined with indirect "sabotage," attempts
at constructive innovation (revision of own
role or of broader structural arrangements),
and the like. The personal role-definition
may thus have varying degrees of fit with
the role-requirements. It may serve in various ways to maintain or to change the social
structure. It may involve a high or a low
degree of self-commitment and personal involvement on the part of the individual.

For certain purposes, it is helpful to make
a sharp distinction between two levels of
adaptation: at a more *ideational* level, we
may speak of a role-conception; at a more
behavioral level, there is a pattern of role-

performance. Each of these has an affective
component. Role-conception and role-performance are independent though related
variables; let us consider them in turn.

INDIVIDUAL (AND MODAL) ROLE-CONCEP-
TIONS The nature of a role-conception may
perhaps be clarified by placing it in relation
to an ideology. The boundary between the
two is certainly not a sharp one. However,
ideology refers most directly to an orientation regarding the entire organizational (or
other) structure—its purposes, its modes of
operation, the prevailing forms of individual
and group relationships, and so on. A role-
conception offers a definition and rationale
for one position within the structure. If
ideology portrays and rationalizes the organizational world, then role-conception delineates the specific functions, values, and
manner of functioning appropriate to one
position within it.

The degree of uniformity or variability in
individual role-conceptions within a given
position will presumably vary from one organization to another. When one or more
types of role-conception are commonly held
(consensual), we may speak of modal types.
The maintenance of structural stability requires that there be at least moderate consensus and that modal role-conceptions be
reasonably congruent with role-requirements.
At the same time, the presence of incongruent modal role-conceptions may, under certain conditions, provide an ideational basis
for major organizational change.

Starting with the primary assumption that
each member "takes over" a structurally defined role, many social scientists tend to assume that there is great uniformity in role-
conception among the members of a given
social position. They hold, in other words,
that for every position there is a *dominant,
modal, role-conception corresponding to the
structural demands*, and that there is relatively little individual deviation from the
modal pattern. Although this state of affairs
may at times obtain, we know that the members of a given social position often have
quite diverse conceptions of their proper
roles. After all, individual role-conceptions
are formed only partially within the present
organizational setting. The individual's ideas
about his occupational role are influenced
by childhood experiences, by his values and

other personality characteristics, by formal education and apprenticeship, and the like. The ideas of various potential reference groups within and outside of the organization are available through reading, informal contacts, etc. There is reason to expect, then, that the role-conceptions of individuals in a given organizational position will vary and will not always conform to official role-requirements. Both the diversities and the modal patterns must be considered in organizational analysis.

INDIVIDUAL (AND MODAL) ROLE-PERFORMANCE This term refers to the overt behavioral aspect of role-definition—to the more or less characteristic ways in which the individual acts as the occupant of a social position. Because role-performance involves immediately observable behavior, its description would seem to present few systematic problems. However, the formulation of adequate variables for the analysis of role-performance is in fact a major theoretical problem and one of the great stumbling blocks in empirical research.

Everyone would agree, I suppose, that role-performance concerns only those aspects of the total stream of behavior that are structurally relevant. But which aspects of behavior are the important ones? And where shall the boundary be drawn between that which is structurally relevant and that which is incidental or idiosyncratic?

One's answer to these questions probably depends, above all, upon his conception of social structure. Those who conceive of social structure rather narrowly in terms of concrete work tasks and normative requirements, are inclined to take a similarly narrow view of role. In this view, role-performance is simply the fulfillment of formal role-norms, and anything else the person does is extraneous to role-performance as such. Its proponents acknowledge that there are variations in "style" of performance but regard these as incidental. What is essential to *role*-performance is the degree to which norms are met.

A more complex and inclusive conception of social structure requires correspondingly multi-dimensional delineation of role-performance. An organization has, from this viewpoint, "latent" as well as "manifest" structure; it has a many-faceted emotional climate; it tends to "demand" varied forms of inter-personal allegiance, friendship, deference, intimidation, ingratiation, rivalry, and the like. If characteristics such as these are considered intrinsic properties of social structure, then they must be included in the characterization of role-performance. My own preference is for the more inclusive view. I regard social structure as having psychological as well as other properties, and I regard as intrinsic to role-performance the varied meanings and feelings which the actor communicates to those about him. Ultimately, we must learn to characterize organizational behavior in a way that takes into account, and helps to illuminate, its functions for the individual, for the others with whom he interacts, and for the organization.

It is commonly assumed that there is great uniformity in role-performance among the members of a given position. Or, in other words, that there is *a dominant, modal pattern of role-performance corresponding to the structural requirements*. The rationale here parallels that given above for role-conceptions. However, where individual variations in patterns of role-performance have been investigated, several modal types rather than a single dominant pattern were found.

Nor is this variability surprising, except to those who have the most simplistic conception of social life. Role-performance, like any form of human behavior, is the resultant of many forces. Some of these forces derive from the organizational matrix; for example, from role-demands and the pressures of authority, from informal group influences, and from impending sanctions. Other determinants lie within the person, as for example his role-conceptions and role-relevant personality characteristics. Except in unusual cases where all forces operate to channel behavior in the same direction, role-performance will reflect the individual's attempts at choice and compromise among diverse external and internal forces.

The relative contributions of various forms of influence to individual or modal role-performance can be determined only *if each set of variables is defined and measured independently of the others*. That is, indeed, one of the major reasons for emphasizing and sharpening the distinctions among role-performance, role-conception, and role-demands. Where these distinctions are not sharply drawn, there is a tendency to study one element and to assume that the others are in close fit. For example, one may learn from the official charter and the administrative authorities how the organization is supposed to work—the formal requirements—and then assume that it in fact operates in this way. Or, conversely, one may observe various regularities in role-performance and then assume that these are structurally determined, without independently assessing the structural requirements. To do this is to make structural explanations purely tautologous.

More careful distinction among these aspects of social structure and role will also, I believe, permit greater use of personality theory in organizational analysis. Let us turn briefly to this question.

Role-Definition, Personality, and Social Structure

Just as social structure presents massive forces which influence the individual from without toward certain forms of adaptation, so does personality present massive forces from within which lead him to select, create, and synthesize certain forms of adaptation rather than others. Role-definition may be seen from one perspective as an aspect of personality. It represents the individual's attempt to structure his social reality, to define his place within it, and to guide his search for meaning and gratification. Role-definition is, in this sense, an *ego achievement*—a reflection of the person's capacity to resolve conflicting demands, to utilize existing opportunities and create new ones, to find some balance between stability and change, conformity and autonomy, the ideal and the feasible, in a complex environment.

The formation of a role-definition is, from a dynamic psychological point of view, an "external function" of the ego. Like the other external (reality-oriented) ego functions, it is influenced by the ways in which the ego carries out its "internal functions" of coping with, and attempting to synthesize, the demands of id, superego, and ego. These internal activities—the "psychodynamics" of personality—include among other things: unconscious fantasies; unconscious moral conceptions and the wishes against which they are directed; the characteristic ways in which unconscious processes are transformed or deflected in more conscious thought, feeling, and behavioral striving; conceptions of self and ways of maintaining or changing these conceptions in the face of changing pressures from within and from the external world.

In viewing role-definition as an aspect of personality, I am suggesting that it is, *to varying degrees*, related to and imbedded within other aspects of personality. An individual's conception of his role in a particular organization is to be seen within a series of wider psychological contexts: his conception of his occupational role generally (occupational identity), his basic values, life-goals, and conception of self (ego identity), and so on. Thus, one's way of relating to authorities in the organization depends in part upon his relation to authority in general, and upon his fantasies, conscious as well as unconscious, about the "good" and the "bad" parental authority. His ways of dealing with the stressful aspects of organizational life are influenced by the impulses, anxieties, and modes of defense that these stresses activate in him.

There are variations in the degree to which personal role-definition is imbedded in, and influenced by, deeper-lying personality characteristics. The importance of individual or modal personality for role-definition is a matter for empirical study and cannot be settled by casual assumption. Traditional sociological theory can be criticized for assuming that individual role-definition is determined almost entirely by social structure. Similarly, dynamic personality theory will not take its rightful place as a crucial element of social psychology until it views the individual within his sociocultural environment. Lacking an adequate recognition and *conceptualization* of the individual's external reality—including the "reality" of social structure—personality researchers tend to assume that individual adaptation is primarily personality-determined and that reality is, for the most part, an amorphous blob structured by the individual to suit his inner needs.

Clearly, individual role-conception and

role-performance do not emanate, fully formed, from the depths of personality. Nor are they simply mirror images of a mold established by social structure. Elsewhere (Levinson, 1954), I have used the term "mirage" theory for the view, frequently held or implied in the psychoanalytic literature, that ideologies, role-conceptions, and behavior are mere epiphenomena or by-products of unconscious fantasies and defenses. Similarly, the term "sponge" theory characterizes the view, commonly forwarded in the sociological literature, in which man is merely a passive, mechanical absorber of the prevailing structural demands.

Our understanding of personal role-definition will remain seriously impaired as long as we fail to place it, analytically, in *both intrapersonal and structural-environmental contexts*. That is to say, we must be concerned with the meaning of role-definition both for the individual personality and for the social system. A given role-definition is influenced by, and has an influence upon, the *psyche* as well as the *socius*. If we are adequately to understand the nature, the determinants, and the consequences of role-definition, we need the double perspective of personality and social structure. The use of these two reference points is, like the use of our two eyes in seeing, necessary for the achievement of depth in our social vision.

Theory and research on organizational roles must consider relationships among at least the following sets of characteristics: structurally given role-demands and opportunities, personal role-definition (including conceptions and performance), and personality in its role-related aspects. Many forms of relationship may exist among them. I shall mention only a few hypothetical possibilities.

In one type of case, the role-requirements are so narrowly defined, and the mechanisms of social control so powerful, that only one form of role-performance can be sustained for any given position. An organization of this type may be able selectively to recruit and retain only individuals who, by virtue of personality, find this system meaningful and gratifying. If a congruent modal personality is achieved, a highly integrated and stable structure may well emerge. I would hypothesize that a structurally congruent modal personality is one condition, though by no means the only one, for the stability of a rigidly integrated system. (In modern times, of course, the rapidity of technological change prevents long-term stabilty in any organizational structure.)

However, an organization of this kind may acquire members who are not initially receptive to the structural order, that is, who are *incongruent* in role-conception or in personality. Here, several alternative developments are possible.

(1) The incongruent members may change so that their role-conceptions and personalities come better to fit the structural requirements.

(2) The incongruent ones may leave the organization, by choice or by expulsion. The high turnover in most of our organizations is due less to technical incompetence than to rejection of the "conditions of life" in the organization.

(3) The incongruent ones may remain, but in a state of apathetic conformity. In this case, the person meets at least the minimal requirements of role-performance but his role-conceptions continue relatively unchanged, he gets little satisfaction from work, and he engages in repeated "sabotage" of organizational aims. This is an uncomfortably frequent occurrence in our society. In the Soviet Union as well, even after 40 years of enveloping social controls, there exist structurally incongruent forms of political ideology, occupational role-definition, and personality (Inkeles, Hanfmann, & Beier, 1958).

(4) The incongruent members may gain sufficient social power to change the organizational structure. This phenomenon is well known, though not well enough understood. For example, in certain of our mental hospitals, schools and prisons over the past 20–30 years, individuals with new ideas and personal characteristics have entered in large enough numbers, and in sufficiently strategic positions, to effect major structural changes. Similar ideological and structural transitions are evident in other types of organization, such as corporate business.

The foregoing are a few of many possible developments in a relatively monolithic structure. A somewhat looser organizational pattern is perhaps more commonly found.

In this setting, structural change becomes a valued aim and innovation is seen as a legitimate function of members at various levels in the organization. To the extent that diversity and innovation are valued (rather than merely given lip-service), variations in individual role-definition are tolerated or even encouraged within relatively wide limits. The role-definitions that develop will reflect various degrees of synthesis and compromise between personal preference and structural demand.

In summary, I have suggested that a primary distinction be made between the structurally given role-demands and the forms of role-definition achieved by the individual members of an organization. Personal role-definition then becomes a linking concept between personality and social structure. It can be seen as a reflection of those aspects of individual personality that are activated and sustained in a given structural-ecological environment. This view is opposed both to the "sociologizing" of individual behavior and to the "psychologizing" of organizational structure. At the same time, it is concerned with both the psychological properties of social structure and the structural properties of individual adaptation.

Finally, we should keep in mind that both personality structure and social structure inevitably have their internal contradictions. No individual is sufficiently all of a piece that he will for long find any form of adaptation, occupational or otherwise, totally satisfying. Whatever the psychic gains stemming from a particular role-definition and social structure, there will also be losses: wishes that must be renounced or made unconscious, values that must be compromised, anxieties to be handled, personal goals that will at best be incompletely met. The organization has equivalent limitations. Its multiple purposes cannot all be optimally achieved. It faces recurrent dilemmas over conflicting requirements: control and freedom; centralization and decentralization of authority; security as against the risk of failure; specialization and diffusion of work function; stability and change; collective unity and diversity. Dilemmas such as these arise anew in different forms at each new step of organizational development, without permanent solution. And perpetual changes in technology, in scientific understanding, in material resources, in the demands and capacities of its members and the surrounding community, present new issues and require continuing organizational readjustment.

In short, every individual and every sociocultural form contains within itself the seeds of its own destruction—or its own reconstruction. To grasp both the sources of stability and the seeds of change in human affairs is one of the great challenges to contemporary social science.

4. *Dilemmas and Contradictions of Status*

EVERETT C. HUGHES

*"Status" for Hughes refers to a social position around which behavioral
expectations in the form of rights and limitations are clustered. Each incumbent
of a status is confronted with social pressures to conform with those behavioral
prescriptions deemed important by his society.*

*In a society such as ours, which values social mobility, it becomes important to
understand factors relevant to whether or not a particular individual has access
to various statuses that are part of the division of labor. When occupational statuses
are viewed, it is apparent that certain task competencies are requirements for an
individual to qualify for a particular status. In addition, there tends to become
associated with a status a complex of what Hughes calls auxiliary characteristics.
These characteristics are expected of a potential incumbent but are not tied to task
ability. Not only do these auxiliary characteristics limit access to specific statuses;
they also may influence the range of persons seeking service from incumbents
in given statuses, depending upon whether or not the incumbents possess those
characteristics. In brief, auxiliary characteristics are the basis for occupational
discrimination.*

It is doubtful whether any society ever had
so great a variety of statuses or recognized
such a large number of status-determining
characteristics as does ours. The combinations
of the latter are, of course, times over more
numerous than the characteristics themselves. In societies where statuses[1] are well
defined and are entered chiefly by birth or a
few well-established sequences of training or
achievement, the particular personal attributes proper to each status are woven into a
whole. They are not thought of as separate
entities. Even in our society, certain statuses
have developed characteristic patterns of
expected personal attributes and a way of
life. To such, in the German language, is
applied the term *Stand.*

From Everett C. Hughes, "Dilemmas and Contradictions of Status," *The American Journal of
Sociology,* March 1945, **50**, 353–359. It is reprinted here with the permission of the author
and publisher.

[1]"Status" is here taken in its strict sense as a
defined social position for whose incumbents
there are defined rights, limitations of rights, and
duties. See the *Oxford Dictionary* and any standard Latin lexicon. Since statuses tend to form a
hierarchy, the term itself has—since Roman times
—had the additional meaning of rank.

Few of the positions in our society, however, have remained fixed long enough for
such an elaboration to occur. We put emphasis on change in the system of positions
which make up our social organization and
upon mobility of the individual by achievement. In the struggle for achievement, individual traits of the person stand out as
separate entities. And they occur in peculiar
combinations which make for confusion,
contradictions, and dilemmas of status.

I shall, in this paper, elaborate the notion of contradictions and dilemmas of
status. Illustrations will be taken from professional and other occupational positions.
The idea was put into a suggestive phrase
by Robert E. Park when he wrote of the
"marginal man." He applied the term to a
special kind of case—the racial hybrid—
who, as a consequence of the fact that races
have become defined as status groups, finds
himself in a status dilemma.

Now there may be, for a given status or
social position, one or more specifically determining characteristics of the person. Some
of them are formal, or even legal. No one,
for example, has the status of physician unless he be duly licensed. A foreman is not

such until appointed by proper authority. The heavy soprano is not a prima donna in more than temperament until formally cast for the part by the director of the opera. For each of these particular positions there is also an expected technical competence. Neither the formal nor the technical qualifications are, in all cases, so clear. Many statuses, such as membership in a social class, are not determined in a formal way. Other statuses are ill-defined both as to the characteristics which determine identification with them and as to their duties and rights.

There tends to grow up about a status, in addition to its specifically determining traits, a complex of auxiliary characteristics which come to be expected of its incumbents. It seems entirely natural to Roman Catholics that all priests should be men, although piety seems more common among women. In this case the expectation is supported by formal rule. Most doctors, engineers, lawyers, professors, managers, and supervisors in industrial plants are men, although no law requires that they be so. If one takes a series of characteristics, other than medical skill and a license to practice it, which individuals in our society may have, and then thinks of physicians possessing them in various combinations, it becomes apparent that some of the combinations seem more natural and are more acceptable than others to the great body of potential patients. Thus a white male Protestant physician of old American stock and of a family of at least moderate social standing would be acceptable to patients of almost any social category in this country. To be sure, a Catholic might prefer a physician of his own faith for reasons of spiritual comfort. A few ardent feminists, a few race-conscious Negroes, a few militant sectarians, might follow their principles to the extent of seeking a physician of their own category. On the other hand, patients who identify themselves with the "old stock" may, in an emergency, take the first physician who turns up.[2]

If the case is serious, patients may seek a specialist of some strange or disliked social category, letting the reputation for special skill override other traits. The line may be crossed also when some physician acquires

such renown that his office becomes something of a shrine, a place of wonderful, last-resort cures. Even the color line is not a complete bar to such a reputation. On the contrary, it may add piquancy to the treatment of a particularly enjoyed malady or lend hope to the quest for a cure of an "incurable" ailment. Allowing for such exceptions, it remains probably true that the white male Protestant physician of old American stock, although he may easily fail to get a clientele at all, is categorically acceptable to a greater variety of patients than is he who departs, in one or more particulars, from this type.

It is more exact to say that, if one were to imagine patients of the various possible combinations of these same characteristics (race, sex, religion, ethnic background, family standing), such a physician could treat patients of any of the resulting categories without a feeling by the physician, patient, or the surrounding social circle that the situation was unusual or shocking. One has only to make a sixteen-box table showing physicians of the possible combinations of race (white and Negro) and sex with patients of the possible combinations to see that the white male is the only resulting kind of physician to whom patients of all the kinds are completely accessible in our society (see Table 1).

One might apply a similar analysis to situations involving other positions, such as the foreman and the worker, the teacher and the pupil. Each case may be compli-

[2] A Negro physician, driving through northern Indiana, came upon a crowd standing around a man just badly injured in a road accident. The physician tended the man and followed the ambulance which took him to the hospital. The hospital authorities tried to prevent the physician from entering the hospital for even long enough to report to staff physicians what he had done for the patient. The same physician, in answer to a Sunday phone call asking him to visit a supposedly very sick woman, went to a house. When the person who answered the door saw that the physician was a Negro, she insisted that they had not called for a doctor and that no one in the house was sick. When he insisted on being paid, the people in the house did so, thereby revealing their lie. In the first instance, an apparently hostile crowd accepted the Negro as a physician because of urgency. In the second, he was refused presumably because the emergency was not great enough.

TABLE 1*

| | PHYSICIAN | | | |
| | White Male | White Female | Negro Male | Negro Female |
PATIENT				
White male				
White female				
Negro male				
Negro female				

*I have not used this table in any study of preferences but should be glad if anyone interested were to do so with selected groups of people.

cated by adding other categories of persons with whom the person of the given position has to deal. The teacher, in practice, has dealings not only with pupils but with parents, school boards, other public functionaries, and, finally, his own colleagues. Immediately one tries to make this analysis, it becomes clear that a characteristic which might not interfere with some of the situations of a given position may interfere with others.

I do not maintain that any considerable proportion of people do consciously put together in a systematic way their expectations of persons of given positions. I suggest, rather, that people carry in their minds a set of expectations concerning the auxiliary traits properly associated with many of the specific positions available in our society. These expectations appear as advantages or disadvantages to persons who, in keeping with American social belief and practice, aspire to positions new to persons of their kinds.

The expected or "natural" combinations of auxiliary characteristics become embodied in the stereotypes of ordinary talk, cartoons, fiction, the radio, and the motion picture. Thus, the American Catholic priest, according to a popular stereotype, is Irish, athletic, and a good sort who with difficulty refrains from profanity in the presence of evil and who may punch someone in the nose if the work of the Lord demands it. Nothing could be farther from the French or French-Canadian stereotype of the good priest. The surgeon, as he appears in advertisements for insurance and pharmaceutical products, is handsome, socially poised, and young of face but gray about the tem-

ples. These public, or publicity, stereotypes —while they do not necessarily correspond to the facts or determine people's expectations—are at least significant in that they rarely let the person in the given position have any strikes against him. Positively, they represent someone's ideal conception; negatively, they take care not to shock, astonish, or put doubts into the mind of a public whose confidence is sought.

If we think especially of occupational status, it is in the colleague-group or fellow-worker group that the expectations concerning appropriate auxiliary characteristics are worked most intricately into sentiment and conduct. They become, in fact, the basis of the colleague-group's definition of its common interests, of its informal code, and of selection of those who become the inner fraternity—three aspects of occupational life so closely related that few people separate them in thought or talk.

The epithets "hen doctor," "boy wonder," "bright young men," and "brain trust" express the hostility of colleagues to persons who deviate from the expected type. The members of a colleague-group have a common interest in the whole configuration of things which control the number of potential candidates for their occupation. Colleagues, be it remembered, are also competitors. A rational demonstration that an individual's chances for continued success are not jeopardized by an extension of the recruiting field for the position he has or hopes to attain, or by some short-cutting of usual lines of promotion, does not, as a rule, liquidate the fear and hostility aroused by such a case. Oswald Hall found that physicians do not like one of their number to become a consultant too soon.[3] Consulting is something for the crowning, easing-off years of a career; something to intervene briefly between high power and high blood-pressure. He who pushes for such practice too early shows an "aggressiveness" which is almost certain to be punished. It is a threat to an order of things which physicians —at least, those of the fraternity of successful men—count upon. Many of the specific rules of the game of an occupation become comprehensible only when viewed as the almost instinctive attempts of a group of people to cushion themselves against the hazards of their careers. The advent of colleague-competitors of some new and peculiar type, or by some new route, is likely to arouse anxieties. For one thing, one cannot be quite sure how "new people"—new in kind—will act in the various contingencies which arise to test the solidarity of the group.[4]

How the expectations of which we are thinking become embodied in codes may be illustrated by the dilemma of a young woman who became a member of that virile profession, engineering. The designer of an airplane is expected to go up on the maiden flight of the first plane built according to the design. He (*sic*) then gives a dinner to the engineers and workmen who worked on the new plane. The dinner is naturally a stag party. The young woman in question designed a plane. Her co-workers urged her not to take the risk—for which, presumably, men only are fit—of the maiden voyage. They were, in effect, asking her to be a lady rather than an engineer. She chose to be an engineer. She then gave the party and paid for it like a man. After food and the first round of toasts, she left like a lady.

Part of the working code of a position is discretion; it allows the colleagues to exchange confidences concerning their relations to other people. Among these

---

[3]Oswald Hall, "The Informal Organization of Medical Practice" (unpublished Ph.D. dissertation, University of Chicago, 1944).

[4]It may be that those whose positions are insecure and whose hopes for the higher goals are already fading express more violent hostility to "new people." Even if so, it must be remembered that those who are secure and successful have the power to exclude or check the careers of such people by merely failing to notice them.

confidences one finds expressions of cynicism concerning their mission, their competence, and the foibles of their superiors, themselves, their clients, their subordinates, and the public at large. Such expressions take the burden from one's shoulders and serve as a defense as well. The unspoken mutual confidence necessary to them rests on two assumptions concerning one's fellows. The first is that the colleague will not misunderstand; the second is that he will not repeat to uninitiated ears. To be sure that a new fellow will not misunderstand requires a sparring match of social gestures. The zealot who turns the sparring match into a real battle, who takes a friendly initiation too seriously, is not likely to be trusted with the lighter sort of comment on one's work or with doubts and misgivings; nor can he learn those parts of the working code which are communicated only by hint and gesture. He is not to be trusted, for though he is not fit for stratagems, he is suspected of being prone to treason. In order that men may communicate freely and confidentially, they must be able to take a good deal of each other's sentiments for granted. They must feel easy about their silences as well as about their utterances. These factors conspire to make colleagues, with a large body of unspoken understandings, uncomfortable in the presence of what they consider odd kinds of fellows. The person who is the first of his kind to attain a certain status is often not drawn into the informal brotherhood in which experiences are exchanged, competence built up, and the formal code elaborated and enforced. He thus remains forever a marginal man.

Now it is a necessary consequence of the high degree of individual mobility in America that there should be large numbers of people of new kinds turning up in various positions. In spite of this and in spite of American heterogeneity, this remains a white, Anglo-Saxon, male Protestant culture in many respects. These are the expected characteristics for many favored statuses and positions. When we speak of racial, religious, sex, and ethnic prejudices, we generally assume that people with these favored qualities are not the objects thereof. In the stereotyped prejudices concerning others, there is usually contained the as-

sumption that these other people are pecu-
liarly adapted to the particular places which
they have held up to the present time; it is
a corollary implication that they are not
quite fit for new positions to which they
may aspire. In general, advance of a new
group—women, Negroes, some ethnic
groups, etc.—to a new level of positions is
not accompanied by complete disappearance
of such stereotypes but only by some modification of them. Thus, in Quebec the idea
that French-Canadians were good only for
unskilled industrial work was followed by
the notion that they were especially good at
certain kinds of skilled work but were not
fit to repair machines or to supervise the
work of others. In this series of modifications
the structure of qualities expected for the
most-favored positions remains intact. But
the forces which make for mobility continue
to create marginal people on new frontiers.

Technical changes also break up configurations of expected status characteristics by
altering the occupations about which they
grow up. A new machine or a new manager-
ial device—such as the assembly line—may
create new positions or break old ones up
into numbers of new ones. The length of
training may be changed thereby and, with
it, the whole traditional method of forming
the person to the social demands of a colleague-group. Thus, a snip of a girl is
trained in a few weeks to be a "machinist"
on a practically foolproof lathe; thereby the
old foolproof machinist, who was initiated
slowly into the skills and attitudes of the
trade, is himself made a fool of in his own
eyes or—worse—in the eyes of his wife,
who hears that a neighbor's daughter is a
machinist who makes nearly as much money
as he. The new positions created by technical changes may, for a time, lack definition as a status. Both the technical and the
auxiliary qualifications may be slow in taking
form. The personnel man offers a good
example. His title is perhaps twenty years
old, but the expectations concerning his
qualities and functions are still in flux.[5]

Suppose we leave aside the problems
which arise from technical changes, as such,
and devote the rest of this discussion to
the consequences of the appearance of new
kinds of people in established positions.
Every such occurrence produces, in some

measure, a status contradiction. It may also
create a status dilemma for the individual
concerned and for other people who have
to deal with him.

The most striking illustration in our
society is offered by the Negro who qualifies
for one of the traditional professions. Membership in the Negro race, as is defined in
American mores and/or law, may be called
a master status-determining trait. It tends
to overpower, in most crucial situations, any
other characteristics which might run counter to it. But professional standing is also a
powerful characteristic—most so in the
specific relationships of professional practice, less so in the general intercourse of
people. In the person of the professionally
qualified Negro these two powerful characteristics clash. The dilemma, for those whites
who meet such a person, is that of having
to choose whether to treat him as a Negro
or as a member of his profession.

The white person in need of professional
services, especially medical, might allow him
to act as doctor in an emergency. Or it may
be allowed that a Negro physician is en-
dowed with some uncanny skill. In either
case, the white client of ordinary American
social views would probably avoid any non-
professional contacts with the Negro physician.[6] In fact, one way of reducing status
conflict is to keep the relationship formal
and specific. This is best done by walking
through a door into a place designed for
the specific relationship, a door which can
be firmly closed when one leaves. A com-

---

[5]The personnel man also illustrates another
problem which I do not propose to discuss in this
paper. It is that of an essential contradiction between the various functions which are united in
one position. The personnel man is expected to
communicate the mind of the workers to management and then to interpret management to the
workers. This is a difficult assignment. The problem is well stated by William F. Whyte, in "Pity
the Personnel Man," *Advanced Management*,
October-December, 1944, pp. 154–58. The
Webbs analyzed the similar dilemma of the official of a successful trade-union in their *History of
Trade-Unionism* (rev. ed.; London: Longmans,
Green, 1920).

[6]The Negro artist can be treated as a celebrity.
It is within the code of social tuft-hunting that
one may entertain, with a kind of affected
Bohemian intimacy, celebrities who, on all counts
other than their artistic accomplishments, would
be beyond the pale.

mon scene in fiction depicts a lady of degree seeking, veiled and alone, the address of the fortuneteller or the midwife of doubtful practice in an obscure corner of the city. The anonymity of certain sections of cities allows people to seek specialized services, legitimate but embarrassing as well as illegitimate, from persons with whom they would not want to be seen by members of their own social circle.

Some professional situations lend themselves more than others to such quarantine. The family physician and the pediatrician cannot be so easily isolated as some other specialists. Certain legal services can be sought indirectly by being delegated to some queer and unacceptable person by the family lawyer. At the other extreme is school teaching, which is done in full view of the community and is generally expected to be accompanied by an active role in community activities. The teacher, unlike the lawyer, is expected to be an example to her charges.

For the white colleagues of the Negro professional man the dilemma is even more severe. The colleague-group is ideally a brotherhood; to have within it people who cannot, given one's other attitudes, be accepted as brothers is very uncomfortable. Furthermore, professional men are much more sensitive than they like to admit about the company in which nonprofessionals see them. The dilemma arises from the fact that, while it is bad for the profession to let laymen see rifts in their ranks, it may be bad for the individual to be associated in the eyes of his actual or potential patients with persons, even colleagues, of so despised a group as the Negro. The favored way of avoiding the dilemma is to shun contacts with the Negro professional. The white physician or surgeon of assured reputation may solve the problem by acting as consultant to Negro colleagues in Negro clinics and hospitals.

For the Negro professional man there is also a dilemma. If he accepts the role of Negro to the extent of appearing content with less than full equality and intimacy with his white colleagues, for the sake of such security and advantage as can be so got, he himself and others may accuse him of sacrificing his race. Given the tendency of whites to say that any Negro who rises to a special position is an exception, there is a strong temptation for such a Negro to seek advantage by fostering the idea that he is unlike others of his race. The devil who specializes in this temptation is a very insinuating fellow; he keeps a mailing list of "marginal men" of all kinds and origins. Incidentally, one of the by-products of American mores is the heavy moral burden which this temptation puts upon the host of Americans who have by great effort risen from (sic) groups which are the objects of prejudice.

There may be cases in which the appearance in a position of one or a few individuals of a kind not expected there immediately dissolves the auxiliary expectations which make him appear odd. This is not, however, the usual consequence. The expectations usually continue to exist, with modifications and with exceptions allowed.

A common solution is some elaboration of social segregation. The woman lawyer may become a lawyer to women clients, or she may specialize in some kind of legal service in keeping with woman's role as guardian of the home and of morals. Women physicians may find a place in those specialties of which only women and children have need. A female electrical engineer was urged by the dean of the school from which she had just been graduated to accept a job whose function was to give the "woman's angle" to design of household electrical appliances. The Negro professional man finds his clients among Negroes. The Negro sociologist generally studies race relations and teaches in a Negro college. A new figure on the American scene is the Negro personnel man in industries which have started employing Negro workers. His functions are to adjust difficulties of Negro workers, settle minor clashes between the races, and to interpret management's policies to the Negro as well as to present and explain the Negro's point of view to management. It is a difficult job. Our interest for the moment, however, is in the fact that the Negro, promoted to this position, acts only with reference to Negro employees. Many industries have had women personnel officials to act with reference to women. In one sense, this is an extension of the earlier and still existing practice of hiring from among a new ethnic group in industry a "straw boss" to look after them. The "straw boss" is the liaison officer reduced to lowest terms.

Another solution, which also results in a kind of isolation if not in segregation, is that of putting the new people in the library or laboratory, where they get the prestige of research people but are out of the way of patients and the public. Recently, industries have hired a good many Negro chemists to work in their testing and research laboratories. The chemist has few contacts with the production organization. Promotion within the laboratory will put the Negro in charge of relatively few people, and those few will be of his own profession. Such positions do not ordinarily lead to the positions of corresponding importance in the production organizations. They offer a career line apart from the main streams of promotion to power and prestige.

These solutions reduce the force of status contradiction by keeping the new person apart from the most troublesome situations. One of the consequences is that it adds new stories to the superstructure of segregation. The Negro hospital and medical school are the formal side of this. The Negro personnel man and foreman show it within the structure of existing institutions. There are evidences that physicians of various ethnic groups are being drawn into a separate medical system of hospitals, clinics, and schools, partly because of the interest of the Roman Catholic church in developing separate institutions but also partly because of the factors here discussed. It is doubtful whether women will develop corresponding separate systems to any great extent. In all of these cases, it looks as if the highest point which a member of these odd groups may attain is determined largely by the number of people of his own group who are in a position to seek his services or in a position such that he may be assigned by other authority to act professionally with reference to them. On the other hand, the kind of segregation involved may lead professional people, or others advanced to special positions, to seek —as compensation—monopoly over such functions with reference to their own group.

Many questions are raised by the order of things here discussed. One is that of the place of these common solutions of status conflict in the evolution of the relations between the sexes, the races, and the ethnic groups of our society. In what circumstances can the person who is accepted formally into a new status, and then informally kept within the limits of the kind mentioned, step out of these limits and become simply a lawyer, foreman, or whatever? Under what circumstances, if ever, is the "hen doctor" simply a doctor? And who are the first to accept her as such—her colleagues or her patients? Will the growth of a separate superstructure over each of the segregated bottom groups of our society tend to perpetuate indefinitely the racial and ethnic division already existing, or will these superstructures lose their identity in the general organization of society? These are the larger questions.

The purpose of the paper, however, is not to answer these large questions. It is rather to call attention to this characteristic phenomenon of our heterogeneous and changing society and to suggest that it become part of the frame of reference of those who are observing special parts of the American social structure.

5. The Role-Set: Problems in Sociological Theory

ROBERT MERTON

In discussing the idea of a social role, it is easy to focus on a specific social position and its accompanying role without considering that particular social position in the context of other social positions to which it is related. Merton introduces the concept of role-set as a vehicle for better understanding some of the important analytical problems that arise when any particular social position is viewed from this broader perspective.

One way of understanding the notion of role-set is to assume that any particular social position may be related to more than one other social position. Thus, the status student is related to the social positions of university administrator, faculty, parents, other students, and so forth. As a result, each of these associated social positions brings to bear certain expectations for any person who is in the capacity of being a student. In circumstances in which these expectations are incongruent, the student faces a behavioral dilemma. Merton suggests several factors that influence how this dilemma may be resolved.

The Problematics of the Role-Set

However much they may differ in other respects, contemporary sociological theorists are largely at one in adopting the premise that social statuses and social roles comprise major building blocks of social structure. This has been the case, since the influential writings of Ralph Linton on the subject, a generation ago. By status, and T. H. Marshall has indicated the great diversity of meanings attached to this term since the time of [Sir Henry] Maine, Linton meant a position in a social system involving designated rights and obligations; by role, the behaviour oriented to these patterned expectations of others. In these terms, status and roles become concepts serving to connect culturally defined expectations with the patterned conduct and relationships which make up a social structure. Linton went on to state the long recognized and basic fact that each person in society inevitably occupies multiple statuses and that

Robert Merton, "The Role-Set: Problems in Sociological Theory," *The British Journal of Sociology,* June 1957, **VIII**, No. 2, 110–118. Reprinted by permission of the author and publisher, Routledge & Kegan Paul Ltd.

each of these statuses has an associated role.

It is at this point that I find it useful to depart from Linton's conception. The difference is initially a small one, some might say so small as not to deserve notice, but it involves a shift in the angle of vision which leads, I believe, to successively greater differences of a fundamental kind. Unlike Linton, I begin with the premise that each social status involves not a single associated role, but an array of roles. This basic feature of social structure can be registered by the distinctive but not formidable term, role-set. To repeat, then, by role-set I mean that complement of role-relationships in which persons are involved by virtue of occupying a particular social status. Thus, in our current studies of medical schools, we have begun with the view that the status of medical student entails not only the role of a student *vis-à-vis* his teachers, but also an array of other roles relating him diversely to other students, physicians, nurses, social workers, medical technicians, and the like. Again, the status of school teacher in the United States has its distinctive role-set, in which are found pupils, colleagues, the school principal and superintendent, the Board of Education, professional associations, and, on occasion, local patriotic organizations.

It should be made plain that the role-set differs from what sociologists have long described as "multiple roles." By established usage, the term multiple role refers not to the complex of roles associated with a single social status, but with the various social statuses (often, in differing institutional spheres) in which people find themselves—for illustration, the statuses of physician, husband, father, professor, church elder, Conservative Party member and army captain. (This complement of distinct statuses of a person, each of these in turn having its own role-set, I would designate as a status-set. This concept gives rise to its own range of analytical problems which cannot be considered here.)

The notion of the role-set reminds us, in the unlikely event that we need to be reminded of this obstinate fact, that even the seemingly simple social structure is fairly complex. All societies face the functional problem of articulating the components of numerous role-sets, the functional problem of managing somehow to organize these so that an appreciable degree of social regularity obtains, sufficient to enable most people most of the time to go about their business of social life, without encountering extreme conflict in their role-sets as the normal, rather than the exceptional, state of affairs.

If this relatively simple idea of role-set has any theoretical worth, it should at the least generate distinctive problems for sociological theory, which come to our attention only from the perspective afforded by this idea, or by one like it. This the notion of role-set does. It raises the general problem of identifying the social mechanisms which serve to articulate the expectations of those in the role-set so that the occupant of a status is confronted with less conflict than would obtain if these mechanisms were not at work. It is to these social mechanisms that I would devote the rest of this discussion.

Before doing so, I should like to recapitulate the argument thus far. We depart from the simple idea, unlike that which has been rather widely assumed, that a single status in society involves, not a single role, but an array of associated roles, relating the status-occupant to diverse others. Secondly, we

note that this structural fact, expressed in the term role-set, gives rise to distinctive analytical problems and to corresponding questions for empirical inquiry. The basic problem, which I deal with here, is that of identifying social mechanisms, that is, processes having designated effects for designated parts of the social structure, which serve to articulate the role-set more nearly than would be the case, if these mechanisms did not operate. Third, unlike the problems centered upon the notion of "multiple roles," this one is concerned with social arrangements integrating the expectations of those in the role-set; it is not primarily concerned with the familiar problem of how the occupant of a status manages to cope with the many, and sometimes conflicting, demands made of him. It is thus a problem of social structure, not an exercise in the no doubt important but different problem of how individuals happen to deal with the complex structures of relations in which they find themselves. Finally, by way of setting the analytical problem, the logic of analysis exhibited in this case is developed wholly in terms of the elements of social structure, rather than in terms of providing historical description of a social system.

All this presupposes, of course, that there is always a *potential* for differing and sometimes conflicting expectations of the conduct appropriate to a status-occupant among those in the role-set. The basic source of this potential for conflict, I suggest—and here we are at one with theorists as disparate as Marx and Spencer, Simmel and Parsons— is that the members of a role-set are, to some degree, apt to hold social positions differing from that of the occupant of the status in question. To the extent that they are diversely located in the social structure, they are apt to have interests and sentiments, values and moral expectations differing from those of the status-occupant himself. This, after all, is one of the principal assumptions of Marxist theory, as it is of all sociological theory: social differentiation generates distinct interests among those variously located in the structure of the society. To continue with one of our examples: the members of a school board are often in social and economic strata which differ greatly from that of the school teacher; and their interests, values and expectations are consequently apt to differ, to some extent, from those of the teacher. The teacher may thus become subject to conflicting role-expectations among such members of his role-set as professional colleagues, influential members of the school board, and, say, the Americanism Committee of the American Legion. What is an educational essential for the one may be judged as an education frill, or as downright subversion, by the other. These disparate and contradictory evaluations by members of the role-set greatly complicate the task of coping with them all. The familiar case of the teacher may be taken as paradigmatic. What holds conspicuously for this one status holds, in varying degree, for the occupants of all other statuses who are structurally related, through their role-set, to others who themselves occupy diverse positions in society.

This, then, is the basic structural basis for potential disturbance of a role-set. And it gives rise, in turn, to a double question: which social mechanisms, if any, operate to counteract such instability of role-sets and, correlatively, under which circumstances do these social mechanisms fail to operate, with resulting confusion and conflict? This is not to say, of course, that role-sets do invariably operate with substantial efficiency. We are concerned here, not with a broad historical generalization to the effect that social order prevails, but with an analytical problem of identifying social mechanisms which produce a greater degree of order than would obtain, if these mechanisms were not called into play. Otherwise put, it is theoretical sociology, not history, which is of interest here.

Social Mechanism Articulating Role-Sets

1. RELATIVE IMPORTANCE OF VARIOUS STATUSES The first of these mechanisms derives from the oft-noticed sociological circumstance that social structures designate certain statuses as having greater importance than others. Family and job obligations, for example, are defined in American society as having priority over membership in voluntary associations. As a result, a particular role-relationship may be of peripheral concern for some; for others it may be central. Our hypothetical teacher, for whom this status holds primary significance, may by this circumstance be better able to withstand the demands for conformity with the differing expectations of those comprising his role-set. For at least some of these others, the relationship has only peripheral significance. This does not mean, of course, that teachers are not vulnerable to demands which are at odds with their own professional commitments. It means only that when powerful members of their role-set are only little concerned with this particular relationship, teachers are less vulnerable than they would otherwise be (or sometimes are). Were all those involved in the role-set *equally* concerned with this relationship, the plight of the teacher would be considerably more sorrowful than it often is. What holds for the particular case of the teacher presumably holds for the occupants of other statuses: the impact upon them of diverse expectations among those in their role-set is mitigated by the basic structural fact of differentials of involvement in the relationship among those comprising their role-set.

2. DIFFERENCES OF POWER OF THOSE IN THE ROLE-SET A second potential mechanism for stabilizing the role-set is found in the distribution of power and authority. By power, in this connection, is meant the observed and predictable capacity to impose one's will in a social action, even against the opposition of others taking part in that action; by authority, the culturally legitimized organization of power.

As a consequence of social stratification, the members of a role-set are not apt to be equally powerful in shaping the behaviour of status-occupants. However, it does not follow that the individuals, group, or stratum in the role-set which are *separately* most powerful uniformly succeed in imposing their demands upon the status-occupant, say, the teacher. This would be so only in the circumstance that the one member of the role-set has either a monopoly of power in the situation or outweighs the combined power of the others. Failing this special but, of course, not infrequent, situation, there may develop *coalitions of power* among some members of the role-set which enable the status-occupants to go their own way. The familiar pattern of a balance of power is of course not confined to the conventionally-defined political realm. In less easily visible form, it can be found in the workings of role-sets generally, as the boy who succeeds in having his father's decision offset his mother's opposed decision has ample occasion to know. To the extent that conflicting powers in his role-set neutralize one another, the status-occupant has relative freedom to proceed as he intended in the first place.

Thus, even in those potentially unstable structures in which the members of a role-set hold contrasting expectations of what the status-occupant should do, the latter is not wholly at the mercy of the most powerful among them. Moreover, the structural variations of engagement in the role-structure, which I have mentioned, can serve to reinforce the relative power of the status-occupant. For to the extent that powerful members of his role-set are not centrally concerned with this particular relationship, they will be the less motivated to exercise their potential power to the full. Within varying margins of his activity, the status-occupant will then be free to act as he would.

Once again, to reiterate that which lends itself to misunderstanding, I do not say that the status-occupant subject to conflicting expectations among members of his role-set is in fact immune to control by them. I suggest only that the power and authority-structure of role-sets is often such that he has a larger measure of autonomy than he would have had if this structure of competing power did not obtain.

3. INSULATION OF ROLE-ACTIVITIES FROM OBSERVABILITY BY MEMBERS OF THE ROLE-SET People do not engage in continuous interaction with all those in their role-sets. This is not an incidental fact, to be ignored because familiar, but one integral to the operation of social structure. Interaction with each member of a role-set tends to be variously intermittent. This fundamental fact allows for role-behaviour which is at odds with the expectations of some in the role-set to proceed without undue stress. For, as I elsewhere suggest at some length, effective social control presupposes social arrangements making for the observability of behaviour. (By observability, a conception which I have borrowed from Simmel and tried to develop, I mean the extent to which social norms and role-performances can readily become known to others in the social system. This is, I believe, a variable crucial to structural analysis, a belief which I cannot, unhappily, undertake to defend here.)

To the extent that the social structure insulates the individual from having his activities known to members of his role-set, he is the less subject to competing pressures. It should be emphasized that we are dealing here with structural arrangements for such insulation, not with the fact that this or that person *happens* to conceal part of his role-behaviour from others. The structural fact is that social statuses differ in the extent to which the conduct of those in them are regularly insulated from observability by members of the role-set. Some have a functionally significant insulation of this kind, as for example, the status of the university teacher, insofar as norms hold that what is said in the classroom is privileged. In this familiar type of case, the norm clearly has the function of maintaining some degree of autonomy for the teacher. For if they were forever subject to observation by all those in the role-set, with their often differing expectations, teachers might be driven to teach not what they know or what the evidence leads them to believe, but to teach what will placate the numerous and diverse people who are ostensibly concerned with "the education of youth." That this sometimes occurs is evident. But it would presumably be more frequent, were it not for the relative exemption from observability by all and sundry who may wish to impose their will upon the instructor.

More broadly, the concept of privileged information and confidential communication in the professions has this same function of insulating clients from observability of their behaviour and beliefs by others in their role-set. Were physicians or priests free to tell all they have learned about the private lives of their clients, the needed information would not be forthcoming and they could not adequately discharge their functions. More generally, if all the facts of one's conducts and beliefs were freely available to anyone, social structures could not operate. What is often described as "the need for privacy"—that is, insulation of actions and beliefs from surveillance by others—is the individual counterpart to the functional requirement of social structure that some measure of exemption from full observability be provided. "Privacy" is not only a personal predilection, though it may be that, too. It is also a requirement of social systems which must provide for a measure, as they say in France, of *quant-à-soi*, a portion of the self which is kept apart, immune from observation by others.

Like other social mechanisms, this one of insulation from full observability can, of course, miscarry. Were the activities of the politician or, if one prefers, the statesman, fully removed from the public spotlight, social control of his behaviour would be correspondingly reduced. And as we all know, anonymous power anonymously exercised does not make for a stable social structure meeting the values of a society. So, too, the teacher or physician who is largely insulated from observability may fail to live up to the minimum requirements of his status. All this means only that some measure of observability of role-performance by members of the role-set is required, if the indispensable social requirement of accountability is to be met. This statement does not contradict an earlier statement to the effect that some measure of insulation from observability is also required for the effective operation of social structures. Instead, the two statements, taken in conjunction, imply that there is an optimum zone of observability, difficult to identify in precise terms and doubtless varying for different social statuses, which will simultaneously make both for an accountability and for substantial autonomy, rather than for a frightened acquiescence with the distribution of power which happens, at a particular moment, to obtain in the role-set.

4. OBSERVABILITY OF CONFLICTING DEMANDS BY MEMBERS OF A ROLE-SET This mechanism is implied by what has been said and therefore needs only passing comment here. As long as members of the role-set are happily ignorant that their demands upon the occupants of a status are incompatible, each member may press his own case. The pattern is then many against one. But when it becomes plain that the demands of some are in full contradiction with the demands of others, it becomes, in part, the task of members of the role-set, rather than that of the status-occupant, to resolve these contradictions, either by a struggle for overriding power or by some degree of compromise.

In such circumstances, the status-occupant subjected to conflicting demands often becomes cast in the role of the *tertius gaudens*, the third (or more often, the nth) party who draws advantage from the conflict of the others. Originally at the focus of the conflict, he can virtually become a bystander whose function it is to highlight the conflicting demands being made by members of his role-set. It becomes a problem for them, rather than for him, to resolve their contradictory demands. At the least, this serves to make evident that it is not wilful misfeasance on his part which keeps him from conforming to all the contradictory expectations imposed upon him. When most effective, this serves to articulate the expectations of those in the role-set beyond a degree which would occur if this mechanism of making contradictory expectations manifest were not at work.

5. MUTUAL SOCIAL SUPPORT AMONG STATUS-OCCUPANTS Whatever he may believe to the contrary, the occupant of a social status is not alone. The very fact that he is placed in a social position means that there are others more or less like-circumstanced. To this extent, the actual or potential experience of facing a conflict of expectations among members of the role-set is variously common to all occupants of the status. The particular persons subject to these conflicts need not, therefore, meet them as wholly private problems which must be coped with in wholly private fashion.

It is this familiar and fundamental fact of social structure, of course, which is the basis for those in the same social status forming the associations intermediate to the individual and the larger society in a pluralistic system. These organizations constitute a structural response to the problems of coping with the (potentially or actually) conflicting demands by those in the role-sets of the status. Whatever the intent, these constitute social formations serving to counter the power of the role-set; of being, not merely amenable to its demands, but of helping to shape them. Such organizations—so familiar a part of the social landscape of differentiated societies—also develop normative systems which are designed to anticipate and thereby to mitigate such conflicting expectations. They provide social support to the individuals in the status under attack. They minimize the need for their improvising personal adjustments to patterned types of conflicting expectations. Emerging codes which state in advance what the socially-supported conduct of the status-occupant should be also serve this social function. This function becomes all the more significant in the structural circumstances when status-occupants are highly vulnerable to pressures from their role-set because they are relatively isolated from one another. Thus, thousands of librarians sparsely distributed among the towns and villages of America and not infrequently subject to censorial pressures received strong support from the code on censorship developed by the American Library Association. This only illustrates the general mechanisms whereby status-peers curb the pressures exerted upon them individually by drawing upon the organizational and normative support of their peers.

6. ABRIDGING THE ROLE-SET There is, of course, a limiting case in the modes of coping with incompatible demands by the role-set. Role-relations are broken off, leaving a greater consensus of role-expectations among those who remain. But this mode of adaptation by amputating the role-set is possible only under special and limited conditions. It can be effectively utilized only in those circumstances where it is still possible for status-occupants to perform their other roles, without the support of those with whom they have discontinued relations. It presupposes that the social structure provides this option. By and large, however, this option is infrequent and limited, since the composition of the role-set is ordinarily not a matter of personal choice but a matter of the social organization in which the status is embedded. More typically, the individual goes, and the social structure remains.

Residual Conflict in the Role-Set

Doubtless, these are only some of the mechanisms which serve to articulate the expectations of those in the role-set. Further inquiry will uncover others, just as it will probably modify the preceding account of those we have provisionally identified. But, however much the substance may change, I believe that the logic of the analysis will remain largely intact. This can be briefly recapitulated.

First, it is assumed that each social status has its organized complement of role-relationships which can be thought of as comprising a role-set. Second, relationships hold not only between the occupant of the particular status and each member of the role-set but always potentially, and often actually, between members of the role-set itself. Third, to the extent that members of the role-set themselves hold substantially differing statuses, they will tend to have some differing expectations (moral and actuarial) of the conduct appropriate for the status-occupant. Fourth, this gives rise to the sociological problem of how their diverse expectations become sufficiently articulated for the status-structure and the role-structure to operate with a modicum of effectiveness. Fifth, inadequate articulation of these role-expectations tends to call one or more social mechanisms into play, which serve to reduce the extent of patterned conflict below the level which would be involved if these mechanisms were not at work.

And now, sixth, finally and importantly, even when these (and probably other) mechanisms are operating, they may not, in particular cases, prove sufficient to reduce the conflict of expectations below the level required for the social structure to operate with substantial effectiveness. This residual conflict within the role-set may be enough to interfere materially with that effective performance of roles by the occupant of the status in question. Indeed, it may well turn out that this condition is the most frequent one—role-systems operating at considerably less than full efficiency. Without trying to draw tempting analogies with other types of systems, I suggest only that this is not unlike the case of engines which cannot fully utilize heat energy. If the analogy lacks force, it may nevertheless have the merit of excluding the utopian figment of a perfectly effective social system.

We do not yet know some of the requirements for fuller articulation of the relations between the occupant of a status and members of his role-set, on the one hand, and for fuller articulation of the values and expectations among those comprising the role-set, on the other. As we have seen, even those requirements which can now be identified are not readily satisfied, without fault, in social systems. To the extent that they are not, social systems are forced to limp along with that measure of ineffectiveness and inefficiency which is often accepted because the realistic prospect of decided improvement seems so remote as sometimes not to be visible at all.

2 *Socialization*

The process of an individual's adjustment to society is known as *socialization*. This adjustment consists primarily of organizing behavior to fit the expectations of other people. The process begins in infancy with an adjustment to particular individuals, especially to parents and other family members. Later socialization includes adjustment to groups as well as to individuals, and to the culture as a whole as well as to particular social settings.

The process of socialization of each individual is unique. No two persons have precisely the same set of social experiences. Furthermore, an individual's socialization is not simply a matter of passive adjustment. The individual resists as well as accepts social influence; even an infant may show rather dramatic resistance. The process of socialization, in other words, is not a simple one-way process; and outcomes of similar influences are different for different individuals.

Nevertheless, there are some general features of socialization that apply to almost every individual. Nearly everyone grows up in a family setting, and in each family, parents play a key role in shaping the child. How do they do this, and with what effects? This is a question indicated by the first two readings of this section. "The Castro Family," by Oscar Lewis, presents a case study of a family whose problems include those of rather unruly children. The article by Urie Bronfenbrenner, "The Changing American Child," discusses possible effects of changing patterns of child rearing in the United States.

Many influences of early child training may not be what parents deliberately intend. Some of these show the subtle shaping of cultural influences, with long-term consequences that sometimes may be surprising to the parents involved. This cultural dimension of the effects of early child training is explored in Project 3, entitled "Cross-Cultural Evidence on Effects of Early Socialization." In this project the student is asked to help test two hypotheses derived from theories about the relationship of culture and personality.

The instructor will give further information about the use and interpretation of Project 4, "Twenty Statements."

Childhood is often considered the main period of socialization. However, socialization is a process that continues throughout life. The induction into adult roles is an especially crucial aspect of socialization, and this is discussed in "Steps to Adulthood" by William N. Stephens. Stephens gives a broad perspective upon this process through a summary of cross-cultural evidence.

6. The Castro Family

OSCAR LEWIS

The Castro family is one of the family case studies included in Five Families *by the anthropologist Oscar Lewis. David Castro, although of humble origins, owns a cement business, two stores, and two apartment houses. His family lives in the wealthiest residential section of Mexico City. Here Isabel, his wife, attempts to manage the household and the children, Rolando (age 14), Manuel (10), Juan (9), and Lourdes (6), the only daughter. Also mentioned in the following excerpts is one of the servants, Josefina.*

The following case study is not presented as "proving" anything. It is presented rather as a "slice of life" that raises important questions about socialization in a concrete setting.

"Shorty," David said to his wife, "you felt hot when I got in last night. Have you got a fever?"

"I don't know," Isabel answered, "but I've felt bad ever since last night. Now I'm going to wake up the children. Listen, why did you come home so late? Another party?"

"Are you beginning that again? I know what I'm doing and that's the end of it. You aren't to complain. Didn't we agree on that?" David spoke deliberately, as usual, pronouncing his words carefully and exaggerating the vowels. He was proud of his ability to speak well, but when he was angry he quickly lapsed into slang and vulgarities, revealing his lower class background.

"All right, but it's just too much. You're a terrible example to your children. That's why they don't respect me."

"They don't respect you because you don't know how to handle them. Where's your psychology? When I'm around they're lambs."

"Yes, you have a very special kind of psychology."

"What do you mean? Do you mean to say I'm an ogre to my children?" David had raised his voice to a yell.

"I didn't say that. But they're afraid of

you because you can take a lot of things away from them and because you're a man. And what about when you're not home? You should train them to obey me. You haven't any idea how much trouble they give me. Especially Rolando. You'd never think I am his mother. But of course they see what goes on between us two."

"Look," David said, "shut up or we'll end up fighting the way we always do and I'm sick of it. I wish we could have a little peace in this damned house. When you're not fighting about money you're fighting because I get home late or for something else. You've always got something to complain about."

Isabel kept quiet. She stood up, putting on a pair of rose-colored silk slippers and a long white bathrobe of Spanish piqué and lace over her transparent pink nylon nightgown. Thirty-four years old and the mother of four children, she was still beautiful and young looking. She was small-boned and had delicate features, a light skin, large brown eyes, and short curly chestnut-colored hair. Fastidious about her person and clothes and careful of her diet, for she tended to gain weight easily, she worked assiduously to keep herself looking young. She never gave her true age when questioned.

Isabel went to her daughter's room where the little girl had been awake for over an hour and playing quietly with her dolls.

Some time before she had started into her parents' room, but when she heard them quarreling she had crept back to bed. Lourdes' room was small but it, too, was expensively furnished with a carpet, a youth bed with a spring mattress, a bureau with drawers, a wardrobe, a night table, and two small chairs. It also had a closet where Lourdes kept all her elaborate toys. When her mother came in, the child began to jump up and down on the bed.

"*Mamacita*, last night I dreamed about a lot of little angels that were flying in a lot of clouds. Why didn't you come to see me sooner?"

"I was talking to your papá, child. Why didn't you come in? Come on, put on your bathrobe and your slippers so we can go down to breakfast. It's very late."

"I was yelling for Josefina but she didn't come. I wanted her to bring me some water."

"Come on. Get up, baby. I'll be right back. I'm going to look in on your brothers to see if they're awake. They're too quiet. I don't know what mischief they're up to."

Just then there was a yell.

"That's Fatty," Isabel said. "They must have hit him." She ran to the boys' room and found a battle under way. Pillows and blankets had been thrown on the floor and the youngest boy, Juan, was sitting in a corner wailing bitterly.

"What's the matter, darling?" Isabel asked.

"Rolando hit me. He hit me hard on the back."

"Yes, I hit him. What of it?" Rolando said. "But just ask him to tell you why. Go ahead, coward, sissy, tell mamá why I hit you. He opened my present, mamá, and if I hadn't seen him he would have taken it out of the box. He's a bastard. He can't take it."

"It's not true. It's not true." The little boy was crying desperately.

Perplexed, not knowing which one to believe, Isabel turned to Manuel, who was hard-of-hearing and wore a hearing aid.

"Tell me, son, you're the most serious one of all. Whose fault was it?"

"Look, mamá, it's true that Fatty unwrapped the present. We were still sleeping and he got up quietly and went to look at all the presents. He opened up his and then he

started in on ours, but Rolando saw him and got up and hit him. Fatty's a hypocrite. He wasn't hit that hard."

Isabel went to the closet and saw that there were indeed several boxes on the floor. One of them was open and its contents, a red sweater, an undershirt, and two pairs of cowboy pants, could be seen; another was half unwrapped. She went back to Juan who was crying more quietly.

"Now, now, son. But what did you do that for? I worked so hard to wrap up the presents and now you can't wait. Be quiet, because if your father hears you he'll come in and beat you all. He's in a bad mood and if he gets angry he won't give us any money to buy a Christmas tree."

*   *   *

[EDITOR'S NOTE: *Later the family sits down to breakfast.*]

Josefina stood beside Isabel ready for orders.

"Listen you, stupid," Juan said to her, "bring me more hotcakes. Don't just stand there like an idiot."

"You see what these boys are like, David?" Isabel said. "They don't respect anybody."

"Leave them alone, woman. That's what we pay for."

Josefina went at once to the kitchen but she could be heard weeping. When she came back with a platter of pancakes her eyes were still wet. She placed the platter near Isabel and returned to the kitchen.

For a moment no one spoke. Suddenly Lourdes gave a yell which made everyone jump.

"What's the matter, baby?" David asked.

"Rolando kicked me under the table, papá," she said and began to cry.

"It's not so, papá, I just stretched out my leg and touched her accidentally."

"Accidentally!" said Isabel, "I don't know what's the matter with that boy. You'd think the devil was in him. He won't stop for anything. He has no consideration for anybody."

"Ay, mamá, don't be that way, it's not true, it's not true," Rolando said petulantly.

"All right, all of you shut up. You're going to make me angry," David said. "If you keep on making trouble I'll take back the train and good-by Christmas presents."

"That's what you should do, old man,"

Isabel said. "Let's see if these little fiends will understand that. But you only threaten—"

"They'll see that it won't be just a threat this time. You just tell me how they behave and they'll see."

Manuel spoke up. "No, papá! It's not our fault. You see, mamá? It's going to be your fault if my papá takes the train back. You're mean."

"Do you hear how they talk to me, David? They don't respect me. Not until I strap them with the belt! You'll see."

* * *

[EDITOR'S NOTE: *After breakfast Isabel hears a great deal of noise upstairs.*]

Upstairs she found that the boys had locked themselves in the bathroom. She knocked on the door but no one opened it. She knocked harder shouting, "If you don't open the door there'll be trouble. You damned boys! You, Rolando, open up because if you don't you'll get it."

She pounded on the door with her fist and at last it was opened. She saw that the bathroom floor was a lake of water, and in one corner Manuel, nude, sat crying.

"And now. What happened? Who hit you? Tell me, boy," Isabel said.

"It was Rolando, mamá. He hit me because I didn't want to give him the soap."

"Yes, mamá, but he was throwing soap in my eyes and wouldn't let me rinse off in the shower and then he pushed me and I slipped."

"Didn't I tell you to bathe one by one? You'll see."

Isabel was angry now, brought out the belt, and hit Rolando with it twice. The boy, furious, began to mutter under his breath.

"Listen, mamá," said Juan, "he is talking back to you."

"Tattle-tale, gossip, old woman. It's not true, mamá. I didn't say anything."

"All right, for the love of God," Isabel said. "None of you loves me. You'll be the death of me. I don't know how to put up with you. You're taking months off my life every day. But you'll see. Next year you're all going to be sent to boarding school. That's going to be your punishment for your bad behavior. I can't stand you any longer. You'll see. I'll give you five minutes to dry yourselves and get into your room."

She slammed the door angrily and went back to her bedroom, saying aloud, "Of course, how can these bastards respect me, with the example set them by their father. Wretched miser! Everything he gives me hurts him. I wish I were dead because these kids are going to kill me off soon anyway. Now I can still manage them, but later? They see how he treats me all the time. Always after women! He even lets the children see him with other women and that is why they don't respect me."

7. The Changing American Child
—A Speculative Analysis

URIE BRONFENBRENNER

What have been the main changes in American child rearing in recent decades, and how have these changes affected the coming generation of adults? Bronfenbrenner deals with these questions in the following article.

A Question of Moment

It is now a matter of scientific record that patterns of child rearing in the United States have changed appreciably over the past twenty-five years (Bronfenbrenner, 1958). Middle class parents especially have moved away from the more rigid and strict styles of care and discipline advocated in the early Twenties and Thirties toward modes of response involving greater tolerance of the child's impulses and desires, freer expression of affection, and increased reliance on "psychological" methods of discipline, such as reasoning and appeals to guilt, as distinguished from more direct techniques like physical punishment. At the same time, the gap between the social classes in their goals and methods of child rearing appears to be narrowing, with working class parents beginning to adopt both the values and techniques of the middle class. Finally, there is dramatic correspondence between these observed shifts in parental values and behavior and the changing character of the attitudes and practices advocated in successive editions of such widely read manuals as the Children's Bureau bulletin on *Infant Care* and Spock's *Baby and Child Care.* Such correspondence should not be taken to mean that the expert has now become the principal instigator and instrument of social change, since the ideas of scientists and professional workers themselves reflect in part

From Urie Bronfenbrenner, "The Changing American Child—A Speculative Analysis," *The Journal of Social Issues,* 1961, **XVII**, No. 1, pp. 6–18, with permission of the author and publisher, The Society For the Psychological Study of Social Issues.

the operation of deep-rooted cultural processes. Nevertheless, the fact remains that changes in values and practices advocated by prestigeful professional figures can be substantially accelerated by rapid and widespread dissemination through the press, mass media of communication, and public discussion.

Given these facts, it becomes especially important to gauge the effect of the changes that are advocated and adopted. Nowhere is this issue more significant, both scientifically and socially, than in the sphere of familial values and behavior. It is certainly no trivial matter to ask whether the changes that have occurred in the attitudes and actions of parents over the past twenty-five years have been such as to affect the personality development of their children, so that the boys and girls of today are somewhat different in character structure from those of a decade or more ago. Or, to put the question more succinctly: has the changing American parent produced a changing American child?

A Strategy of Inference

Do we have any basis for answering this intriguing question? To begin with, do we have any evidence of changes in the behavior of children in successive decades analogous to those we have already been able to find for parents? If so, we could take an important first step toward a solution of the problem. Unfortunately, in contrast to his gratifying experience in seeking and finding appropriate data on parents, the present writer has, to date, been unable to locate enough instances in which comparable methods of behavioral assessment have been employed with different groups of children of similaɪ ages over an extended period of time. Although the absence of such material precludes any direct and unequivocal approach to the question at hand, it is nevertheless possible, through a series of inferences from facts already known, to arrive at some estimate of what the answer might be. Specifically, although as yet we have no comparable data on the relation between parental and child behavior for different families at successive points in time, we do have facts on the influence of parental treatment on child behavior at a given point in time; that is, we know that certain variations in parental behavior tend to be accompanied by systematic differences in the personality characteristics of children. If we are willing to assume that these same relationships obtained not only at a given moment but across different points in time, we are in a position to infer the possible effects on children of changing patterns of child rearing over the years. It is this strategy that we propose to follow.

The Changing American Parent

We have already noted the major changes in parental behavior discerned in a recent analysis of data reported over a twenty-five year period. These secular trends may be summarized as follows:

(1) Greater permissiveness toward the child's spontaneous desires

(2) Freer expression of affection

(3) Increased reliance on indirect "psychological" techniques of discipline (such as reasoning or appeals to guilt) vs. direct methods (like physical punishment, scolding, or threats)

(4) In consequence of the above shifts in the direction of what are predominantly middle class values and techniques, a narrowing of the gap between social classes in their patterns of child rearing.

Since the above analysis was published, a new study has documented an additional trend. Bronson, Katten, and Livson (1959) have compared patterns of paternal and maternal authority and affection in two generations of families from the California Guidance Study. Unfortunately, the time span surveyed overlaps only partially with the twenty-five year period covered in our

own analysis, the first California generation having been raised in the early 1900's and the second in the late '20's and early '30's. Accordingly, if we are to consider the California results along with the others cited above, we must make the somewhat risky assumption that a trend discerned in the first three decades of the century has continued in the same direction through the early 1950's. With this important qualification, an examination of the data cited by Bronson *et al.* (1959) points to still another, secular trend—a shift over the years in the pattern of parental role differentiation within the family. Specifically:

(5) In succeeding generations the relative position of the father vis-à-vis the mother is shifting with the former becoming increasingly more affectionate and less authoritarian, and the latter becoming relatively more important as the agent of discipline, especially for boys.

"Psychological" Techniques of Discipline and Their Effects

In pursuing our analytic strategy, we next seek evidence of the effects on the behavior of children of variations in parental treatment of the type noted in our inventory. We may begin by noting that the variables involved in the first three secular trends constitute a complex that has received considerable attention in recent research in parent-child relationships. Within the last three years, two sets of investigators, working independently, have called attention to the greater efficacy of "love-oriented" or "psychological" techniques in bringing about desired behavior in the child (Sears, Maccoby, and Levin, 1957; Miller and Swanson, 1958; 1960). The present writer, noting that such methods are especially favored by middle class parents, offered the following analysis of the nature of these techniques and the reasons for their effectiveness.

Such parents are, in the first place, more likely to overlook offenses, and when they do punish, they are less likely to ridicule or inflict physical pain. Instead, they reason with the youngster, isolate him, appeal to guilt, show disappointment —in short, convey in a variety of ways, on the one hand, the kind of behavior that is expected of the child; on the other, the realization that transgression means the interruption of a mutually valued relationship. . . .

These findings [of greater efficacy] mean that middle class parents, though in one sense more lenient in their discipline techniques, are using methods that are actually more compelling. Moreover, the compelling power of these practices is probably enhanced by the more permissive treatment accorded to middle class children in the early years of life. The successful use of withdrawal of love as a discipline technique implies the prior existence of a gratifying relationship; the more love present in the first instance, the greater the threat implied in its withdrawal (Bronfenbrenner, 1958).

It is now a well established fact that children from middle class families tend to excel those from lower class in many characteristics ordinarily regarded as desirable, such as self-control, achievement, responsibility, leadership, popularity, and adjustment in general.* If, as seems plausible, such differences in behavior are attributable at least in part to class-linked variations in parental treatment, the strategy of inference we have adopted would appear on first blush to lead to a rather optimistic conclusion. Since, over the years, increasing numbers of parents have been adopting the more effective socialization techniques typically employed by the middle class, does it not follow that successive generations of children should show gains in the development of effective behavior and desirable personality characteristics?

Unfortunately, this welcome conclusion, however logical, is premature, for it fails to take into account all of the available facts.

Sex, Socialization, and Social Class

To begin with, the parental behaviors we have been discussing are differentially distributed not only by socio-economic status but also by sex. As we have pointed out elsewhere (Bronfenbrenner, 1961a), girls are exposed to more affection and less punish-

*For a summary of findings on social class differences in children's behavior and personality characteristics, see Mussen, P. H., and Conger, J. J., *Child Development and Personality*. New York: Harper, 1956.

ment than boys, but at the same time are more likely to be subjected to "love-oriented" discipline of the type which encourages the development of internalized controls. And, consistent with our line of reasoning, girls are found repeatedly to be "more obedient, cooperative, and in general better socialized than boys at comparable age levels." But this is not the whole story.

. . . At the same time, the research results indicate that girls tend to be more anxious, timid, dependent, and sensitive to rejection. If these differences are a function of differential treatment by parents, then it would seem that the more "efficient" methods of child rearing employed with girls involve some risk of what might be called "oversocialization" (Bronfenbrenner, 1961a).

One could argue, of course, that the contrasting behaviors of boys and girls have less to do with differential parental treatment than with genetically-based maturational influences. Nevertheless, two independent lines of evidence suggest that socialization techniques do contribute to individual differences, *within the same sex*, precisely in the types of personality characteristics noted above. In the first place, variations in child behavior and parental treatment strikingly similar to those we have cited for the two sexes are reported in a recent comprehensive study of differences between first and later born children (Schachter, 1959). Like girls, first children receive more attention, are more likely to be exposed to "psychological" discipline, and end up more anxious and dependent, whereas later children, like boys, are more aggressive and self-confident.

A second line of evidence comes from our own current research. We have been concerned with the role of parents in the development of such "constructive" personality characteristics as responsibility and leadership among adolescent boys and girls. Our findings reveal not only the usual differences in adolescents' and parents' behaviors associated with the sex of the child, but also a striking contrast in the relationship between parental and child behaviors for the two sexes. To start on firm and familiar ground, girls are rated by their teachers as more responsible than boys, whereas the latter obtain scores on leadership. Expected differences similarly appear in the realm of parental behavior: girls receive more affection, praise, and companionship; boys are subjected to more physical punishment and achievement demands. Quite unanticipated, however, at least by us, was the finding that both parental affection and discipline appeared to facilitate effective psychological functioning in boys, but to impede the development of such constructive behavior in girls. Closer examination of our data indicated that both extremes of either affection or discipline were deleterious for all children, but that the process of socialization entailed somewhat different risks for the two sexes. Girls were especially susceptible to the detrimental influence of overprotection; boys to the ill effects of insufficient parental discipline and support. Or, to put it in more colloquial terms: boys suffered more often from too little taming, girls from too much.

In an attempt to account for this contrasting pattern of relationships, we proposed the notion of differential optimal levels of affection and authority for the two sexes.

The qualities of independence, initiative, and self-sufficiency, which are especially valued for boys in our culture, apparently require for their development a somewhat different balance of authority and affection than is found in the "love-oriented" strategy characteristically applied with girls. While an affectional context is important for the socialization of boys, it must evidently be accompanied by and be compatible with a strong component of parental discipline. Otherwise, the boy finds himself in the same situation as the girl, who, having received greater affection, is more sensitive to its withdrawal, with the result that a little discipline goes a long way and strong authority is constricting rather than constructive (Bronfenbrenner, 1960).

What is more, available data suggest that this very process may already be operating for boys from upper middle class homes. To begin with, differential treatment of the sexes is at a minimum for these families. Contrasting parental attitudes and behaviors toward boys and girls are pronounced only at lower class levels, and decrease as one moves up the socio-economic scale (Kohn, 1959; Bronfenbrenner, 1960). Thus our own results show that it is primarily at lower

middle class levels that boys get more punishment than girls, and the latter receive greater warmth and attention. With an increase in family's social position, direct discipline drops off, especially for boys, and indulgence and protectiveness decrease for girls. As a result, patterns of parental treatment for the two sexes begin to converge. In like manner, we find that the differential effects of parental behavior on the two sexes are marked only in the lower middle class. It is here that girls especially risk being overprotected and boys not receiving sufficient discipline and support. In upper middle-class the picture changes. Girls are not as readily debilitated by parental affection and power; nor is parental discipline as effective in fostering the development of responsibility and leadership in boys.

All these trends point to the conclusion that the "risks" experienced by each sex during the process of socialization tend to be somewhat different at different social class levels. Thus the danger of overprotection for girls is especially great in lower class families, but lower in upper middle class because of the decreased likelihood of overprotection. Analogously, boys are in greater danger of suffering from inadequate discipline and support in lower middle than in upper middle class. But the upper middle class boy, unlike the girl, exchanges one hazard for another. Since at this upper level the more potent "psychological" techniques of discipline are likely to be employed with both sexes, the boy presumably now too runs the risk of being "oversocialized," of losing some of his capacity for independent aggressive accomplishment.

Accordingly, if our line of reasoning is correct, we should expect a changing pattern of sex differences at successive socio-economic levels. Specifically, aspects of effective psychological functioning favoring girls should be most pronounced in the upper middle class; those favoring boys in the lower middle. A recent analysis of some of our data bears out this expectation. Girls excel boys on such variables as *responsibility* and *social acceptance* primarily at the higher socio-economic levels. In contrast, boys surpass girls on such traits as *leadership, level of aspiration*, and *competitiveness* almost exclusively in lower middle class. Indeed, with a rise in a family's social position, the differences tend to reverse themselves with girls now excelling boys.*

Trends in Personality Development: A First Approximation

The implications for our original line of inquiry are clear. We are suggesting that the "love-oriented" socialization techniques, which over the past twenty-five years have been employed in increasing degree by American middle class families, may have negative as well as constructive aspects. While fostering the internalization of adult standards and the development of socialized behavior, they may also have the effect of undermining capacities for initiative and independence, particularly in boys. Males exposed to this "modern" pattern of child rearing might be expected to differ from their counterparts of a quarter century ago in being somewhat more conforming and anxious, less enterprising and self-sufficient, and, in general, possessing more of the virtues and liabilities commonly associated with feminine character structure.†

At long last, then, our strategy of inference has led us to a first major conclusion. The term "major" is appropriate since the conclusion takes as its points of departure and return four of the secular trends which served as the impetus for our inquiry. Specifically, through a series of empirical links and theoretical extrapolations, we have arrived at an estimate of the effects on children of the tendency of successive generations of parents to become progressively more permissive, to express affection more freely, to utilize "psychological" techniques of discipline, and by moving in these directions to narrow the gap between the social classes in their patterns of child rearing.

*These shifts in sex difference with a rise in class status are significant at the 5% level of confidence (one-tailed test).

† Strikingly similar conclusions were reached almost fifteen years ago in a provocative essay by Arnold Green ("The Middle Class Male Child and Neurosis," *American Sociological Review*, 1946, 11, 31–41). With little to go on beyond scattered clinical observations and impressions, Green was able to detect many of the same trends which we have begun to discern in more recent systematic empirical data.

Family Structure and Personality Development

But one other secular trend remains to be considered: what of the changing pattern of parental role differentiation during the first three decades of the century? If our extrapolation is correct, the balance of power within the family has continued to shift with fathers yielding parental authority to mothers and taking on some of the nurturant and affectional functions traditionally associated with the maternal role. Again we have no direct evidence of the effects of such secular changes on successive generations of children, and must look for leads to analogous data on contemporaneous relationships.

We may begin by considering the contribution of each parent to the socialization processes we have examined thus far. Our data indicate that it is primarily mothers who tend to employ "love-oriented" techniques of discipline and fathers who rely on more direct methods like physical punishment. The above statement must be qualified, however, by reference to the sex of the child, for it is only in relation to boys that fathers use direct punishment more than mothers. More generally, . . . the results reveal a tendency for each parent to be somewhat more active, firm, and demanding with a child of the same sex, more lenient and indulgent with a child of the opposite sex. . . . The reversal is most complete with respect to discipline, with fathers being stricter with boys, mothers with girls. In the spheres of affection and protectiveness, there is no actual shift in preference, but the tendency to be especially warm and solicitous with girls is much more pronounced among fathers than among mothers. In fact, generally speaking, it is the father who is more likely to treat children of the two sexes differently (Bronfenbrenner, 1960).

Consistent with this pattern of results, it is primarily the behavior of fathers that accounts for the differential effects of parental behavior on the two sexes and for the individual differences within each sex. In other words, it is paternal authority and affection that tend especially to be salutary for sons but detrimental for daughters. But as might be anticipated from what we already know, these trends are pronounced only in the lower middle class; with a rise in the family's social status, both parents tend to have similar effects on their children, both within and across sexes. Such a trend is entirely to be expected since parental role differentiation tends to decrease markedly as one ascends the socio-economic ladder. It is almost exclusively in lower middle class homes that fathers are more strict with boys and mothers with girls. To the extent that direct discipline is employed in upper middle class families, it tends to be exercised by both parents equally. Here again we see a parallelism between shifts in parental behavior across time and social class in the direction of forms (in this instance of family structure) favored by the upper middle class group.

What kinds of children, then, can we expect to develop in families in which the father plays a predominantly affectionate role, and a relatively low level of discipline is exercised equally by both parents? A tentative answer to this question is supplied by a preliminary analysis of our data in which the relation between parental role structure and adolescent behavior was examined with controls for the family's social class position. The results of this analysis are summarized as follows: . . . Both responsibility and leadership are fostered by the relatively greater salience of the parent of the same sex. . . . Boys tend to be more responsible when the father rather than the mother is the principal disciplinarian; girls are more dependable when the mother is the major authority figure. . . . In short, boys thrive in a patriarchal context, girls in a matriarchal. . . . The most dependent and least dependable adolescents describe family arrangements that are neither patriarchal nor matriarchal, but equalitarian. To state the issue in more provocative form, our data suggest that the democratic family, which for so many years has been held up and aspired to as a model by professionals and enlightened laymen, tends to produce young people who "do not take initiative," look to others for direction and decision," and "cannot be counted on to fulfill obligations" (Bronfenbrenner, 1960).

In the wake of so sweeping a conclusion, it is important to call attention to the tentative, if not tenuous, character of our findings. The results were based on a single study employing crude questionnaire methods and rating scales. Also, our interpretation is limited by the somewhat "attenuated" character of most of the families classified as patriarchal or matriarchal in our sample. Extreme concentrations of power in one or another parent were comparatively rare. Had they been more frequent, we suspect the data would have shown that such extreme asymmetrical patterns of authority were detrimental rather than salutary for effective psychological development, perhaps even more disorganizing than equalitarian forms.

Nevertheless, our findings do find some peripheral support in the work of others. A number of investigators, for example, point to the special importance of the father in the socialization of boys (Bandura and Walters, 1959; Mussen and Distler, 1959). Further corroborative evidence appears in the growing series of studies of effects of paternal absence (Bach, 1946; Sears, Pintler and Sears, 1946; Lynn and Sawrey, 1959; Tiller, 1958). The absence of the father apparently not only affects the behavior of the child directly but also influences the mother in the direction of greater over-protectiveness. The effect of both these tendencies is especially critical for male children; boys from father-absent homes tend to be markedly more submissive and dependent. Studies dealing explicitly with the influence of parental role structure in intact families are few and far between. Papanek (1957), in an unpublished doctoral dissertation reports greater sex-role differentiation among children from homes in which the parental roles were differentiated. And in a carefully controlled study, Kohn and Clausen (1956) find that "schizophrenic patients more frequently than normal persons report that their mothers played a very strong authority role and the father a very weak authority role." Finally, what might best be called complementary evidence for our inferences regarding trends in family structure and their effects comes from the work of Miller, Swanson, and their associates (1958; 1960) on the differing patterns of behavior exhibited by families from *bureaucratic* and *entrepreneurial* work settings. These investigators argue that the entrepreneurial-bureaucratic dichotomy represents a new cleavage in

American social structure that cuts across and overrides social class influences and carries with it its own characteristic patterns of family structure and socialization. Thus one investigation (Gold and Slater, 1958) contrasts the exercise of power in families of husbands employed in two kinds of job situations: (a) those working in large organizations with three or more levels of supervision; (b) those self-employed or working in small organizations with few levels of supervision. With appropriate controls for social class, equalitarian families were found more frequently in the bureaucratic groups; patriarchal and, to a lesser extent, matriarchal in the entrepreneurial setting. Another study (Miller and Swanson, 1958) shows that, in line with Miller and Swanson's hypotheses, parents from these same two groups tend to favor rather different ends of socialization, with entrepreneurial families putting considerably more emphasis on the development of independence and mastery and on the use of "psychological" techniques of discipline. These differences appear at both upper and lower middle class levels but are less prounounced in higher socio-economic strata. It is Miller and Swanson's belief, however, that the trend is toward the bureaucratic way of life, with its less structured patterns of family organization and child rearing. The evidence we have cited on secular changes in family structure and the inferences we have drawn regarding their possible effects on personality development are on the whole consistent with their views.

Looking Forward

If Miller and Swanson are correct in the prediction that America is moving toward a bureaucratic society that emphasizes, to put it colloquially, "getting along" rather than "getting ahead," then presumably we can look forward to ever increasing numbers of equalitarian families who, in turn, will produce successive generations of ever more adaptable but unaggressive "organization men." But recent signs do not all point in this direction. In our review of secular trends in child rearing practices we detected in the data from the more recent studies a slowing up in the headlong rush toward greater per-

missiveness and toward reliance on indirect methods of discipline. We pointed out also that if the most recent editions of well-thumbed guidebooks on child care are as reliable harbingers of the future as they have been in the past, we can anticipate something of a return to the more explicit discipline techniques of an earlier era. Perhaps the most important forces, however, acting to redirect both the aims and methods of child rearing in America emanate from behind the Iron Curtain. With the firing of the first Sputnik, Achievement began to replace Adjustment as the highest goal of the American way of life. We have become concerned—perhaps even obsessed—with "education for excellence" and the maximal utilization of our intellectual resources. Already, ability grouping, and the guidance counsellor who is its prophet, have moved down from the junior high to the elementary school, and parents can be counted on to do their part in preparing their youngsters for survival in the new competitive world of applications and achievement tests.

But if a new trend in parental behavior is to develop, it must do so in the context of changes already under way. And if the focus of parental authority is shifting from husband to wife, then perhaps we should anticipate that pressures for achievement will be imposed primarily by mothers rather than fathers. Moreover, the mother's continuing strong emotional investment in the child should provide her with a powerful lever for evoking desired performance. It is noteworthy in this connection that recent studies of the familial origins of need-achievement point to the matriarchy as the optimal context for development of the motive to excel (Strodtbeck, 1958; Rosen and D'Andrade, 1959).

The prospect of a society in which socialization techniques are directed toward maximizing achievement drive is not altogether a pleasant one. As a number of investigators have shown (Baldwin, Kalhorn and Breese, 1945; Baldwin, 1948; Haggard, 1957; Winterbottom, 1958; Rosen and D'Andrade, 1959), high achievement motivation appears to flourish in a family atmosphere of "cold democracy" in which initial high levels of maternal involvement are followed by pressures for independence and accomplishmcnt.* Nor docs thc product of this process give ground for reassurance. True, children from achievement-oriented homes excel in planfulness and performance, but they are also more aggressive, tense, domineering, and cruel (Baldwin, Kalhorn and Breese, 1945; Baldwin, 1948; Haggard, 1957). It would appear that education for excellence if pursued single-mindedly may entail some sobering social costs.

But by now we are in danger of having stretched our chain of inference beyond the strength of its weakest link. Our speculative analysis has become far more speculative

*Cold democracy under female administration appears to foster the development of achievement not only in the home but in the classroom as well. In a review of research on teaching effectiveness, Ackerman reports that teachers most successful in bringing about gains in achievement score for their pupils were judged "least considerate," while those thought friendly and congenial were least effective. (Ackerman, W. I., "Teacher Competence and Pupil Change," *Harvard Educational Review*, 1954, 24, 273–289.)

than analytic and to pursue it further would bring us past the bounds of science into the realms of science fiction. In concluding our discussion, we would re-emphasize that speculations should, by their very nature, be held suspect. It is for good reason that, like "damn Yankees," they too carry their almost inseparable sobriquets: speculations are either "idle" or "wild." Given the scientific and social importance of the issues we have raised, we would dismiss the first of these labels out of hand, but the second cannot be disposed of so easily. Like the impetuous child, the "wild" speculation responds best to the sobering influence of friendly but firm discipline, in this instance from the hand of the behavioral scientist. As we look ahead to the next twenty-five years of human socialization, let us hope that the "optimal levels" of involvement and discipline can be achieved not only by the parent who is unavoidably engaged in the process, but also by the scientist who attempts to understand its working, and who—also unavoidably—contributes to shaping its course.

8. *Steps to Adulthood*

WILLIAM N. STEPHENS

The transition from childhood to adult roles is an especially important part of the process of socialization. Anthropologist William N. Stephens gives a cross-cultural perspective upon this process, in the process pointing out how nontypical American culture is in these aspects of socialization. Does the reader see any special problems of American society rooted in these unusual patterns of delayed occupational maturity and delayed marriage—combined with sudden emancipation from parental authority?

The road from childhood to adulthood is marked by many little signposts. For a boy in our society, these may include being allowed to cross the street alone, the first

From William N. Stephens, Chapter Eight, "Child Rearing," from *The Family in Cross-Cultural Perspective.* Copyright © 1963 by Holt, Rinehart and Winston, Inc. Reprinted by permission of Holt, Rinehart and Winston, Inc.

bicycle, the first long pants, the first date, the first part-time job, driver's license, school graduation, and—eventually—full-time job, marriage, and parenthood. These steps, these points in the transition from child role to adult role, I would divide into three categories:

(1) Those having to do with work and the adult occupational role.

(2) Those having to do with marriage and parenthood: the transition in family roles, from a child in the family of orientation to spouse-parent in one's (newly founded) family of procreation.

(3) Those having to do with the child's "emancipation" from his parents' authority: the transition from a situation in which the child must "mind" his parent and must account to them for his actions, while they are "responsible" for him, to one where the child is autonomous, is no longer his parents' responsibility, and is no longer subject to their authority.

In this matter of transition from child to adult role our society is, again, quite deviant compared with other societies. In regard to category 3, our society is unusual for the sudden, radical nature of the child's emancipation from his parents' authority. As far as category 2 is concerned, age of marriage and parenthood is apparently rather late in America—although a generation ago our society was much more unusual in this respect. Regarding the first category, "going to work" and assumption of the adult occupational role, we are definitely odd.

In nearly all the societies in my ethnographic notes, children are put to work by the age of ten. Typically, work begins somewhere between the ages of three and six, the load of duties and responsibilities is gradually increased, and sometime between the ages of nine and fifteen the child becomes — occupationally speaking — a fully functioning adult. Some of these children's duties are strictly "children's work," and will have little carry-over to adulthood—errand-running, for example. However, in nearly all cases, the bulk of children's work is a clearcut, specific apprenticeship to the adult occupational role. That is, typically a little girl works at being a little mother (a child-nurse), a little housekeeper, a cook, and a farmer (in societies where women do agricultural work); little boys work at being herdsmen (in herding societies), farm workers (in societies where men do farm work), and, in hunting and gathering societies, boys work (or play) at being hunters.

* * *

In our society childhood work is largely replaced by going to school. Schooling is, to be sure, preparation for adult work, especially in the cases of boys. However, it is not, in itself, adult work. Transition to the adult role in the occupational sphere is extraordinarily retarded in our society. . . . This is a most unusual condition of child rearing which, quite possibly, fosters personality characteristics distinctive to our culture.

* * *

In regard to age of marriage, my cross-cultural data are rather scanty. There are eleven cases in my notes in which the age of marriage appears to be pretty early—by our standards, at least. Opposed to these, there are three cases of apparent late marriage.

* * *

The data suggest (merely suggest, since the evidence is so fragmentary) that primitive societies and peasant societies tend to have quite early marriages, and that girls are frequently married at an earlier age than boys. Why should there be this age differential between the sexes? Two possibilities have already been suggested. The first possible reason, advanced by Murdock, is polygyny. One way to "correct" the sex ratio in a polygynous society is early marriage for girls and later marriage for boys. A second possible reason is marriage finance. Since bride-price payments are usually greater than dowry payments, this may pose added obstacles to a boy's marriage.

As to the reason for the generally early age of marriage—why not? As we have seen, work apprenticeship begins during early childhood in these societies. By puberty, most of these people are functioning as adults in the work and economic spheres. If they can do a man's work (or a woman's work) at puberty, why shouldn't they get married?

So it appears that in most of the known cases an individual is married some time between the ages of twelve and eighteen, and makes a basic family-role transition; he (she) moves from the status of child in the family of orientation, to spouse in his (her) new family of procreation. Actual "procreation" —parenthood—does, I imagine, follow soon afterward, and by the age of twenty, perhaps the full cycle of family roles has been completed: from child to spouse to parent.

Age of marriage evokes the third general area of role transition from childhood to adulthood—"emancipation," the transition from childhood subservience to parents' authority to the autonomy, the freedom from parents' authority, of adulthood. In this area our society also appears to be unusual, but in this case it is not because we are "late." Rather, it is because emancipation is so sudden, radical, and early in our society.

Everywhere, no doubt, emancipation is to some extent a gradual process. As the child "grows" and accumulates skills and knowledge, he is given greater and greater latitude for independent decision making, more responsibility, and greater freedom. Emancipation ordinarily occurs gradually; it is also a matter of degree. Many people, in most societies, do not become fully "emancipated" until their parents' (or at least father's) death. Perhaps even then they are not fully emancipated; that is, even then they may play a sort of child role (authority-wise) vis-á-vis some surviving older kinsmen —elder brothers, and uncles, for example. This delayed emancipation is due to two widespread social conditions: (1) deference customs, which in many societies are due elder male kin as long as they live; and (2) the extended family.

In regard to the extended family: about one-fourth of the societies in Murdock's *World Ethnographic Sample* are characterized by extended-family households. Many additional societies—typically, African societies—have extended-family compounds. In such a situation, some married people (the in-married spouses) continue to live with their parents. It is my impression that in such cases a young person, even after his (or her) marriage, still is somewhat subordinate to parents and older kin. Status-wise, he is to some extent a married child.

* * *

In any event, because of the rarity of the isolated nuclear household throughout most of the world, "emancipation" is gradual and often, apparently, never complete. A person is not suddenly set free of parental authority as the result of marriage. Our society is unusual in this area since, as the result of our high frequency of neolocal residence and nuclear families, marriage usually marks a sudden, radical, and fairly complete emancipation from parental authority. In other words, in our society two of the major "steps to adulthood"—marriage and emancipation from parental authority—are joined; marriage automatically brings emancipation. In most other societies this is not the case: marriage does not end the parents' authority; after marriage, one continues in a quasi childlike authority relationship either with one's own elder kin or in relation to one's spouse's kin (in the case of out-marrying). In the words of the Irish countryman, "You can be a boy forever, as long as the old fellow is alive."

To summarize this discussion of the steps to adulthood, and the comparison of the United States with the rest of the world:

(1) In the occupational sphere, maturity is extraordinarily retarded in our society. We have little or nothing in the way of an early work apprenticeship. Instead, we merely send our children to school.

(2) In the area of family role transition, marriage and parenthood seem to occur relatively late in our society.

(3) In regard to breaking the bonds of parental authority, our society is unusual in the joining of marriage with sudden, radical emancipation.

③ *Identity in Interaction*

As the infant grows and develops, part of his world of experiences becomes differentiated as self. Not only does the child form impressions about objects external to himself, but he also arrives at a set of impressions about himself. For some there is a great deal of stability and persistence in their self-image; for others self remains elusive.

The great Russian novelist Boris Pasternak captures one of the more stable social psychological considerations about self-images when he suggests that impressions about oneself emerge out of interaction with other people. This is also the basic perspective represented by Cooley's concept of the "looking-glass self," in which the responses of other people to an individual form the basis of his self-concept.

Ralph Ellison writing as a black man living in the United States, vividly reflects the premise that a man's self-concept emerges through his interactions with others. Ellison writes, "I am invisible, understand, simply because people refuse to see me. . . . When they approach me they see only my surroundings, themselves, or figments of their imagination—indeed, everything and anything except me." Assuredly, the black man's quest for identity is underwritten by the need of all men to "know thyself."

Beginning with his book, *Client-Centered Therapy*, Carl Rogers has made an enormous impact on American psychology. His principal contention is that psychological adjustment exists when there is congruence between how an individual perceives himself and the image that person holds of what he ought to be like. Psychotherapy from this perspective is an attempt to aid the individual in achieving congruence between these two dimensions of self.

With Carl Rogers' article in mind, Project 5 addresses itself to the problem of how self-esteem can be measured. Self-esteem is seen as a function of the relationship between an individual's actual and ideal self-concepts. Basically, the greater the discrepancy between what an individual thinks he is and what he thinks he should be, the less his feelings of self-esteem. Placed in the framework of Carl Rogers, the less the self-esteem the greater the psychological maladjustment.

Stephen Crane captures brilliantly this problem of self-esteem in his novel *The Red Badge of Courage*. With the American Civil War as a background, Crane employs his genius to portray the struggle of a young soldier to regain his self-esteem after fleeing from the enemy.

Shailer Thomas, *et al.*, provides material that illuminates at least one way in which the term self-concept can be used instrumentally to modify behavior. Project 6 allows the student to extend the research of Thomas, *et al.*, to his own experiences.

9. *Identity: You in Others*

BORIS PASTERNAK

In the following passage from Dr. Zhivago, Boris Pasternak suggests that knowledge about self is revealed in the external manifestations of a person. He is expressing the essential dependency between self-images and social interaction.

"Well, what are you? What is it about you that you have always known as yourself? What are you conscious of in yourself: your kidneys, your liver, your blood vessels? No. However far back you go in your memory it is always some external manifestation of yourself where you come across your identity: in the work of your hands, in your family, in other people. And now, listen carefully. You in others—this is what you are, this is what your consciousness has breathed, and lived on, and enjoyed throughout your life, your soul, your immortality—YOUR LIFE IN OTHERS."

From *Dr. Zhivago*, a novel by Boris Pasternak.

10. *The Looking-Glass Self*

CHARLES HORTON COOLEY

Charles Horton Cooley was an early sociologist who was instrumental in promoting the proposition that self-awareness can arise only in society. He proposes that it is through our imagination of how we appear to other people that we arrive at perceptions about ourselves.

. . . We think of the body as "I" when it comes to have social function or significance, as when we say "I am looking well to-day," or "I am taller than you are." We bring it into the social world, for the time being, and for that reason put our self-consciousness into it. Now it is curious, though natural, that in precisely the same way we may call any inanimate object "I" with which we are identifying our will and purpose. This is notable in games, like golf or croquet, where the ball is the embodiment of the player's fortunes. You will hear a man say, "I am in the long grass down by the third tee," or "I am in position for the middle arch." So a boy flying a kite will say "I am higher than you," or one shooting at a mark will declare that he is just below the bullseye.

In a very large and interesting class of cases the social reference takes the form of a somewhat definite imagination of how one's self—that is any idea he appropriates —appears in a particular mind, and the kind of self-feeling one has is determined by the attitude toward this attributed to that other mind. A social self of this sort might be called the reflected or looking-glass self:

From *Human Nature and the Social Order* by Charles Horton Cooley. Charles Scribner's Sons, 1922.

"Each to each a looking-glass
Reflects the other that doth pass."

As we see our face, figure, and dress in the glass, and are interested in them because they are ours, and pleased or otherwise with them according as they do or do not answer to what we should like them to be; so in imagination we perceive in another's mind some thought of our appearance, manners, aims, deeds, character, friends, and so on, and are variously affected by it.

A self-idea of this sort seems to have three principal elements: the imagination of our appearance to the other person; the imagination of his judgment of that appearance, and some sort of self-feeling, such as pride or mortification. The comparison with a looking-glass hardly suggests the second element, the imagined judgment, which is quite essential. The thing that moves us to pride or shame is not the mere mechanical reflection of ourselves, but an imputed sentiment, the imagined effect of this reflection upon another's mind. This is evident from the fact that the character and weight of that other, in whose mind we see ourselves, makes all the difference with our feeling. We are ashamed to seem evasive in the presence of a straightforward man, cowardly in the presence of a brave one, gross in the eyes of a refined one, and so on. We always imagine, and in imagining share, the judgments of the other mind. A man will boast to one person of an action—say some sharp transaction in trade—which he would be ashamed to own to another.

II. *Invisible Man*

RALPH ELLISON

Ralph Ellison writes sensitively about the interrelationship that exists between an individual's experiences with other people and his own images of himself. For the black man existing within a predominately white society, the frustration often resides not in the fact that he may obtain an unfavorable image of himself, but rather that by being treated as a nonperson, an invisible man, he may have no image at all. In the words of the author, "Or again, you often doubt if you really exist. You wonder whether you aren't simply a phantom in other people's minds."

I am an invisible man. No, I am not a spook like those who haunted Edgar Allan Poe; nor am I one of your Hollywood-movie ectoplasms. I am a man of substance, of flesh and bone, fiber and liquids—and I might even be said to possess a mind. I am invisible, understand, simply because people refuse to see me. Like the bodiless heads you see sometimes in circus sideshows, it is as though I have been surrounded by mirrors of hard, distorting glass. When they approach me they see only my surroundings, themselves, or figments of their imagination—indeed, everything and anything except me.

Nor is my invisibility exactly a matter of a bio-chemical accident to my epidermis. That invisibility to which I refer occurs because of a peculiar disposition of the eyes of those with whom I come in contact. A matter of the construction of their *inner* eyes, those eyes with which they look through their physical eyes upon reality. I am not complaining, nor am I protesting either. It is sometimes advantageous to be unseen, although it is most often rather wearing on the nerves. Then too, you're constantly being bumped against by those of poor vision. Or

Excerpted from Ralph Ellison, *Invisible Man*, New York: Random House, 1952, by permission of the publisher.

again, you often doubt if you really exist. You wonder whether you aren't simply a phantom in other people's minds. Say, a figure in a nightmare which the sleeper tries with all his strength to destroy. It's when you feel like this that, out of resentment, you begin to bump people back. And, let me confess, you feel that way most of the time. You ache with the need to convince yourself that you do exist in the real world, that you're a part of all the sound and anguish, and you strike out with your fists, you curse and you swear to make them recognize you. And, alas, it's seldom successful.

* * *

It goes a long way back, some twenty years. All my life I had been looking for something, and everywhere I turned someone tried to tell me what it was. I accepted their answers too, though they were often in contradition and even self-contradictory. I was naive. I was looking for myself and asking everyone except myself questions which I, and only I, could answer. It took me a long time and much painful boomeranging of my expectations to achieve a realization everyone else appears to have been born with: That I am nobody but myself. But first I had to discover that I am an invisible man!

And yet I am no freak of nature, nor of history. I was in the cards, other things having been equal (or unequal) eighty-five years ago. I am not ashamed of my grandparents for having been slaves. I am only ashamed of myself for having at one time been ashamed. About eighty-five years ago they were told that they were free, united with others of our country in everything pertaining to the common good, and, in everything social, separate like the fingers of the hand. And they believed it. They exulted in it. They stayed in their place, worked hard, and brought up my father to do the same. But my grandfather is the one. He was an odd old guy, my grandfather, and I am told I take after him. It was he who caused the trouble. On his deathbed he called my father to him and said, "Son, after I'm gone I want you to keep up the good fight. I never told you, but our life is a war and I have been a traitor all my born days, a spy in the enemy's country ever since I give up my gun back in the Reconstruction. Live with your head in the lion's mouth. I

want you to overcome 'em with yesses, undermine 'em with grins, agree 'em to death and destruction, let 'em swoller you till they vomit or bust wide open." They thought the old man had gone out of his mind. He had been the meekest of men. The younger children were rushed from the room, the shades drawn and the flame of the lamp turned so low that it sputtered on the wick like the old man's breathing. "Learn it to the younguns," he whispered fiercely; then he died.

But my folks were more alarmed over his last words than over his dying. It was as though he had not died at all, his words caused so much anxiety. I was warned emphatically to forget what he had said and, indeed, this is the first time it has been mentioned outside the family circle. It had a tremendous effect upon me, however. I could never be sure of what he meant. Grandfather had been a quiet old man who never made any trouble, yet on his deathbed he had called himself a traitor and a spy, and he had spoken of his meekness as a dangerous activity. It became a constant puzzle which lay unanswered in the back of my mind. And whenever things went well for me I remembered my grandfather and felt guilty and uncomfortable. It was as though I was carrying out his advice in spite of myself. And to make it worse, everyone loved me for it. I was praised by the most lily-white men of the town. I was considered an example of desirable conduct—just as my grandfather had been. And what puzzled me was that the old man had defined it as *treachery*. When I was praised for my conduct I felt a guilt that in some way I was doing something that was really against the wishes of the white folks, that if they had understood they would have desired me to act just the opposite, that I should have been sulky and mean, and that that really would have been what they wanted, even though they were fooled and thought they wanted me to act as I did. It made me afraid that some day they would look upon me as a traitor and I would be lost. Still I was more afraid to act any other way because they didn't like that at all. The old man's words were like a curse. On my graduation day I delivered an oration in which I showed that humility was the secret, the very essence of progress. (Not that I believed this—how could I, remembering my grandfather?—I only believed that it worked.) It was a great success. Everyone praised me and I was invited to give the speech at a gathering of the town's leading white citizens. It was a triumph for our whole community.

* * *

So there, you have all of it that's important. Or at least you *almost* have it. I'm an invisible man and it placed me in a hole— or showed me the hole I was in, if you will— and I reluctantly accepted the fact. What else could I have done? Once you get used to it, reality is as irresistible as a club, and I was clubbed into the cellar before I caught the hint. Perhaps that's the way it had to be; I don't know. Nor do I know whether accepting the lesson has placed me in the rear or in the *avant-garde. That*, perhaps, is a lesson for history, and I'll leave such decisions to Jack and his ilk while I try belatedly to study the lesson of my own life.

Let me be honest with you—a feat which, by the way, I find of the utmost difficulty. When one is invisible he finds such problems as good and evil, honesty and dishonesty, of such shifting shapes that he confuses one with the other, depending upon who happens to be looking through him at the time. Well, now I've been trying to look through myself, and there's a risk in it. I was never more hated than when I tried to be honest. Or when, even as just now, I've tried to articulate exactly what I felt to be the truth. No one was satisfied—not even I. On the other hand, I've never been more loved and appreciated than when I tried to "justify" and affirm someone's mistaken beliefs; or when I've tried to give my friends the incorrect, absurd answers they wished to hear. In my presence they could talk and agree with themselves, the world was nailed down, and they loved it. They received a feeling of security. But here was the rub: Too often, in order to justify *them,* I had to take myself by the throat and choke myself until my eyes bulged and my tongue hung out and wagged like the door of an empty house in a high wind. Oh, yes, it made them happy and it made me sick. So I became ill of affirmation, of saying "yes" against the naysaying of my stomach—not to mention my brain.

There is, by the way, an area in which a man's feelings are more rational than his mind, and it is precisely in that area that his will is pulled in several directions at the same time. You might sneer at this, but I know now. I was pulled this way and that for longer than I can remember. And my problem was that I always tried to go in everyone's way but my own. I have also been called one thing and then another while no one really wished to hear what I called myself. So after years of trying to adopt the opinions of others I finally rebelled. I am an *invisible* man. Thus I have come a long way and returned and boomeranged a long way from the point in society toward which I originally aspired.

So I took to the cellar; I hibernated. I got away from it all. But that wasn't enough. I couldn't be still even in hibernation. Because, damn it, there's the mind, the *mind.* It wouldn't let me rest. Gin, jazz and dreams were not enough. Books were not enough. My belated appreciation of the crude joke that had kept me running was not enough. And my mind revolved again and again back to my grandfather. And, despite the farce that ended my attempt to say "yes" to the Brotherhood, I'm still plagued by his deathbed advice . . . Perhaps he hid his meaning deeper than I thought, perhaps his anger threw me off—I can't decide. Could he have meant—hell, he *must* have meant the principle, that we were to affirm the principle on which the country was built and not the men, or at least not the men who did the violence. Did he mean say "yes" because he knew that the principle was greater than the men, greater than the numbers and the vicious power and all the methods used to corrupt its name? Did he mean to affirm the principle, which they themselves had dreamed into being out of the chaos and darkness of the feudal past, and which they had violated and compromised to the point of absurdity even in their own corrupt minds? Or did he mean that we had to take the responsibilty·for all of it, for the men as well as the principle, because we were the heirs who must use the principle because no other fitted our needs? Not for the power or for vindication, but because we, with the given circumstance of our origin, could only thus find transcendence? Was it that we of all, we, most of all, had to affirm the principle, the plan in whose name we had been brutalized and sacrificed —not because we would always be weak nor because we were afraid or opportunistic, but because we were older than they, in the sense of what it took to live in the world with others and because they had exhausted in us, some—not much, but some—of the human greed and smallness, yes, and the fear and superstition that had kept them running. (Oh, yes, they're running too, running all over themselves.) Or was it, did he mean that we should affirm the principle because we, through no fault of our own, were linked to all the others in the loud, clamoring semi-visible world, that world seen only as a fertile field for exploitation by Jack and his kind, and with condescension by Norton and his, who were tired of being the mere pawns in the futile game of "making history"? Had he seen that for these too we had to say "yes" to the principle, lest they turn upon us to destroy both it and us?

"Agree 'em to death and destruction," grandfather had advised. Hell, weren't they their own death and their own destruction except as the principle lived in them and in us? And here's the cream of the joke: Weren't we *part of them* as well as apart from them and subject to die when they died? I can't figure it out; it escapes me. But what do *I* really want, I've asked myself. Certainly not the freedom of a Rinehart or the power of a Jack, nor simply the freedom not to run. No, but the next step I couldn't make, so I've remained in the hole.

I'm not blaming anyone for this state of affairs, mind you; nor merely crying *mea culpa*. The fact is that you carry part of your sickness within you, at least I do as an invisible man. I carried my sickness and though for a long time I tried to place it in the outside world, the attempt to write it down shows me that at least half of it lay within me. It came upon me slowly, like that strange disease that affects those black men whom you see turning slowly from black to albino, their pigment disappearing as under the radiation of some cruel, invisible ray. You go along for years knowing something is wrong, then suddenly you discover that you're as transparent as air. At first you tell

yourself that it's all a dirty joke, or that it's due to the "political situation." But deep down you come to suspect that you're yourself to blame, and you stand naked and shivering before the millions of eyes who look through you unseeingly. *That* is the real soul-sickness, the spear in the side, the drag by the neck through the mob-angry town, the Grand Inquisition, the embrace of the Maiden, the rip in the belly with the guts spilling out, the trip to the chamber with the deadly gas that ends in the oven so hygienically clean—only it's worse because you continue stupidly to live. But live you must, and you can either make passive love to your sickness or burn it out and go on to the next conflicting phase.

Yes, but what *is* the next phase? How often have I tried to find it! Over and over again I've gone up above to seek it out. For, like almost everyone in our country, I started out with my share of optimism. I believed in hard work and progress and action, but now, after first being "for" society and then "against" it, I assign myself no rank or any limit, and such an attitude is very much against the trend of the times. But my world has become one of infinite possibilities. What a phrase—still it's a good phrase and a good view of life, and a man shouldn't accept any other; that much I've learned underground. Until some gang succeeds in putting the world in a strait jacket, its definition is possibility. Step outside the narrow borders of what men call reality and you step into chaos—ask Rinehart, he's a master of it—or imagination. That too I've learned in the cellar and not by deadening my sense of perception; I'm invisible, not blind.

No indeed, the world is just as concrete, ornery, vile and sublimely wonderful as before, only now I better understand my relation to it and it to me. I've come a long way from those days when, full of illusion, I lived a public life and attempted to function under the assumption that the world was solid and all the relationships therein. Now I know men are different and that all life is divided and that only in division is there true health. Hence again I have stayed in my hole, because up above there's an increasing passion to make men conform to a pattern. Just as in my nightmare, Jack and the boys are waiting with their knives, looking for the slightest excuse to . . . well, to "ball the jack," and I do not refer to the old dance step, although what they're doing is making the old eagle rock dangerously.

Whence all this passion toward conformity anyway?—diversity is the word. Let man keep his many parts and you'll have no tyrant states. Why, if they follow this conformity business they'll end up by forcing me, an invisible man, to become white, which is not a color but the lack of one. Must I strive toward colorlessness? But seriously, and without snobbery, think of what the world would lose if that should happen. America is woven of many strands; I would recognize them and let it so remain. It's "winner take nothing" that is the great truth of our country or of any country. Life is to be lived, not controlled; and humanity is won by continuing to play in face of certain defeat. Our fate is to become one, and yet many—This is not prophecy, but description. Thus one of the greatest jokes in the world is the spectacle of the whites busy escaping blackness and becoming blacker every day, and the blacks striving toward whiteness, becoming quite dull and gray. None of us seems to know who he is or where he's going.

Which reminds me of something that occurred the other day in the subway. At first I saw only an old gentleman who for the moment was lost. I knew he was lost, for as I looked down the platform I saw him approach several people and turn away without speaking. He's lost, I thought and he'll keep coming until he sees me, then he'll ask his direction. Maybe there's an embarrassment in it if he admits he's lost to a strange white man. Perhaps to lose a sense of *where* you are implies the danger of losing a sense of *who* you are. That must be it, I thought—to lose your direction is to lose your face. So here he comes to ask his direction from the lost, the invisible. Very well, I've learned to live without direction. Let him ask.

But then he was only a few feet away and I recognized him; it was Mr. Norton. The old gentleman was thinner and wrinkled now but as dapper as ever. And seeing him made all the old life live in me for an instant, and

I smiled with tear-stinging eyes. Then it was over, dead, and when he asked me how to get to Centre Street, I regarded him with mixed feelings.

"Don't you know me?" I said.

"Should I?" he said.

"You see me?" I said, watching him tensely.

"Why, of course—Sir, do you know the way to Centre Street?"

"So. Last time it was the Golden Day, now it's Centre Street. You've retrenched, sir. But don't you really know who I am?"

"Young man, I'm in a hurry," he said, cupping a hand to his ear. "Why should I know you?"

"Because I'm your destiny."

"My destiny, did you say?" He gave me a puzzled stare, backing away. "Young man, are you well? Which train did you say I should take?"

"I didn't say," I said, shaking my head. "Now, aren't you ashamed?"

"Ashamed? ASHAMED!" he said indignantly.

I laughed, suddenly taken by the idea. "Because, Mr. Norton, if you don't know *where* you are, you probably don't know *who* you are. So you come to me out of shame. You are ashamed, now aren't you?"

"Young man, I've lived too long in this world to be ashamed of anything. Are you light-headed from hunger? How do you know my name?"

"But I'm your destiny, I made you. Why shouldn't I know you?" I said, walking closer and seeing him back against a pillar. He looked around like a cornered animal. He thought I was mad.

"Don't be afraid, Mr. Norton," I said. "There's a guard down the platform there. You're safe. Take any train; they all go to the Golden D—"

But now an express had rolled up and the old man was disappearing quite spryly inside one of its doors. I stood there laughing hysterically. I laughed all the way back to my hole.

But after I had laughed I was thrown back on my thoughts—how had it all happened? And I asked myself if it were only a joke and I couldn't answer. Since then I've sometimes been overcome with a passion to return into that "heart of darkness" across the Mason-Dixon line, but then I remind myself that the true darkness lies within my own mind, and the idea loses itself in the gloom. Still the passion persists. Sometimes I feel the need to reaffirm all of it, the whole unhappy territory and all the things loved and unlovable in it, for all of it is part of me. Till now, however, this is as far as I've ever gotten, for all life seen from the hole of invisibility is absurd.

So why do I write, torturing myself to put it down? Because in spite of myself I've learned some things. Without the possibility of action, all knowledge comes to one labeled "file and forget," and I can neither file nor forget. Nor will certain ideas forget me; they keep filing away at my lethargy, my complacency. Why should I be the one to dream this nightmare? Why should I be dedicated and set aside—yes, if not to at least *tell* a few people about it? There seems to be no escape. Here I've set out to throw my anger into the world's face, but now that I've tried to put it all down the old fascination with playing a role returns, and I'm drawn upward again. So that even before I finish I've failed (maybe my anger is too heavy; perhaps, being a talker, I've used too many words). But I've failed. The very act of trying to put it all down has confused me and negated some of the anger and some of the bitterness. So it is that now I denounce and defend, or feel prepared to defend. I condemn and affirm, say no and say yes, say yes and say no. I denounce because though implicated and partially responsible, I have been hurt to the point of abysmal pain, hurt to the point of invisibility. And I defend because in spite of all I find that I love. In order to get some of it down I *have* to love. I sell you no phony forgiveness, I'm a desperate man—but too much of your life will be lost, its meaning lost, unless you approach it as much through love as through hate. So I approach it through division. So I denounce and I defend and I hate and I love.

Perhaps that makes me a little bit as human as my grandfather. Once I thought my grandfather incapable of thoughts about humanity, but I was wrong. Why should an old slave use such a phrase as, "This and this or this has made me more human," as I did in my arena speech? Hell, he never had

any doubts about his humanity—that was left to his "free" offspring. He accepted his humanity just as he accepted the principle. It was his, and the principle lives on in all its human and absurd diversity. So now having tried to put it down I have disarmed myself in the process. You won't believe in my invisibility and you'll fail to see how any principle that applies to you could apply to me. You'll fail to see it even though death waits for both of us if you don't. Nevertheless, the very disarmament has brought me to a decision. The hibernation is over. I must shake off the old skin and come up for breath. There's a stench in the air which, from this distance underground, might be the smell either of death or of spring—I hope of spring. But don't let me trick you, there *is* a death in the smell of spring and in the smell of thee as in the smell of me. And if nothing more, invisibility has taught my nose to classify the stenches of death.

In going underground, I whipped it all except the mind, the *mind*. And the mind that has conceived a plan of living must never lose sight of the chaos against which that pattern was conceived. That goes for societies as well as for individuals. Thus, having tried to give pattern to the chaos which lives within the pattern of your certainties, I must come out, I must emerge. And there's still a conflict within me: With Louis Armstrong one half of me says, "Open the window and let the foul air out," while the other says, "It was good green corn before the harvest." Of course Louie was kidding, *he* wouldn't have thrown old Bad Air out, because it would have broken up the music and the dance, when it was the good music that came from the bell of old Bad Air's horn that counted. Old Bad Air is still around with his music and his dancing and his diversity, and I'll be up and around with mine. And, as I said before, a decision has been made. I'm shaking off the old skin and I'll leave it here in the hole. I'm coming out, no less invisible without it, but coming out nevertheless. And I suppose it's damn well time. Even hibernations can be overdone, come to think of it. Perhaps that's my greatest social crime, I've overstayed my hibernation, since there's a possibility that even an invisible man has a socially responsible role to play.

"Ah," I can hear you say, "so it was all a build-up to bore us with his buggy jiving. He only wanted us to listen to him rave!" But only partially true: Being invisible and without substance, a disembodied voice, as it were, what else could I do? What else but try to tell you what was really happening when your eyes were looking through? And it is this which frightens me:

Who knows but that, on the lower frequencies, I speak for you?

12. *A Theory of Personality and Behavior*

CARL ROGERS

Carl Rogers is first and foremost a man deeply concerned about developing methods by which therapy can further benefit the psychological adjustment of individuals. The material excerpted below represents some of the essential implications about personality and behavior that have emerged out of the therapeutic experiences of Rogers and his colleagues. Critical to this intellectual framework are considerations about an individual's perception of himself and the relationship between these perceptions and psychological adjustment.

Behavior is basically the goal-directed attempt of the organism to satisfy its needs as experienced, in the field as perceived....

It is noted that behavior is postulated as a reaction to the field as perceived. This point, like some of the other propositions, is often overlooked. The reaction is not to reality, but to the perception of reality. A horse, sensing danger, will try to reach the safety and security which he perceives in his stall, even though the barn may be in flames. A man in the desert will struggle just as hard to reach the "lake" which he perceives in a mirage, as to reach a real water hole. At a more complex level, a man may strive for money because he perceives money as the source of emotional security, even though in fact it may not satisfy his need. Often, of course, the perception has a high degree of correspondence with reality, but it is important to recognize that it is the perception,

This material has been excerpted from a broader theoretical statement that appears in Carl Rogers, *Client-Centered Therapy*, Boston: Houghton Mifflin Company, 1951, by permission of the author.

not the reality, which is crucial in determining behavior.

It should also be mentioned that in this concept of motivation all the effective elements exist in the present. Behavior is not "caused" by something which occurred in the past. Present tensions and present needs are the only ones which the organism endeavors to reduce or satisfy. While it is true that past experience has certainly served to modify the meaning which will be perceived in present experiences, yet there is no behavior except to meet a present need....

A portion of the total perceptual field gradually becomes differentiated as the self.

Mead, Cooley, Angyal, Lecky, and others have helped to advance our knowledge of the development and functioning of the self. We shall have much to say about various aspects of the operation of the self. For the present the point is made that gradually, as the infant develops, a portion of the total private world becomes recognized as "me," "I," "myself." There are many puzzling and unanswered questions in regard to the dawning concept of the self. We shall try to point out some of these.

Is social interaction necessary in order for a self to develop? Would the hypothetical person reared alone upon a desert island have a self? Is the self primarily a product of the process of symbolization? Is it the fact that experiences may be not only directly experienced, but symbolized and manipulated in thought, that makes the self possible? Is the self simply the symbolized portion of experience? These are some of the questions which shrewd research may be able to answer.

Another point which needs to be made in regard to the development of a conscious self is the fact that it is not necessarily co-existent with the physical organism. Angyal points out that there is no possibility of a sharp line between organism and environment, and that there is likewise no sharp limit between the experience of the self and of the outside world. Whether or not an object or an experience is regarded as a part of the self depends to a considerable extent upon whether or not it is perceived as within the control of the self. Those elements which we control are regarded as a part of self, but when even such an object as a part of our body is out of control, it is experienced as being less a part of the self. The way in which, when a foot "goes to sleep" from lack of circulation, it becomes an object to us rather than a part of self, may be a sufficient illustration. Perhaps it is this "gradient of autonomy" which first gives the infant the awareness of self, as he is for the first time aware of a feeling of control over some aspect of his world of experience.

It should be clear from the foregoing that though some authors use the term "self" as synonomous with "organism" it is here being used in a more restricted sense, namely, the awareness of being, of functioning.

As a result of interaction with the environment, and particularly as a result of evaluational interaction with others, the structure of self is formed—an organized, fluid, but consistent conceptual pattern of perceptions of characteristics and relationships of the "I" or the "me," together with values attached to these concepts.

The values attached to experience, and the values which are a part of the self structure, in some instances are values experienced directly by the organism, and in some instances are values introjected or taken over from others, but perceived in distorted fashion, as if they had been experienced directly.

It will probably be best to discuss these two important propositions together. In the past few years they have been revised and reworded so many different times by the author that is is quite certain the present statement is inadequate also. Yet within the range of experience which these propositions attempt to symbolize, there seem clearly to be some highly important learnings for the personality theorist.

As the infant interacts with his environment he gradually builds up concepts about himself, about the environment, and about himself in relation to his environment. While these concepts are nonverbal, and may not be present in consciousness, this is no barrier to their functioning as guiding principles, as Leeper has shown. Intimately associated with all these experiences is a direct organismic valuing which appears highly important for understanding later development. The very young infant has little uncertainty in valuing. At the same time that there is the dawning awareness of "I experience," there is also the awareness that "I like," "I dislike." "I am cold, and I dislike it," "I am cuddled and I like it," "I can reach my toes and find this enjoyable"— these statements appear to be adequate descriptions of the infant's experience, though he does not have the verbal symbols which we have used. He appears to value those experiences which he perceives as enhancing himself, and to place a negative value on those experiences which seem to threaten himself or which do not maintain or enhance himself.

There soon enters into this picture the evaluation of self by others. "You're a good child," "You're a naughty boy"—these and similar evaluations of himself and of his behavior by his parents and others come to form a large and significant part of the infant's perceptual field. Social experiences, social evaluations by others, become a part of his phenomenal field along with experiences not involving others—for example, that radiators are hot, stairs are dangerous, and candy tastes good. . . .

As experiences occur in the life of the individual, they are either (a) symbolized, perceived, and organized into some relationship to the self, (b) ignored because there is no perceived relationship to the self-structure, (c) denied symbolization or given a distorted symbolization because the experience is inconsistent with the structure of the self. . . . Psychological maladjustment exists when the organism denies to awareness significant sensory and visceral experiences, which consequently are not symbolized and organized into the gestalt of the self-structure. When this situation exists, there is a basic or potential psychological tension.

The basis for this proposition has become evident in the preceding statements. If we think of the structure of the self as being a symbolic elaboration of a portion of the private experiential world of the organism, we may realize that when much of this private world is denied symbolization, certain basic tensions result. We find, then, that there is a very real discrepancy between the experiencing organism as it exists, and the concept of self which exerts such a governing influence upon behavior. This self is now very inadequately representative of the experience of the organism. Conscious control becomes more difficult as the organism strives to satisfy needs which are not consciously admitted, and to react to experiences which are denied by the conscious self. Tension then exists, and if the individual becomes to any degree aware of this tension or discrepancy, he feels anxious, feels that he is not united or integrated, that he is unsure of his direction. Such statements may not be the surface account of the maladjustment, such surface account having more often to do with the environmental difficulties being faced, but the feeling of inner lack of integration is usually communicated as the individual feels free to reveal more of the field of perception which is available to his consciousness. Thus, such statements as "I don't know what I'm afraid of," "I don't know

what I want," "I can't decide on anything," "I don't have any real goal" are very frequent in counseling cases and indicate the lack of any integrated purposeful direction in which the individual is moving. . . .

Psychological adjustment exists when the concept of the self is such that all the sensory and visceral experiences of the organism are, or may be, assimilated on a symbolic level into a consistent relationship with the concept of self.

This proposition may be put in several different ways. We may say that freedom from inner tension, or psychological adjustment, exists when the concept of self is at least roughly congruent with all the experiences of the organism. To use some of the illustrations previously given, the woman who perceives and accepts her own sexual cravings, and also perceives and accepts as a part of her reality the cultural values placed upon suppression of these cravings, will be accepting and assimilating all the sensory evidence experienced by the organism in this connection. This is possible only if her concept of self in this area is broad enough to include both her sex desires and her desire to live in some harmony with her culture. The mother who "rejects" her child can lose the inner tensions connected with her relationship to her child if she has a concept of self which permits her to accept her feelings of dislike for the child, as well as her feelings of affection and liking.

The feeling of reduction of inner tension is something that clients experience as they make progress in "being the real me" or in developing a "new feeling about myself." One client, after gradually giving up the notion that much of her behavior was "not acting like myself" and accepting the fact that her self could include these experiences and behaviors which she had hitherto excluded, expressed her feeling in these words: "I can remember an organic feeling of relaxation. I did not have to keep up the struggle to cover up and hide this shameful person." The cost of maintaining an alertness of defense to prevent various experiences from being symbolized in consciousness is obviously great.

13. *The Red Badge Of Courage*

STEPHEN CRANE

Stephen Crane writes perceptively about the struggle a young Union soldier undergoes as he is confronted with his own cowardice in battle. Since he has imagined himself glorious in battle, the self-doubts raised when he flees an enemy charge provide the primary theme of this excellent Civil War novel. The artistry of Crane's prose graphically portrays the intensity with which this individual searches for his identity.

The youth was in a little trance of astonishment. So they were at last going to fight. On the morrow, perhaps, there would be a battle, and he would be in it. For a time he was obliged to labor to make himself believe. He could not accept with assurance an omen that he was about to mingle in one of those great affairs of the earth.

He had, of course, dreamed of battles all his life—of vague and bloody conflicts that had thrilled him with their sweep and fire. In visions he had seen himself in many struggles. He had imagined peoples secure in the shadow of his eagle-eyed prowess. . . .

However, he perceived now that it did not greatly matter what kind of soldiers he was going to fight, so long as they fought, which fact no one disputed. There was a more serious problem. He lay in his bunk pondering upon it. He tried to mathematically prove to himself that he would not run from a battle.

Previously he had never felt obliged to wrestle too seriously with this question. In his life he had taken certain things for granted, never challenging his belief in ultimate success, and bothering little about means and roads. But here he was confronted with a thing of moment. It had suddenly appeared to him that perhaps in a battle he might run. He was forced to admit that as far as war was concerned he knew nothing of himself.

* * *

Excerpted from the novel by Stephen Crane, *The Red Badge of Courage*, New York: D. Appleton and Company, 1925.

[EDITOR'S NOTE: *The young soldier's questioning about his own response to battle comes out later in a discussion with his fellow soldiers.*]

The youth watched him for a moment in silence. When he finally spoke his voice was as bitter as dregs. "Oh, you're going to do great things, I s'pose!"

The loud soldier blew a thoughtful cloud of smoke from his pipe. "Oh, I don't know," he remarked with dignity; "I don't know. I s'pose I'll do as well as the rest. I'm going to try like thunder." He evidently complimented himself upon the modesty of this statement.

"How do you know you won't run when the time comes?" asked the youth.

"Run?" said the loud one; "run?—of course not!" He laughed.

"Well," continued the youth, "lots of good-a-'nough men have thought they was going to do great things before the fight, but when the time come they skedaddled."

"Oh, that's all true, I s'pose," replied the other; "but I'm not going to skeddadle. The man that bets on my running will lose his money, that's all." He nodded confidently.

"Oh, shucks!" said the youth. "You ain't the bravest man in the world, are you?"

"No, I ain't," exclaimed the loud soldier indignantly; "and I didn't say I was the bravest man in the world, neither. I said I was going to do my share of fighting—that's what I said. And I am, too. Who are you, anyhow? You talk as if you thought you was Napoleon Bonaparte." He glared at the youth for a moment, and then strode away.

The youth called in a savage voice after his comrade: "Well, you needn't git mad about it!" But the other continued on his way and made no reply.

He felt alone in space when his injured comrade had disappeared. His failure to discover any mite of resemblance in their viewpoints made him more miserable than before. No one seemed to be wrestling with such a terrific personal problem. He was a mental outcast.

He went slowly to his tent and stretched himself on a blanket by the side of the snoring tall soldier. In the darkness he saw visions of a thousand-tongued fear that would babble at his back and cause him to flee, while others were going coolly about their country's business.

* * *

The youth had been taught that a man became another thing in a battle. He saw his salvation in such a change. Hence this waiting was an ordeal to him. He was in a fever of impatience. . . .

So it was over at last! The supreme trial had been passed. The red, formidable difficulties of war had been vanquished.

He went into an ecstasy of self-satisfaction. He had the most delightful sensations of his life. Standing as if apart from himself, he viewed that last scene. He perceived that the man who had fought thus was magnificent.

He felt that he was a fine fellow. He saw himself even with those ideals which he had considered as far beyond him. He smiled in deep gratification.

Upon his fellows he beamed tenderness and good will. "Gee! ain't it hot, hey?" he said affably to a man who was polishing his streaming face with his coat sleeves.

"You bet!" said the other, grinning sociably. "I never seen sech dumb hotness." He sprawled out luxuriously on the ground. "Gee, yes! An' I hope we don't have no more fightin' till a week from Monday."

There were some handshakings and deep speeches with men whose features were familiar, but with whom the youth now felt the bonds of tied hearts. He helped a cursing comrade to bind up a wound of the shin.

But, of a sudden, cries of amazement broke out along the ranks of the new regiment. "Here they come ag'in! Here they come ag'in!" The man who had sprawled upon the ground started up and said "Gosh!"

The youth turned quick eyes upon the field. He discerned forms begin to swell in masses out of a distant wood. He again saw the tilted flag speeding forward. . . .

[EDITOR'S NOTE: *The youth is speaking.*]

"Say, this is too much of a good thing! What do they take us for—why don't they send supports? I didn't come here to fight the hull damned rebel army."

He began to exaggerate the endurance, the skill, and the valor of those who were coming. Himself reeling from exhaustion, he was astonished beyond measure at such persistency. They must be machines of steel. It was very gloomy struggling against such affairs, wound up perhaps to fight until sundown.

He slowly lifted his rifle and catching a glimpse of the thickspread field he blazed at a cantering cluster. He stopped then and began to peer as best he could through the smoke. He caught changing views of the ground covered with men who were all running like pursued imps, and yelling.

To the youth it was an onslaught of redoubtable dragons. He became like the man who lost his legs at the approach of the red and green monster. He waited in a sort of a horrified, listening attitude. He seemed to shut his eyes and waited to be gobbled.

A man near him who up to this time had been working feverishly at his rifle suddenly stopped and ran with howls. A lad whose face had borne an expression of exalted courage, the majesty of he who dares give his life, was, at an instant, smitten abject. He blanched like one who has come to the edge of a cliff at midnight and is suddenly made aware. There was a revelation. He, too, threw down his gun and fled. There was no shame in his face. He ran like a rabbit. . . .

[EDITOR'S NOTE: *Having fled, the youth spent some time wandering around. Upon returning to his lines he was horrified to find that others had not run and in fact had successfully met the enemy.*]

The youth cringed as if discovered in a crime. By heavens, they had won after all!

The imbecile line had remained and become victors. He could hear cheering.

He lifted himself upon his toes and looked in the direction of the fight. A yellow fog lay wallowing on the treetops. From beneath it come the clatter of musketry. Hoarse cries told of an advance.

He turned away amazed and angry. He felt that he had been wronged.

He had fled, he told himself, because annihilation approached. He had done a good part in saving himself, who was a little piece of the army. He had considered the time, he said, to be one in which it was the duty of every little piece to rescue itself if possible. Later the officers could fit the little pieces together again, and make a battle front. If none of the little pieces were wise enough to save themselves from the flurry of death at such a time, why, then, where would be the army? It was all plain that he had proceeded according to very correct and commendable rules. His actions had been sagacious things. They had been full of strategy. They were the work of a master's legs.

Thoughts of his comrades came to him. The brittle blue line had withstood the blows and won. He grew bitter over it. It seemed that the blind ignorance and stupidity of those little pieces had betrayed him. He had been overturned and crushed by their lack of sense in holding the position, when intelligent deliberation would have convinced them that it was impossible. He, the enlightened man who looks afar in the dark, had fled because of his superior perceptions and knowledge. He felt a great anger against his comrades. He knew it could be proved that they had been fools.

He wondered what they would remark when later he appeared in camp. His mind heard howls of derision. Their destiny would not enable them to understand his sharper point of view.

He began to pity himself acutely. He was ill used. He was trodden beneath the feet of an iron injustice. He had proceeded with wisdom and from the most righteous motives under heaven's blue only to be frustrated by hateful circumstances. . . .

He wondered what those men had eaten that they could be in such haste to force their way to grim chances of death. As he watched, his envy grew until he thought that he wished to change lives with one of them. He would have liked to have used a tremendous force, he said, throw off himself and become a better. Swift pictures of himself, apart, yet in himself, came to him—a blue desperate figure leading lurid charges with one knee forward and a broken blade high— a blue, determined figure standing before a crimson and steel assault, getting calmly killed on a high place before the eyes of all. He thought of the magnificent pathos of his dead body. . . .

[EDITOR'S NOTE: *Upon rejoining his regiment, he realized that his fears were unfounded, because his friends were unaware that he had fled from battle.*]

His self-pride was now entirely restored. In the shade of its flourishing growth he stood with braced and self-confident legs, and since nothing could now be discovered he did not shrink from an encounter with the eyes of judges, and allowed no thoughts of his own to keep him from an attitude of manfulness. He had performed his mistakes in the dark, so he was still a man.

14. *An Experiment to Modify Self-Concept and School Performance*

SHAILER THOMAS, WILBUR B. BROOKOVER, JEAN M.
LEPERE, DON E. HAMACHEK, AND EDSEL L. ERICKSON

*A basic assumption that is generally supported by the literature on self-concept
argues that an individual's self-concept has a directive influence on his behavior.
This, taken in conjunction with the proposal that the actual evaluations of others
form the basis for an individual's self-concept, would yield the expectation that if
the evaluations of others could be modified, there would be a corresponding change
in the self-concept and behavior of the individual. The following material
summarizes a research effort that supports this basic expectation.*

Research which utilizes a self-concept orientation is a consistent focus in social psychology. The ideas of George H. Mead, which provided the initial impetus for sociological writers, have been operationalized in a variety of fields such as delinquency, education, and family. The contemporary orientation has been formalized by Kinch (1963), Secord and Backman (1961), Sherwood (1965), and Stryker (1962).

In Kinch's (1963) terms, the theoretical orientation states that the actual evaluations of others (A) are perceived (P) by the subject and form the basis for his self-concept (S); the self-concept directs his behavior (B).

	$P{\to}S$	postulate 1
and	$S{\to}B$	postulate 2
then	$P{\to}B$	postulate 4

This may be summarized as:

$$A{\to}P{\to}S{\to}B \quad \text{(Kinch, 1963)}*$$

Research generally has supported several of the relationships between these elements. It has been established that there is a relationship between perceived evaluations of others and self-concept (Reeder, *et. al.*, 1960; Miyamoto and Dornbush, 1956; Sher-wood, 1965, 1967; Brookover *et. al.*, 1964; Couch, 1958; Couch and Murray, 1963). There is also an established relationship between self-concept and behavior (Brookover, *et. al.*, 1964, 1965; McPartland *et. al.*, 1961; Wylie, 1961).

Moreover as Secord and Backman (1961), Backman *et. al.* (1963) and Kinch (1963) have stated, there is the explicit notion of congruency between the elements of this formulation. The individual attempts to structure his relationships with others in order to maintain stability between evaluations, self, and behavior. When lack of congruency occurs there is activity to achieve congruency. Therefore if there are changes in evaluations of others there should also be a change in self-concept. If there is a change in self-concept there should be a change in behavior.

This study is concerned with this aspect

This material is reprinted in slightly abridged form from an unpublished article by Shailer Thomas, *et al.*, entitled, "An Experiment to Modify Self-Concept and School Performance," by permission of the authors.

* The theoretical orientation does not "dead-end" here. However, in this paper we will be concerned with this part of the orientation. An attempt will be made to modify the actual evaluation of significant others (A), and assess resulting changes in S and B.

of self-concept theory. It tests the hypothesis that changes in a self-concept are related to changes in behavior. Several studies have concerned themselves with changes in evaluation or expectations and self-concept (Videbeck, 1960; Maehr *et. al.*, 1962; Backman *et. al.*, 1963). Or in terms of the foregoing paradigm, A→S.

Recently there has been an increased interest in the influence of expectations on behavior (Rosenthal and Jacobson, 1968), i.e. A→B. Though the S→B aspect is found in the paradigm above, it has not been demonstrated that changes in self-concept are reflected in changes in behavior.

This research attempts to work through established "significant others" to modify self-concept in students and to assess changes in school performance. The self-concept is operationalized as self-concept of ability to perform in school, the performance variable is school achievement. (GPA [Grade Point Average])

The almost universal identification of parents as "significant others" by students (Brookover *et. al.*, 1965) was the basis for their selection as "significant others" whose changed expectations might affect the self-concept of ability and subsequently the achievement of low-achieving students.

Procedures

An experimental design was used to evaluate the effects of attempted modifications of parental expectations and definitions of their children. The subjects were parents of low-achieving ninth grade students in an urban school system.

Sample

All white ninth grade students in a single school who had been achieving below the mean grade point average (computed on the subjects of Math, English, Social Studies, and Science) for the previous two semesters were defined as low-achievers. From this low-achieving population three groups of students were randomly selected. The groups were randomly designated an experimental group, a placebo group, and a control group. The parents of the experimental and control group students were contacted and involved

in a series of meetings. Since the experiment depended on this cooperation of parents, some changes in the original random samples were necessary. Three uncooperative parents of experimental group students were randomly replaced. The placebo group remained intact as a random sample.

Instruments

Self-Concept of Ability Scale: In a previous investigation of the relationship of self-concept of ability and school performance, a scale assessing the student's self-concept of academic ability was developed (Brookover *et. al.*, 1964). The scale, consisting of eight multiple choice items, originally formed a Guttman scale with coefficients of reproducibility of .95 for males and .96 for females for 1050 seventh grade students. In the eighth and ninth grades, random samples of thirty-five males and thirty-five females indicated these items retained a scale form with reproducibilities of .96 and .97 for males in the two years and .92 and .93 for females in the same two years. In addition, the scale has an average reliability calculated by Hoyt's Analysis of Variance of .88 for males for the three years and .82 for females for the three years. The test-retest reliability of the scale over a twelve-month period is .75 for 446 males and .77 for 508 females.

This scale along with others was administered to the total school population. Grades were obtained as a measure of performance.

Questionnaires which paralleled those answered by the students were administered to the parents of the low-achieving students involved in the experiment.

Pre- and post-treatment assessments were made of the sample of low-achieving students, and of their parents. A follow-up was made six months after the experiment ended.

Analysis of Samples

The groups randomly selected in the experiment were compared by Analysis of Variance on the variables of GPA for two previous semesters, measured intelligence, socio-economic status, self-concept, perceived parental image, perceived teacher image, and importance of grades. These comparisons were carried out on the random samples prior to contact with them or their parents.

Except for self-concept of ability, all groups within the experiment were not significantly different from each other at the time of selection.

Treatment and Analysis

The experiment proceeded with the orientation that positive parental evaluations and expectations for students would affect their self-concept of ability in school and that changes would be reflected in school achievement. Parents of the experimental and the placebo groups met separately one evening per month during the school year with the research staff.

Experimental Group

At the first meeting parents in the experimental group were introduced to the program they were to participate in. The goals of the seminar for experimental group parents were outlined as follows:

(1) To help the child develop a more positive perception of himself in the school setting.

(2) To develop a recognition that low-achievement in school could be improved.

(3) To develop parental feelings of responsibility for achievement in school.

The parents responded to a questionnaire concerning their perceptions and evaluations of the child. A presentation concerning self-concept theory, and the role of parents as "significant others" was made. The second meeting for the experimental group involved a discussion of school achievement and a film* demonstrating the impact of family interaction and evaluations on school achievement.

Following the film parents expressed some interesting interpretations of the role of parents in influencing their children.

(1) Many parents did not accept the role of "significant other" for their child in terms of effecting his self-concept and his achievement. Some specifically rejected the idea

*The Development of Individual Differences (Young American Film, Inc.)

that parents had any influence on the child.

(2) Scapegoats for parental responsibility and low-achievement were found in past school training, teachers, subject-matter content, lack of reading ability, and laziness of the child.

(3) The parents became somewhat hostile and defensive. One father stated that *he* had *his* life to live and was *not* going back to relive his school years to get his son through school. He asserted that it was none of his (the father's) business if his son wanted to waste his own life. This reaction was not atypical among the parents.

The initial resistance of the parents and the avoidance of parent responsibility for pupil achievement was unanticipated.

At the third meeting a taped interview between a counselor and a ninth grade student was presented. At this meeting most of the parents had moved to a more positive attitude toward the child and the parent's influence on the child. They appeared to accept their influence on the self-concept of their children.

During December and January, individual conferences were scheduled with all parents.

After these conferences with parents, four more group meetings were held. Topics for these were:

(1) The development of potential
   a. Intelligence tests
   b. Inaccurate perceptions of "significant others"
   c. Aspiration levels
   d. Expectations of "significant others"

(2) A panel of college students who discussed self-concept in relation to achievement, the role of parents as "significant others" in their lives

(3) A reading diagnostician who used a self-concept approach

(4) The final meeting summarized the year. Parents again responded to the questionnaire.

Placebo Group

Placebo parents were told that their assistance was being solicited in a study of the problems of junior high schools in America today. The number and format of the meetings for this group were the same as for the experimental group. No individual conferences were held, however, with this group. General topics for their meetings included: problems of adolescence, dating, school, guidance in the school, ability grouping, and reading material for adolescents. This group spent three of the last four meetings discussing ability grouping in the school. A primary focus of their attention was on the "gifted" student rather than on low achievement.

Analysis of Student Data

Analysis of all subjects whose parents participated in this experiment revealed that *prior* to treatment there were significant differences among the three groups on self-concept of ability.

The post-treatment sign test indicated that there was a significant proportion of changers in the experimental group on self-concept of ability and on GPA at the end of ninth grade. There was not a significant proportion of changers on these variables in the placebo or control group.

This study indicated that improvement of self-concept of ability can be affected by working with parents as "significant others," and that this improvement in self-perception tends to reflect itself in improved academic performance as assessed by grades. Furthermore, analysis of data for the children of placebo group parents indicated that involvement of parents in discussions of general school problems does not result in changes in self-concept or achievement among their children.

Analysis of Parents

In addition to assessing changes in the self-concept of ability and performance of the students, an assessment was made of changes among the parents. Parents in pre- and post-treatment assessments responded to questionnaires which paralleled those administered to their children.

It was evident that following the sessions with the research staff the parents in the experimental group had significantly higher evaluations of their child's academic ability, their perceptions of how teachers evaluated their child, and how they thought their child evaluated himself. These significant changes

support and parallel the changes found among the students. Changes among the parents in the placebo group were not significant.

A Follow-up

To assess the long-range effects of the experiment, data was gathered the following year when the students were in tenth grade. The analysis (not presented here) indicates that the effects of the experiment were not continued into the following year.

Summary and Conclusions

Working with parents of low-achieving students significantly raised the self-concept of ability of such students. In addition a significant proportion of students changed in a positive direction on achievement; the experimental group showed significant improvement on GPA while the placebo and control group did not. These effects, however, did not persist in the following year. Data from the parents indicated positive changes in their perceptions and evaluations of their children.

Two other experiments utilizing a counselor, who counseled low-achieving students, and an expert who made formal presentations to a group of low-achieving students were carried out at the same time. Both of these experiments failed to induce change in either self-concept of ability or school performance. These results (Brookover *et. al.*, 1965) indicate that attempts to modify self-conceptions by persons who are not established "significant others" are not as successful as attempts by established "significant others."

For these samples of students the family was an established and positive reference group. This research suggests that when changes are made in established reference groups, changes may be induced in self-attitudes and in some forms of behavior. If this is correct, then other studies which did not use established reference groups (Backman, *et. al.*, 1963, Videbeck, 1960; and Maehr *et. al.*, 1962) might not have succeeded in modifying behavior.

Another interpretation is that if extreme parental indifference is related to low self esteem (Rosenberg, 1963), then an experimental treatment which directs the parents to pay attention to their children may have the effect of modifying self-attitudes. In this research the placebo parents exhibited a high level of interest; the data, however, indicated the parents and their children did not significantly change on the variables measured.

The results reported here are similar to other work dealing with labeling or the influence of expectations on behavior (Rosenthal and Jacobson, 1968). Rosenthal and Jacobson (1968:94) indicate that in some case histories, those children who benefited most from favorable teacher expectations had parents who seemed especially interested in their child's academic progress. Rosenthal's research revealed the impact of teacher expectations on intelligence test scores; this research demonstrates the impact of parent expectations on self-concept and achievement. Both researchers indicate the importance of "significant others" and the impact of modification of expectations on self-concept and performance.

In addition Rosenthal and Jacobson (1968) demonstrate that the effect of changed expectations is greatest in the primary grades. The use of ninth grade students in this study demonstrates that some changes can be affected in later years as well, though the change obtained is not large, or long lasting.

An unanswered question concerns the technique of how parental expectations or definitions of a child are transmitted to the child so as to elicit the expected behavior. Or, in this particular experimental design (since it was not a double-blind design), how were the expectations of the research staff transmitted to the experimental group of parents so as to affect a change in the parents' behavior and attitudes which were then presumably transmitted to the child and elicited changes in his self-attitudes and behavior?

This research indicates that programs with natural subjects in a field setting do have an effect on parental attitudes; that changes in attitudes of "significant others" are transmitted to the children and affect their self-attitudes and to a lesser extent their performance. These results are consistent with symbolic interaction theoretical formulations, and they give tentative support to the proposition that self-concept changes are related to behavior changes. This research does not, however, furnish insight into the techniques by which changes in expectations are communicated to the subjects.

In terms of Kinch's (1963) paradigm, changes in actual evaluations (A) of parents as assessed by questionnaires are reflected in self-attitudes (S) of children, and have a slight momentary impact on performance (B) of their children.

Attitude Formation and Change

An attitude represents a mental state that predisposes an individual to experience aspects of his world in a particular manner. This predisposition to experience includes (1) affective states, suggesting feelings of liking or disliking, and (2) beliefs, which are assertions the individual holds regarding the characteristics of the attitude object. In general, both the affective and belief predispositions are seen as motivating behavior in relation to the attitude object. However, most theories do not clearly articulate the precise nature of this assumed relationship.

To discover the determinants or correlates of particular attitudes, social psychologists have taken several different paths. One approach seeks to locate the relationship between types of attitudes and social factors. Accordingly, the selection from *Personal Influence* by Elihu Katz and Paul Lazarsfeld indicates how the mass media may influence voting behavior. The authors posit a two-step flow of communication, in which the mass media directly influence opinion leaders, who in turn exert personal influence over less active segments of the voting population. It should be understood that while many studies correlating social factors to types of attitudes deal with political attitudes, this is not necessary. For instance, one can study the relation between social factors and social attitudes about issues such as socialization or international relations or whatever. Project 7 provides the opportunity for students to engage directly in some attitude research.

Functionalism represents another orientation to the study of attitudes. It proceeds from the assumption that the attitudes an individual holds are an integral part of his personality. This perspective addresses itself to the problem of what psychological functions are served by holding an attitude. Daniel Katz argues in his article, "The Functional Approach to the Study of Attitudes," that to understand the reasons for holding or changing an attitude, one must understand the underlying psychological functions they perform for the individual. To appreciate the difference between a demographic and functional approach to the study of attitudes, the reader is directed to the fact that the former looks for determinants and correlates of attitudes at the interpersonal level, while the latter seeks determinants and correlates of attitudes at the intrapersonal level.

Like functionalism, the final approach to the study of attitudes discussed here focuses at the intrapersonal level. This is the *structural* method of understanding attitude organization and change. The most basic assumption is that the structures or components relevant to an attitude object must be consistent. These structures include affective states, knowledge or beliefs about the attitude object, and behavior. A state of balance or congruity is said to exist if these structures stand in a consistent relationship to each other.

Attitude change occurs for an individual when one of these structures changes, and as a consequence, a general reorganization of the orientation to the attitude object in question is required. Robert Zajonc's article provides an excellent introduction to the structural approach to the study of attitudes. Rosenberg's work reflects structural analysis in that it attempts to delineate a relationship between the affective and cognitive (belief) components of an attitude.

15. *Two-Step Flow of Communication*

ELIHU KATZ AND PAUL F. LAZARSFELD

One of the earliest systematic studies of voter preference concentrated on the Presidential election of 1940, the contest between Roosevelt and Wilkie.* An important aspect of that research was concerned with the process by which the mass media influenced voting patterns. A later book, from which the material included here is excerpted, elaborates on this process. Essentially, the mass media was seen as not directly influencing all voters but instead affecting informed opinion leaders, who in turn exerted their influence through primary group involvements. This finding suggests the importance of understanding primary group phenomena for students of propaganda and other topics associated with the mass media.

During the course of studying the presidential election campaign of 1940, it became clear that certain people in every stratum of a community serve relay roles in the mass communication of election information and influence (Lazarsfeld, Berelson, and Gaudet, 1948).

This "discovery" began with the finding that radio and the printed page seemed to have only negligible effects on actual vote decisions and particularly minute effects on *changes* in vote decisions. Here, then, was another of those findings which reduce belief in the magic of mass media influence. But the authors were not content to report only this unexpected negative finding. They were interested in how people make up their

minds, and why they change them, and in effect, they asked, if the mass media are not major determinants of an individual's vote decision, then what is?†

† The authors could ask themselves this question because they were equipped with more than just the standard gear of mass communications research. They were equipped to study both mass communications effects and what we might call "decision-making." There is an interesting difference between these two approaches: Communications research begins with a communication' and then attempts to track down the influence it has had, while a decision-making study begins at the other end with an "effect," that is, with a decision—about a career, about moving from one house to another, about marketing and fashion purchases, etc—and tries to locate all of the influences—whatever they happen to be—that went into the making of that decision. *The People's Choice*, the study which we are discussing, seems to have been the first academically legitimated report of the wedding of these two traditions of social research: the tradition of mass media research and the tradition of decision-making studies.

* See Paul F. Lazarsfeld, Bernard Berelson, and Hazel Gaudet, *The People's Choice* (New York: Columbia University Press, 1948).

The Opinion Leader Idea and the Two-Step Flow of Communication

To investigate this problem, particular attention was paid to those people who changed their vote intentions during the course of the campaign. When these people were asked what had contributed to their decision, their answer was: other people. The one source of influence that seemed to be far ahead of all others in determining the way people made up their minds was personal influence. Given this clue from the testimony of the voters themselves, other data and hypotheses fell into line. People tend to vote, it seems, the way their associates vote: wives like husbands, club members with their clubs, workers with fellow employees, etc. Furthermore, looked at in this way, the data implied (although they were not completely adequate for this new purpose) that there were people who exerted a disproportionately great influence on the vote intentions of their fellows. And it could be shown that these "opinion leaders"—as they were dubbed—were not at all identical with those who are thought of traditionally as the wielders of influence; opinion leaders seemed to be distributed in all occupational groups, and on every social and economic level.

The next question was obvious: Who or what influences the influentials? Here is where the mass media re-entered the picture. For the leaders reported much more than the non-opinion leaders that for them, the mass media were influential. Pieced together this way, a new idea emerged—the suggestion of a "two-step flow of communication." The suggestion basically was this: that ideas, often, seem to flow *from* radio and print *to* opinion leaders and *from them* to the less active sections of the population.

The study presented as the major part of this volume represents an attempt to test and further extend these ideas. Other studies with similar bearing, and the ways in which they are linked to one another, are set forth briefly in the Introduction [of this article].

These studies all tend to bear out the validity of the opinion leader idea, in one way or another, and to make quite explicit that the traditional image of the mass persuasion process must make room for

"people" as intervening factors between the stimuli of the media and resultant opinions, decisions and actions. These studies contribute not only to the validation of the apparent relevance of this new intervening factor, but also to a more fruitful formulation of the opinion leader idea itself. We might say, perhaps, that as a result of investigating and thinking about the opinion leader, mass communications research has now joined those fields of social research which, in the last years, have been "rediscovering" the primary group.* And if we are correct, the "rediscovery" seems to have taken place in two steps. First of all, the phenomenon of opinion leadership was discovered. But then, study of the widespread distribution of opinion leaders throughout the population and analysis of the character of their relations with those for whom they were influential (family, friends, co-workers) soon led to a second idea. This was the idea that opinion leaders are not a group set apart, and that opinion leadership is not a trait which some people have and others do not, but rather that opinion leadership is an integral part of the give-and-take of everyday personal relationships. It is being suggested, in other words, that all interpersonal relations are potential networks of communication and that an opinion leader can best be thought of as a group member playing a key communications role. It is this elaboration—that is the tying of opinion leaders to the specific others with whom they are in contact—that completes the "rediscovery."

* * *

The previous chapters make two basic assertions: First, that communications research, to date, has been studying short run mass media *effects*; second, that the intellectual history of this research is best charac-

* The "rediscovery" of the primary group is an accepted term by now, referring to the belated recognition that researchers in many fields have given to the importance of informal, interpersonal relations within situations formerly conceptualized as strictly formal and atomistic. It is "rediscovery" in the sense that the primary group was dealt with so explicitly (though descriptively and apart from any institutional context) in the work of pioneering American sociologists and social psychologists and then was systematically overlooked by empirical social research until its several dramatic "rediscoveries."

terized as a successive taking account of those factors which *intervene* between the mass media and their audience and, thus, which modify mass media effects. The central focus of Section One [of *Personal Influence*] had to do with the introduction of the intervening variable of interpersonal relations.

In the four chapters of the present section we want to scrutinize this notion of interpersonal relations, asking ourselves which elements of such social ties have most bearing on communications effectiveness. We shall try, in other words, to single out and examine those ingredients of informal primary groups which are, so to speak, the "active ingredients" as far as the mass communications process is concerned.

Our purpose, of course, is to try to point the way for the planning of research on the transmission of mass persuasion via the mass media—and, particularly, for the incorporation of a concern with interpersonal relations into the design of such research. By attempting to specify exactly which elements of person-to-person interaction might be relevant for mass media effectiveness, and by exploring what social science knows about the workings of these elements, we shall contribute, perhaps, to a more complex—yet, more realistic—formulation of a "model" for the study of mass persuasion campaigns.

Let us take as our starting point the several illustrations from mass media research set down above, and the thinking and research which constitutes the opinion leader tradition. If we reflect on these, and try to speculate about the specific ways in which interpersonal relationships might be said to affect the response of an individual to a communications campaign, we are led to two characteristics of interpersonal relations, each one of which seems to be a major key to our problem:

1. Interpersonal relationships seem to be *"anchorage" points for individual opinions, attitudes, habits and values*. That is, interacting individuals seem collectively and continuously to *generate* and *to maintain* common ideas and behavior patterns which they are reluctant to surrender or to modify unilaterally. If this is the case, and if many, or most, of the ostensibly individual opinions and attitudes which mass media campaigns seek to modify are anchored in small groups, then the bearing of this aspect of group relations on the effectiveness of such campaigns will be well worth our attention.

2. Interpersonal relationships imply *networks of interpersonal communication*, and this characteristic seems to be relevant for campaign effectiveness in several interlocking ways: The "two-step flow" hypothesis suggests, in the first place, that these interpersonal networks are linked to the mass media networks in such a way that some people, who are relatively more exposed, pass on what they see, or hear, or read, to others with whom they are in contact who are less exposed. Primary groups, in other words, may serve as channels for mass media transmission; this might be called the *relay function* of interpersonal relations. Secondly, it is implied, person-to-person influences may coincide with mass media messages and thus either counteract or reinforce their message. This might be called the *reinforcement function*; and, there is substantial reason to suspect, when the reinforcement is positive, the communication in question is likely to be particularly effective..

It is our guess that these two characteristics of small, intimate groups—(1) person-to-person *sharing of opinions and attitudes* (which we shall often refer to as "group norms") and (2) person-to-person *communications networks*—are the keys to an adequate understanding of the intervening role played by interpersonal relations in the mass communications process.

16. The Functional Approach to the Study of Attitudes

DANIEL KATZ

In the following article Katz articulates the essence of the functional approach to the study of attitudes. Attitudes are seen as expressing certain underlying psychological regularities. The most important question asked by the functionalist is, in brief, what functions attitudes serve for the individual. To understand the conditions under which attitudes are acquired, one must refer to the psychological needs being served by those attitudes. Similarly, to understand attitude change, one must focus on the psychological functions served by the change.

Katz not only introduces a broad orientation to the functional approach to attitudes but also provides a typology of functions served by different kinds of attitudes.

The study of opinion formation and attitude change is basic to an understanding of the public opinion process even though it should not be equated with this process. The public opinion process is one phase of the influencing of collective decisions, and its investigation involves knowledge of channels of communication, of the power structures of a society, of the character of mass media, of the relation between elites, factions and masses, of the role of formal and informal leaders, of the institutionalized access to officials. But the raw material out of which public opinion develops is to be found in the attitudes of individuals, whether they be followers or leaders and whether these attitudes be at the general level of tendencies to conform to legitimate authority or majority opinion or at the specific level of favoring or opposing the particular aspects of the issue under consideration. The nature of the organization of attitudes within the personality and the processes which account for attitude change are thus critical areas for the understanding of the collective product known as public opinion.

*   *   *

Excerpted from an article by Daniel Katz in *The Public Opinion Quarterly*, 1960, **24**, 163–204, by permission of the author and publisher.

Nature of Attitudes: Their Dimensions

Attitude is the predisposition of the individual to evaluate some symbol or object or aspect of his world in a favorable or unfavorable manner. Opinion is the verbal expression of an attitude, but attitudes can also be expressed in nonverbal behavior. Attitudes include both the affective, or feeling core of liking or disliking, and the cognitive, or belief, elements which describe the object of the attitude, its characteristics, and its relations to other objects. All attitudes thus include beliefs, but not all beliefs are attitudes. When specific attitudes are organized into a hierarchical structure, they comprise *value systems*. Thus a person may not only hold specific attitudes against deficit spending and unbalanced budgets but may also have a systematic organization of such beliefs and attitudes in the form of a value system of economic conservatism.

The dimensions of attitudes can be stated more precisely if the above distinctions between beliefs and feelings and attitudes and value systems are kept in mind. The *intensity* of an attitude refers to the strength of the *affective* component. In fact, rating scales and even Thurstone scales deal primarily with the intensity of feeling of the individual for or against some social object.

The cognitive, or belief, component suggests two additional dimensions, the *specificity* or *generality* of the attitude and the *degree of differentiation* of the beliefs. Differentiation refers to the number of beliefs or cognitive items contained in the attitude, and the general assumption is that the simpler the attitude in cognitive structure the easier it is to change. For simple structures there is no defense in depth, and once a single item of belief has been changed the attitude will change. A rather different dimension of attitude is the *number and strength of its linkages to a related value system*. If an attitude favoring budget balancing by the Federal government is tied in strongly with a value system of economic conservatism, it will be more difficult to change than if it were a fairly isolated attitude of the person. Finally, the relation of the value system to the personality is a consideration of first importance. If an attitude is tied to a value system which is closely related to, or which consists of, the individual's conception of himself, then the appropriate change procedures become more complex. The *centrality* of an attitude refers to its role as part of a value system which is closely related to the individual's self-concept.

An additional aspect of attitudes is not clearly described in most theories, namely, their relation to action or overt behavior. Though behavior related to the attitude has other determinants than the attitude itself, it is also true that some attitudes in themselves have more of what Cartwright calls an action structure than do others. Brewster Smith refers to this dimension as policy orientation and Katz and Stotland speak of it as the action component. For example, while many people have attitudes of approval toward one or the other of the two political parties, these attitudes will differ in their structure with respect to relevant action. One man may be prepared to vote on election day and will know where and when he should vote and will go to the polls no matter what the weather or how great the inconvenience. Another man will only vote if a party worker calls for him in a car. Himmelstrand's work is concerned with all aspects of the relationship between attitude and behavior, but he deals with the action

structure of the attitude itself by distinguishing between attitudes where the affect is tied to verbal expression and attitudes where the affect is tied to behavior concerned with more objective referents of the attitude. In the first case an individual derives satisfaction from talking about a problem; in the second case he derives satisfaction from taking some form of concrete action.

Attempts to change attitudes can be directed primarily at the belief component or at the feeling, or affective, component. Rosenberg theorizes that an effective change in one component will result in changes in the other component and presents experimental evidence to confirm this hypothesis. For example, a political candidate will often attempt to win people by making them like him and dislike his opponent, and thus communicate affect rather than ideas. If he is successful, people will not only like him but entertain favorable beliefs about him. Another candidate may deal primarily with ideas and hope that, if he can change people's beliefs about an issue, their feelings will also change.

Four Functions Which Attitudes Perform for the Individual

The major functions which attitudes perform for the personality can be grouped according to their motivational basis:

(1) *The instrumental, adjustive, or utilitarian function* upon which Jeremy Bentham and the utilitarians constructed their model of man. A modern expression of this approach can be found in behavioristic learning theory.

(2) *The ego-defensive function* in which the person protects himself from acknowledging the basic truths about himself or the harsh realities in his external world. Freudian psychology and neo-Freudian thinking have been preoccupied with this type of motivation and its outcomes.

(3) *The value-expressive function* in which the individual derives satisfactions from expressing attitudes appropriate to his personal values and to his concept of himself. This function is central to doctrines of ego psychology which stress the importance of self-expression, self-development, and self-realization.

(4) *The knowledge function* based upon the individual's need to give adequate structure to his universe. The search for meaning, the need to understand, the trend toward better organization of perceptions and beliefs to provide clarity and consistency for the individual, are other descriptions of this function. The development of principles about perceptual and cognitive structure has been the contribution of Gestalt psychology.

Stated simply, the functional approach is the attempt to understand the reasons people hold the attitudes they do. The reasons, however, are at the level of psychological motivations and not of the accidents of external events and circumstances. Unless we know the psychological need which is met by the holding of an attitude we are in a poor position to predict when and how it will change. Moreover, the same attitude expressed toward a political candidate may not perform the same function for all the people who express it. And while many attitudes are predominantly in the service of a single type of motivational process, as described above, other attitudes may serve more than one purpose for the individual. A fuller discussion of how attitudes serve the above four functions is in order.

1. THE ADJUSTMENT FUNCTION Essentially this function is a recognition of the fact that people strive to maximize the rewards in their external environment and to minimize the penalties. The child develops favorable attitudes toward the objects in his world which are associated with the satisfactions of his needs and unfavorable attitudes toward objects which thwart him or punish him. Attitudes acquired in the service of the adjustment function are either the means for reaching the desired goal or avoiding the undesirable one, or are affective associations based upon experiences in attaining motive satisfactions. The attitudes of the worker favoring a political party which will advance his economic lot are an example of the first type of utilitarian attitude. The pleasant image one has of one's favorite food is an example of the second type of utilitarian attitude.

In general, then, the dynamics of attitude formation with respect to the adjustment function are dependent upon present or past perceptions of the utility of the attitudinal object for the individual. The clarity, consistency, and nearness of rewards and punishments, as they relate to the individual's activities and goals, are important factors in the acquisition of such attitudes. Both attitudes and habits are formed toward specific objects, people, and symbols as they satisfy specific needs. The closer these objects are to actual need satisfaction and the more they are clearly perceived as relevant to need satisfaction, the greater are the probabilities of positive attitude formation. These principles of attitude formation are often observed in the breach rather than the compliance. In industry, management frequently expects to create favorable attitudes toward job performance through programs for making the company more attractive to the worker, such as providing recreational facilities and fringe benefits. Such programs, however, are much more likely to produce favorable attitudes toward the company as a desirable place to work than toward performance on the job. The company benefits and advantages are applied across the board to all employees and are not specifically relevant to increased effort in task performance by the individual worker.

Consistency of reward and punishment also contributes to the clarity of the instrumental object for goal attainment. If a political party bestows recognition and favors on party workers in an unpredictable and inconsistent fashion, it will destroy the favorable evaluation of the importance of working hard for the party among those whose motivation is of the utilitarian sort. But, curiously, while consistency of reward needs to be observed, 100 per cent consistency is not as effective as a pattern which is usually consistent but in which there are some lapses. When animal or human subjects are invariably rewarded for a correct performance, they do not retain their learned responses as well as when the reward is sometimes skipped.

2. THE EGO-DEFENSIVE FUNCTION People not only seek to make the most of their external world and what it offers, but they also expend a great deal of their energy on living with themselves. The mechanisms by which the individual protects his ego from his own unacceptable impulses and from the knowledge of threatening forces from with-

out, and the methods by which he reduces his anxieties created by such problems, are known as mechanisms of ego defense. A more complete account of their origin and nature will be found in Sarnoff (1960). They include the devices by which the individual avoids facing either the inner reality of the kind of person he is, or the outer reality of the dangers the world holds for him. They stem basically from internal conflict with its resulting insecurities. In one sense the mechanisms of defense are adaptive in temporarily removing the sharp edges of conflict and in saving the individual from complete disaster. In another sense they are not adaptive in that they handicap the individual in his social adjustments and in obtaining the maximum satisfactions available to him from the world in which he lives. The worker who persistently quarrels with his boss and with his fellow workers, because he is acting out some of his own internal conflicts, may in this manner relieve himself of some of the emotional tensions which beset him. He is not, however, solving his problem of adjusting to his work situation and thus may deprive himself of advancement or even of steady employment.

Defense mechanisms, Miller and Swanson point out, may be classified into two families on the basis of the more or less primitive nature of the devices employed. The first family, more primitive in nature, are more socially handicapping and consist of denial and complete avoidance. The individual in such cases obliterates through withdrawal and denial the realities which confront him. The exaggerated case of such primitive mechanisms is the fantasy world of the paranoiac. The second type of defense is less handicapping and makes for distortion rather than denial. It includes rationalization, projection, and displacement.

Many of our attitudes have the function of defending our self-image. When we cannot admit to ourselves that we have deep feelings of inferiority we may project those feelings onto some convenient minority group and bolster our egos by attitudes of superiority toward this underprivileged group. The formation of such defensive attitudes differs in essential ways from the formation of attitudes which serve the adjustment function. They proceed from within the person, and the objects and situation to which they are attached are merely convenient outlets for their expression. Not all targets are equally satisfactory for a given defense mechanism, but the point is that the attitude is not created by the target but by the individual's emotional conflicts. And when no convenient target exists the individual will create one. Utilitarian attitudes, on the other hand, are formed with specific reference to the nature of the attitudinal object. They are thus appropriate to the nature of the social world to which they are geared. The high school student who values high grades because he wants to be admitted to a good college has a utilitarian attitude appropriate to the situation to which it is related.

All people employ defense mechanisms, but they differ with respect to the extent that they use them and some of their attitudes may be more defensive in function than others. It follows that the techniques and conditions for attitude change will not be the same for ego-defensive as for utilitarian attitudes.

Moreover, though people are ordinarily unaware of their defense mechanisms, especially at the time of employing them, they differ with respect to the amount of insight they may show at some later time about their use of defenses. In some cases they recognize that they have been protecting their egos without knowing the reason why. In other cases they may not even be aware of the devices they have been using to delude themselves.

3. THE VALUE-EXPRESSIVE FUNCTION While many attitudes have the function of preventing the individual from revealing to himself and others his true nature, other attitudes have the function of giving positive expression to his central values and to the type of person he conceives himself to be. A man may consider himself to be an enlightened conservative or an internationalist or a liberal, and will hold attitudes which are the appropriate indication of his central values. Thus we need to take account of the fact that not all behavior has the negative function of reducing the tensions of biological drives or of internal conflicts. Satisfactions also accrue to the person from the expression of attitudes which reflect his cherished be-

liefs and his self-image. The reward to the person in these instances is not so much a matter of gaining social recognition or monetary rewards as of establishing his self-identity and confirming his notion of the sort of person he sees himself to be. The gratifications obtained from value expression may go beyond the confirmation of self-identity. Just as we find satisfaction in the exercise of our talents and abilities, so we find reward in the expression of any attributes associated with our egos.

Value-expressive attitudes not only give clarity to the self-image but also mold that self-image closer to the heart's desire. The teenager who by dress and speech establishes his identity as similar to his own peer group may appear to the outsider a weakling and a craven conformer. To himself he is asserting his independence of the adult world to which he has rendered childlike subservience and conformity all his life. Very early in the development of the personality the need for clarity of self-image is important—the need to know "who I am." Later it may be even more important to know that in some measure I am the type of person I want to be. Even as adults, however, the clarity and stability of the self-image is of primary significance. Just as the kind, considerate person will cover over his acts of selfishness, so too will the ruthless individualist become confused and embarrassed by his acts of sympathetic compassion. One reason it is difficult to change the character of the adult is that he is not comfortable with the new "me." Group support for such personality change is almost a necessity, as in Alcoholics Anonymous, so that the individual is aware of approval of his new self by people who are like him.

The socialization process during the formative years sets the basic outlines for the individual's self-concept. Parents constantly hold up before the child the model of the good character they want him to be. A good boy eats his spinach, does not hit girls, etc. The candy and the stick are less in evidence in training the child than the constant appeal to his notion of his own character. It is small wonder, then, that children reflect the acceptance of this model by inquiring about the characters of the actors in every drama, whether it be a television play, a political

context, or a war, wanting to know who are the "good guys" and who are the "bad guys." Even as adults we persist in labeling others in the terms of such character images. Joe McCarthy and his cause collapsed in fantastic fashion when the telecast of the Army hearings showed him in the role of the villain attacking the gentle, good man represented by Joseph Welch.

A related but somewhat different process from childhood socialization takes place when individuals enter a new group or organization. The individual will often take over and internalize the values of the group. What acounts, however, for the fact that sometimes this occurs and sometimes it does not? Four factors are probably operative, and some combination of them may be necessary for internalization. (1) The values of the new group may be highly consistent with existing values central to the personality. The girl who enters the nursing profession finds it congenial to consider herself a good nurse because of previous values of the importance of contributing to the welfare of others. (2) The new group may in its ideology have a clear model of what the good group member should be like and may persistently indoctrinate group members in these terms. One of the reasons for the code of conduct for members of the armed forces, devised after the revelations about the conduct of American prisoners in the Korean War, was to attempt to establish a model for what a good soldier does and does not do. (3) The activities of the group in moving toward its goal permit the individual genuine opportunity for participation. To become ego-involved so that he can internalize group values, the new member must find one of two conditions. The group activity open to him must tap his talents and abilities so that his chance to show what he is worth can be tied into the group effort. Or else the activities of the group must give him an active voice in group decisions. His particular talents and abilities may not be tapped but he does have the opportunity to enter into group decisions, and thus his need for self-determination is satisfied. He then identifies with the group in which such opportunities for ego-involvement are available. It is not necessary that opportunities for self-expression and self-determination be of great magnitude in an objective sense, so long as they are important for the psychological economy of the individuals themselves. (4) Finally, the individual may come to see himself as a group member if he can share in the rewards of group activity which includes his own efforts. The worker may not play much of a part in building a ship or make any decisions in the process of building it. Nevertheless, if he and his fellow workers are given a share in every boat they build and a return on the proceeds from the earnings of the ship, they may soon come to identify with the ship-building company and see themselves as builders of ships.

4. THE KNOWLEDGE FUNCTION Individuals not only acquire beliefs in the interest of satisfying various specific needs; they also seek knowledge to give meaning to what would otherwise be an unorganized chaotic universe. People need standards or frames of reference for understanding their world, and attitudes help to supply such standards. The problem of understanding, as John Dewey made clear years ago, is one "of introducing (1) *definiteness* and *distinction* and (2) *consistency* and *stability* of meaning into what is otherwise vague and wavering." The definiteness and stability are provided in good measure by the norms of our culture, which give the otherwise perplexed individual ready-made attitudes for comprehending his universe. Walter Lippmann's classical contribution to the study of opinions and attitudes was his description of stereotypes and the way they provided order and clarity for a bewildering set of complexities. The most interesting finding

in Herzog's familiar study of the gratifications obtained by housewives in listening to daytime serials was the unsuspected role of information and advice. The stories were liked "because they explained things to the inarticulate listener."

The need to know does not of course imply that people are driven by a thirst for universal knowledge. The American public's appalling lack of political information has been documented many times. In 1956, for example, only 13 per cent of the people in Detroit could correctly name the two United States Senators from the state of Michigan and only 18 per cent knew the name of their own Congressman. People are not avid seekers after knowledge as judged by what the educator or social reformer would desire. But they do want to understand the events which impinge directly on their own life. Moreover, many of the attitudes they have already acquired give them sufficient basis for interpreting much of what they perceive to be important for them. Our already existing stereotypes, in Lippmann's language, "are an ordered, more or less consistent picture of the world, to which our habits, our tastes, our capacities, our comforts and our hopes have adjusted themselves. They may not be a complete picture of the world, but they are a picture of a possible world to which we are adapted." It follows that new information will not modify old attitudes unless there is some inadequacy or incompleteness or inconsistency in the existing attitudinal structure as it relates to the perceptions of new situations.

17. The Concepts of Balance, Congruity, and Dissonance

ROBERT B. ZAJONC

The term homeostasis *was appropriated from the biological sciences early in the development of psychology to further explain the concept of drive. The term refers to processes that restore equilibrium when an organism experiences biological disturbances. It is not surprising that psychologists concerned with understanding factors relevant to attitude formation and change would also borrow this concept and attempt to integrate it into their theories.*

The concepts of balance, congruity, and dissonance are all related to a basic homeostatic perspective. Attitude change is seen to occur under conditions of disequilibrium in which a fundamental inconsistency exists between certain factors related to the same or similar attitude objects. Disequilibrium is seen as motivating the individual to achieve equilibrium, or in the terms of Zajonc, consistency.

Common to the concepts of balance, congruity, and dissonance is the notion that thoughts, beliefs, attitudes, and behavior tend to organize themselves in meaningful and sensible ways. Members of the White Citizens Council do not ordinarily contribute to NAACP. Adherents of the New Deal seldom support Republican candidates. Christian Scientists do not enroll in medical schools. And people who live in glass houses apparently do not throw stones. In this respect the concept of consistency underscores and presumes human *rationality*. It holds that behavior and attitudes are not only consistent to the objective observer, but that individuals try to appear consistent to themselves. It assumes that inconsistency is a noxious state setting up pressures to eliminate it or reduce it. But in the *ways* that consistency in human behavior and attitudes is achieved we see rather often a striking lack of rationality. A heavy smoker cannot readily accept evidence relating cancer to smoking; a socialist, told that Hoover's endorsement of certain political slogans agreed perfectly with his own, calls him a "typical hypocrite and a liar." Allport illustrates this irration-

Excerpted from an article by Robert Zajonc in *The Public Opinion Quarterly*, 1960, **24**, 280–296, by permission of the author and publisher.

ality in the following conversation:

MR. X: The trouble with Jews is that they only take care of their own group.

MR. Y: But the record of the Community Chest shows that they give more generously than non-Jews.

MR. X: That shows that they are always trying to buy favor and intrude in Christian affairs. They think of nothing but money; that is why there are so many Jewish bankers.

MR. Y: But a recent study shows that the per cent of Jews in banking is proportionally much smaller than the per cent of non-Jews.

MR. X: That's just it. They don't go in for respectable business. They would rather run night clubs.

Thus, while the concept of consistency acknowledges man's rationality, observation of the means of its achievement simultaneously unveils his irrationality. The psychoanalytic notion of rationalization is a literal example of a concept which assumes both rationality and irrationality—it holds, namely, that man strives to understand and justify painful experiences and to make them sensible and rational, but he employs completely irrational methods to achieve this end.

The concepts of consistency are not novel. Nor are they indigenous to the study of attitudes, behavior, or personality. These concepts have appeared in various forms in almost all sciences. It has been argued by some that it is the existence of consistencies in the universe that made science possible, and by others that consistencies in the universe are a proof of divine power. There is, of course, a question of whether consistencies are "real" or mere products of ingenious abstraction and conceptualization. For it would be entirely possible to categorize natural phenomena in such a haphazard way that instead of order, unity, and consistency, one would see a picture of utter chaos. If we were to eliminate one of the spatial dimensions from the conception of the physical world, the consistencies we now know and the consistencies which allow us to make reliable predictions would be vastly depleted.

The concept of consistency in man is, then, a special case of the concept of universal consistency. The fascination with this concept led some psychologists to rather extreme positions. Franke, for instance, wrote, ". . . the unity of a person can be traced in each instant of his life. There is nothing in character that contradicts itself. If a person who is known to us seems to be incongruous with himself that is only an indication of the inadequacy and superficiality of our previous observations." This sort of hypothesis is, of course, incapable of either verification or disproof and therefore has no significant consequences.

Empirical investigations employing the concepts of consistency have been carried out for many years. Not until recently, however, has there been a programmatic and systematic effort to explore with precision and detail their particular consequences for behavior and attitudes. The greatest impetus to the study of attitudinal consistency was given recently by Festinger and his students. In addition to those already named, other related contributions in this area are those of Newcomb, who introduced the concept of "strain toward symmetry," and of Cartwright and Harary, who expressed the notions of balance and symmetry in a mathematical form. These notions all assume inconsistency to be a painful or at least psychologically uncomfortable state, but they differ in the generality of application. The most restrictive and specific is the principle of congruity, since it restricts itself to the problems of the effects of information about objects and events on the attitudes toward the source of information. The most general is the notion of cognitive dissonance, since it considers consistency among any cognitions. In between are the notions of balance and symmetry, which consider attitudes toward people and objects in relation to one another, either within one person's cognitive structure, as in the case of Heider's theory of balance, or among a given group of individuals, as in the case of Newcomb's strain toward symmetry. It is the purpose of this paper to survey these concepts and to consider their implications for theory and research on attitudes.

The Concepts of Balance and Strain Toward Symmetry

The earliest formalization of consistency is attributed to Heider, who was concerned with the way relations among persons involving some impersonal entity are cognitively experienced by the individual. The consistencies in which Heider was interested were those to be found in the ways people view their relations with other people and with the environment. The analysis was limited to two persons, labeled P and O, with P as the focus of the analysis and with O representing some other person, and to one impersonal entity, which could be a physical object, an idea, an event, or the like, labeled X. The object of Heider's inquiry was to discover how relations among P, O, and X are organized in P's cognitive structure, and whether there exist recurrent and systematic tendencies in the way these relations are experienced. Two types of relation, liking (L) and so-called U, or unit, relations (such as possession, cause, similarity, and the like) were distinguished. On the basis of incidental observations and intuitive judgment, probably, Heider proposed that the person's (P's) cognitive structure representing relations among P, O, and X are either what he termed "balanced" or "unbalanced." In particular, he proposed, "In the case of three entities, a balanced state exists if all three relations are positive in all respects or if two are negative and one posi-

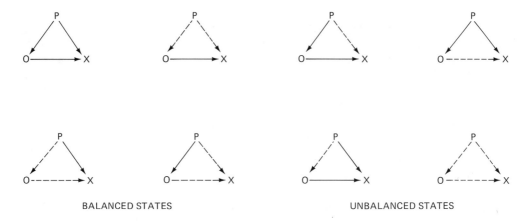

BALANCED STATES　　　　　　　　　　UNBALANCED STATES

FIGURE 1. Examples of balanced and unbalanced states, according to Heider's definition of balance. Solid lines represent positive, and broken lines negative, relations.

tive." Thus a balanced state is obtained when, for instance, P likes O, P likes X, and O likes X; or when P likes O, P dislikes X, and O dislikes X; or when P dislikes O, P likes X, and O dislikes X (see Figure 1). It should be noted that within Heider's conception a relation may be either positive or negative; degrees of liking cannot be represented. The fundamental assumption of balance theory is that an unbalanced state produces tension and generates forces to restore balance. This hypothesis was tested by Jordan. He presented subjects with hypothetical situations involving two persons and an impersonal entity to rate for "pleasantness." Half the situations were by Heider's definition balanced and half unbalanced. Jordan's data showed somewhat higher unpleasantness ratings for the unbalanced than the balanced situations.

Cartwright and Harary have cast Heider's formulations in graph-theoretical terms and derived some interesting consequences beyond those stated by Heider. Heider's concept allows either a balanced or an unbalanced state. Cartwright and Harary have constructed a more general definition of balance, with balance treated as a matter of degree, ranging from 0 to 1. Furthermore, their formulation of balance theory extended the notion to any number of entities, and an experiment by Morrissette similar in design to that of Jordan obtained evidence for Cartwright and Harary's derivations.

A notion very similar to balance was ad-

vanced by Newcomb in 1953. In addition to substituting A for P, and B for O, Newcomb took Heider's notion of balance out of one person's head and applied it to communication among people. Newcomb postulates a "strain toward symmetry" which leads to a communality of attitudes of two people (A and B) oriented toward an object (X). The strain toward symmetry influences communication between A and B so as to bring their attitudes toward X into congruence. Newcomb cites a study in which a questionnaire was administered to college students in 1951 following the dismissal of General MacArthur by President Truman. Data were obtained on students' attitudes toward Truman's decision and their perception of the attitudes of their closest friends. Of the pro-Truman subjects 48 said that their closest friends favored Truman and none that their closest friends were opposed to his decision. Of the anti-Truman subjects only 2 said that their friends were generally pro-Truman and 34 that they were anti-Truman. In a longitudinal study, considerable more convincing evidence was obtained in support of the strain-toward-symmetry hypothesis. In 1954 Newcomb set up a house at the University of Michigan which offered free rent for one semester for seventeen students who would serve as subjects. The residents of the house were observed, questioned, and rated for four to five hours a week during the entire semester. The study was then repeated with another set of seventeen students. The findings revealed a tendency for those who were attracted to one another to agree on many matters, including the way they perceived their own selves and their ideal selves, and their attractions for other group members. Moreover, in line with the prediction, these similarities, real as well as perceived, seemed to increase over time.

Newcomb also cites the work of Festinger and his associates on social communication in support of his hypothesis. Festinger's studies on communication have clearly shown that the tendency to influence other group members toward one's own opinion increases with the degree of attraction. More recently Burdick and Burnes reported two experiments in which measures of skin resistance (GSR) were obtained as an index of emotional reaction in the presence of balanced and unbalanced situations. They observed significant differences in skin resistance depending on whether the subjects agreed or disagreed with a "well-liked experimenter." In the second experiment Burdick and Burnes found that subjects who liked the experimenter tended to change their opinions toward greater agreement with his, and those who disliked him, toward greater disagreement. There are, of course, many other studies to show that the attitudes toward the communicator determines his persuasive effectiveness. Hovland and his co-workers have demonstrated these effects in several studies. They have also shown, however, that these effects are fleeting; that is, the attitude change produced by the communication seems to dissipate over time. Their interpretation is that over time subjects tend to dissociate the source from the message and are therefore subsequently less influenced by the prestige of the communicator. This proposition was substantiated by Kelman and Hovland, who produced attitude changes with a prestigeful communicator and retested subjects after a four-week interval with and without reminding the subjects about the communicator. The results showed that the permanence of the attitude change depended on the association with the source.

In general, the consequences of balance theories have up to now been rather limited. Except for Newcomb's longitudinal study, the experimental situations dealt mostly with subjects who responded to hypothetical situations, and direct evidence is scarce. The Burdick and Burnes experiment is the only one bearing more directly on the assumption that imbalance or asymmetry produces tension. Cartwright and Harary's mathematization of the concept of balance should, however, lead to important empirical and theoretical developments. One difficulty is that there really has not been a serious experimental attempt to *disprove* the theory. It is conceivable that some situations defined by the theory as unbalanced may in fact remain stable and produce no signficant pressures toward balance. Festinger once inquired in a jocular mood if it followed from balance theory that since he likes chicken, and since chickens like chicken feed, he must also like chicken feed or else experience the tension of imbalance. While this counterexample is, of course, not to be taken seriously, it does point to some difficulties in the concepts of balance. It is not clear from Heider's theory of balance and Newcomb's theory of symmetry what predictions are to be made when attraction of both P and O toward X exists but when the origin and nature of these attractions are different. In other words, suppose both P and O like X but for different reasons and in entirely different ways, as was the case with Festinger and the chickens. Are the consequences of balance theory the same then as in the case where P and O like X for the same reasons and in the same way? It is also not clear, incidentally, what the consequences are when the relation between P and O is cooperative and when it is competitive. Two men vying for the hand of the same fair maiden might experience tension whether they are close friends or deadly enemies.

In a yet unpublished study conducted by Harburg and Price at the University of Michigan, students were asked to name two of their best friends. When those named were of opposite sexes, subjects reported they would feel uneasy if the two friends liked one another. In a subsequent experiment subjects were asked whether they desired their good friends to like, be neutral to, or dislike one of their strongly disliked acquaintances, and whether they desired the disliked acquaintance to like or dislike the friend. It will be recalled that in either case

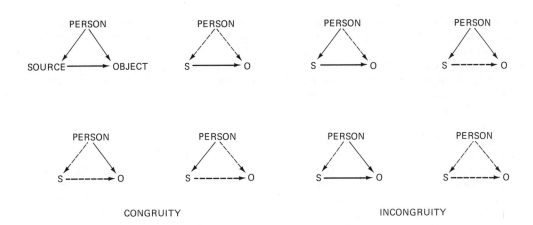

FIGURE 2. Examples of congruity and incongruity. Heavy lines represent assertions, light lines attitudes. Solid heavy lines represent assertions which imply a positive attitude on the part of the source, and broken heavy lines negative attitudes. Solid light lines represent positive, and broken light lines negative, attitudes.

a balanced state obtains only if the two persons are negatively related to one another. However, Harburg and Price found that 39 per cent desired their friend to be liked by the disliked acquaintance, and only 24 per cent to be disliked. Moreover, faced with the alternative that the disliked acquaintance dislikes their friend, 55 per cent as opposed to 25 per cent expressed uneasiness. These results are quite inconsistent with balance theory. Although one may want one's friends to dislike one's enemies, one may not want the enemies to dislike one's friends. The reason for the latter may be simply a concern for the friend's welfare.

Osgood and Tannenbaum's Principle of Congruity

The principle of congruity, which is in fact a special case of balance, was advanced by Osgood and Tannenbaum in 1955. It deals specifically with the problem of *direction* of attitude change. The authors assume that "judgmental frames of reference tend toward maximal simplicity." Thus, since extreme "black-and-white," "all-or-nothing," judgments are simpler than refined ones, valuations tend to move toward extremes or, in the words of the authors, there is "a continuing pressure toward polarization." Together with the notion of maximization of simplicity is the assumption of identity as being less com-

plex than the discrimination of fine differences. Therefore, related "concepts" will tend to be evaluated in a similar manner. Given these assumptions, the principle of congruity holds that when change in evaluation or attitude occurs it always occurs in the direction of increased congruity with the prevailing frame of reference. The paradigm of congruity is that of an individual who is confronted with an assertion regarding a particular matter about which he believes and feels in a certain way, made by a person toward whom he also has some attitude. Given that Eisenhower is evaluated positively and freedom of the press also positively, and given that Eisenhower (+) comes out in favor of freedom of the press (+), congruity is said to exist. But given that the *Daily Worker* is evaluated negatively, and given that the *Daily Worker* (−) comes out in favor of freedom of the press (+), incongruity is said to exist. Examples of congruity and incongruity are shown in Figure 2. The diagram shows the attitudes of a given individual toward the source and the object of the assertion. The assertions represented by heavy lines imply either positive or negative attitudes of the source toward the object. It is clear from a comparison of Figures 1 and 2 that in terms of their formal properties, the definitions of balance and congruity are identical. Thus, incongruity is said to exist when the attitudes toward the source and the object are similar and the assertion is negative, or when they are dissimilar and the assertion is positive. In comparison, unbalanced states are defined as having either one or all negative relations, which is of course equivalent to the above. To the extent that the person's attitudes are congruent with those implied in the assertion, a stable state exists. When the attitudes toward the person and the assertion are incongruent, there will be a tendency to change the attitudes toward the person and the object of the assertion in the direction of increased congruity. Tannenbaum obtained measures on 405 college students regarding their attitudes toward labor leaders, the *Chicago Tribune*, and Senator Robert Taft as sources, and toward legalized gambling, abstract art, and accelerated college programs as objects. Some time after the attitude scores were obtained, the subjects were presented with "highly realistic" newspaper clippings involving assertions made by the various sources regarding the concepts. In general, when the original attitudes toward the source and the concept were both positive and the assertion presented in the newspaper clippings was also positive, no significant attitude changes were observed in the results. When the original attitudes toward the source and the concept were negative and the assertion was positive, again no changes were obtained. As predicted, however, when a positively valued source was seen as making a positive assertion about a negatively valued concept, the attitude toward the source became less favorable, and toward the concept more favorable. Conversely, when a negatively

valued source was seen as making a positive assertion about a positively valued concept, attitudes toward the source became more favorable and toward the concept less favorable. The entire gamut of predicted changes was confirmed in Tannenbaum's data; it is summarized in the accompanying table, in which the direction of change is represented by either a plus or a minus sign, and the extent of change by either one or two such signs.

A further derivation of the congruity principle is that incongruity does not invariably produce attitude change, but that it may at times lead to incredulity on the part of the individual. When confronted by an assertion which stands in an incongruous relation to the person who made it, there will be a tendency not to believe that the person made the assertion, thus reducing incongruity.

There is a good deal of evidence supporting Osgood and Tannenbaum's principle of congruity. As early as 1921, H. T. Moore had subjects judge statements for their grammar, ethical infringements for their seriousness, and resolutions of the dominant seventh chord for their dissonance. After two and one-half months the subjects returned and were presented with judgments of "experts." This experimental manipulation resulted in 62 per cent reversals of judgments on grammar, 50 per cent of ethical judgments, and 43 per cent of musical judgments. And in 1935 in a study on a similar problem of prestige suggestion, Sherif let subjects rank sixteen authors for their literary merit. Subsequently, the subjects were given sixteen passages presumably written by the various

CHANGE OF ATTITUDE TOWARD THE SOURCE AND THE OBJECT WHEN POSITIVE
AND NEGATIVE ASSERTIONS ARE MADE BY THE SOURCE

ORIGINAL ATTITUDE TOWARD THE SOURCE	POSITIVE ASSERTION ABOUT AN OBJECT TOWARD WHICH THE ATTITUDE IS		NEGATIVE ASSERTION ABOUT AN OBJECT TOWARD WHICH THE ATTITUDE IS	
	POSITIVE	NEGATIVE	POSITIVE	NEGATIVE
Change of Attitude Toward the Source				
Positive	+	− −	− −	+
Negative	+ +	−	−	+ +
Change of Attitude Toward the Object				
Positive	+	+ +	− −	−
Negative	− −	−	+	+ +

authors previously ranked. The subjects were asked to rank-order the passages for literary merit. Although in actuality *all* the passages were written by Robert Louis Stevenson, the subjects were able to rank the passages. Moreover, the correlations between the merit of the author and the merit of the passage ranged from between .33 to .53. These correlations are not very dramatic, yet they do represent some impact of attitude toward the source on attitude toward the passage.

With respect to incredulity, an interesting experiment was conducted recently by Jones and Kohler in which subjects learned statements which either supported their attitudes or were in disagreement with them. Some of the statements were plausible and some implausible. The results were rather striking. Subjects whose attitudes favored segregation learned plausible pro-segregation statements and implausible anti-segregation statements much more rapidly than plausible anti-segregation and implausible pro-segregation statements. The reverse was of course true for subjects whose attitudes favored desegregation.

While the principle of congruity presents no new ideas, it has a great advantage over the earlier attempts in its precision. Osgood and Tannenbaum have formulated the principle of congruity in quantitative terms allowing for precise predictions regarding the extent and direction of attitude change—predictions which in their studies were fairly well confirmed. While balance theory allows merely a dichotomy of attitudes, either positive or negative, the principle of congruity allows refined measurements using Osgood's method of the semantic differential. Moreover, while it is not clear from Heider's statement of balance in just what direction changes will occur when an unbalanced state exists, such predictions can be made on the basis of the congruity principle.

Festinger's Theory of Cognitive Dissonance

Perhaps the largest systematic body of data is that collected in the realm of Festinger's dissonance theory. The statement of the dissonance principle is simple. It holds that two elements of knowledge ". . . are in dissonant relation if, considering these two alone, the obverse of one element would follow from the other." It further holds that dissonance ". . . being psychologically uncomfortable, will motivate the person to try to reduce dissonance and achieve consonance" and ". . . in addition to trying to reduce it, the person will actively avoid situations and information which would likely increase the dissonance." A number of rather interesting and provocative consequences follow from Festinger's dissonance hypothesis.

First, it is predicted that all decisions or choices result in dissonance to the extent that the alternative not chosen contains positive features which make it attractive also, and the alternative chosen contains features which might have resulted in rejecting it. Hence after making a choice people seek evidence to confirm their decision and so reduce dissonance. In the Ehrlich experiment cited by Cohen in this issue the finding was that new car owners noticed and read ads about the cars they had recently purchased more than ads about other cars.

Post-decision dissonance was also shown to result in a change of attractiveness of the alternative involved in a decision. Brehm had female subjects rate eight appliances for desirability. Subsequently, the subjects were given a choice between two of the eight products, given the chosen product, and after some interpolated activity (consisting of reading research reports about four of the appliances) were asked to rate the products again. Half the subjects were given a choice between products which they rated in a similar manner, and half between products on which the ratings differed. Thus in the first case higher dissonance was to be expected than in the second. The prediction from dissonance theory that there should be an increase in the attractiveness of the chosen alternative and decrease in the attractiveness of the rejected alternative was on the whole confirmed. Moreover, the further implication was also confirmed that the pressure to reduce dissonance (which was accomplished in the above experiment by changes in attractiveness of the alternatives) varies directly with the extent of dissonance.

Another body of data accounted for by the dissonance hypothesis deals with situations in which the person is forced (either by reward or punishment) to express an opinion publicly or make a public judgment or statement which is contrary to his own opinions and beliefs. In cases where the person actually makes such a judgment or expresses an opinion contrary to his own as a result of a promised reward or threat, dissonance exists between the knowledge of the overt behavior of the person and his privately held beliefs. Festinger also argues that in the case of non-compliance dissonance will exist between the knowledge of overt behavior and the anticipation of reward and punishment.

An example of how dissonance theory accounts for forced-compliance data is given by Brehm. Brehm offered prizes to eighth-graders for eating disliked vegetables and obtained measures of how well the children liked the vegetables. Children who ate the vegetables increased their liking for them. Of course, one might argue that a simpler explanation of the results is that the attractiveness of the prize generalized to the vegetable, or that, even more simply, the vegetables increased in utility because a reward came with them. However, this argument would also lead one to predict that the increment in attraction under such conditions is a *direct* function of the magnitude of the reward. Dissonance theory makes the opposite prediction, and therefore a test of the validity of the two explanations is possible. Data collected by Festinger and Carlsmith and by Aronson and Mills support the dissonance point of view. In Festinger and Carlsmith's experiment subjects were offered either $20 or $1 for telling someone that an experience which had actually been quite boring had been rather enjoyable and interesting. When measures of the subjects' private opinions about their actual enjoyment of the task were taken, those who were to be paid only $1 for the false testimony showed considerably higher scores than those who were to be paid $20. Aronson and Mills, on the other hand, tested the effects of negative incentive. They invited college women to join a group requiring them to go through a process of initiation. For some women the initiation was quite severe, for others it was mild. The prediction from dissonance theory that those who had to undergo severe initiation would increase their attraction for the group more than those having no initiation or mild initiation was borne out.

A third set of consequences of the theory of dissonance deals with exposure to information. Since dissonance occurs between cognitive elements, and since information may lead to change in these elements, the principle of dissonance should have a close bearing on the individual's commerce with information. In particular, the assumption that dissonance is a psychologically uncomfortable state leads to the prediction that individuals will seek out information reducing dissonance and avoid information increasing it. The study on automobile-advertising readership described above is a demonstration of this hypothesis. In another study Mills, Aronson, and Robinson gave college students a choice between an objective and an essay examination. Following the decision, the subjects were given articles about examinations presumably written by experts, and they were asked if they would like to read them. In addition, in order to vary the intensity of dissonance, half the subjects were told that the examination counted 70 per cent toward the final grade, and half that it counted only 5 per cent. The data were obtained in the form of rankings of the articles for preference. While there was a clear preference for reading articles containing positive information about the alternative chosen, no significant selective effects were found when the articles presented arguments against the given type of examination. Also, the authors failed to demonstrate effects relating selectivity in exposure to information to the magnitude of dissonance, in that no significant differences were found between subjects for whom the examination was quite important (70 per cent of the final grade) and those for whom it was relatively unimportant (5 per cent of the final grade).

Festinger was able to account for many other results by means of the dissonance principle, and in general his theory is rather successful in organizing a diverse body of empirical knowledge by means of a limited number of fairly reasonable assumptions. Moreover, from these reasonable assumptions dissonance theory generated several nontrivial and nonobvious consequences. The negative relationship between the magnitude of incentive and attraction of the object of false testimony is not at all obvious. Also not obvious is the prediction of an increase in proselytizing for a mystical belief following an event that clearly contradicts it. Festinger, Riecken, and Schachter studied a group of "Seekers"—people who presumably received a message from outer space informing them of an incipient major flood. When the flood failed to materialize on the critical date, instead of quietly withdrawing from the public scene, as one would expect, the "Seekers" summoned press representatives, gave extended interviews, and invited the public to visit them and be informed of the details of the whole affair. In a very recent study by Brehm, a "nonobvious" derivation from dissonance theory was tested. Brehm predicted that when forced to engage in an unpleasant activity, an individual's liking for this activity will increase more when he receives information essentially berating the activity than when he receives information promoting it. The results tended to support Brehm's prediction. Since negative information is said to increase dissonance, and since increased dissonance leads to an increased tendency to reduce it, and since the only means of dissonance reduction was increasing the attrac-tiveness of the activity, such an increase would in fact be expected.

Conclusions

The theories and empirical work dealing with consistencies are mainly concerned with intra-individual phenomena, be it with relationships between one attitude and another, between attitudes and values, or information, or perception, or behavior, or the like. One exception is Newcomb's concept of "strain toward symmetry." Here the concern is primarily with the interplay of forces among individuals which results in uniformities or consistencies among them. There is no question that the concepts of consistency, and especially the theory of congitive dissonance, account for many varied attitudinal phenomena. Of course, the various formulations of consistency do not pretend, nor are they able, to account completely for the phenomena they examine. Principles of consistency, like all other principles, are prefaced by the *ceteris paribus* preamble. . . .

18. *A Structural Theory of Attitude Dynamics*

MILTON ROSENBERG

Rosenberg's structural orientation to the understanding of attitude formation and change is one of several theories identified with the consistency perspective. Inconsistency between the cognitive and affective components of an individual's orientation toward an attitude object is seen as creating disequilibrium within that individual. This state of inconsistency or disequilibrium results in the individual's attempting to achieve consistency between the cognitive and affective components of his general attitude toward that object.

Common insight suggests that when stable feelings and beliefs refer to the same object they tend toward congruence with one another. This paper reports a structural theory of attitude dynamics which has been de-

Excerpted from an article by Milton Rosenberg in *The Public Opinion Quarterly*, 1960, **24**, 319–340, by permission of the author and publisher.

veloped through elaboration and extension of this insight. The theory is "structural" because it is not so much concerned with conditions and variables influencing the erection or reorganization of attitudes as with the problem of what attitudes *are* and the related problem of what happens "inside" them as they undergo change.

In support of the theory, a few experimental studies are briefly reviewed and one recent experiment is presented in greater detail. The last section of this report examines the theory for its bearing upon some problems in attitude measurement and persuasion.

Theory and Data

Most, though by no means all, definitions of the attitude concept have been restricted to the notion of emotional *"einstellung"*: when some object or class of objects regularly and dependably elicits an affective evaluative set that can be characterized as either "pro" or "con," "positive" or "negative," the individual is said to hold an attitude.

The theory outlined here flows from the contention that typically such stable affective sets are integrated with other psychological processes and that a more useful approach to attitude is one in which these processes are somehow represented. (Among the writers who have discussed this point are Chein, Katz and Stotland, Krech and Crutchfield, Peak, and Tolman.) One convenient way to do this is to conceive of an attitude as consisting of a *cognitive* as well as an affective component. Of the many possible kinds of cognitions about attitude objects one variety is here singled out as requiring representation in the minimum definition of the attitude concept: these are beliefs about the relations between the attitude object and other "objects" of affective significance to the individual. Thus a physician's negative attitude toward Federal medical insurance involves not only the fact of his affectively colored opposition but also the fact that he believes that Federal medical insurance, if instituted, would lead to "socialism" and "debasement of medical standards," which for him are negatively evaluated conditions, and that it would tend also to defeat, or reduce the likelihood of, such positively valued conditions as "professional freedom" and "maintenance of my income."

It will be argued in a later section of this paper that the elicitation and measurement of such attitudinal cognitions would help to reduce some of the major problems encountered in survey and experimental studies of social attitudes. But the full relevance and import of this argument will be apparent only if it is first demonstrated that a concern with both the affective and cognitive components of attitudes leads to a useful clarification of their structural properties and to a useful formulation of the attitude-change process.

ATTITUDE STRUCTURE As employed by behavioral scientists the word "structure" usually denotes some constellation of component events or processes so related to one another that the irreversible alteration of the quality or magnitude of a particular component will set in motion comparable changes in the other components. If the structure of an attitude is simply conceptualized in terms of two major components, the affective and the cognitive, confirmation of this conceptualization can be obtained by demonstrating that these components co-vary in close relation to each other. Evidence of such co-variation may be sought either with regard to stable attitudes or with regard to attitudes undergoing change.

The first-mentioned case is exemplified by a group of studies which show that within a population of persons varying in their attitudinal affects toward some social object there exist correlate and consistent variations in *beliefs* about the object. A similar study was conducted by the author in which the attitudinal affects of a large number of subjects were measured with regard to two separate social issues. One month later these same subjects took a "test of cognitive structure" requiring them to rate a group of "values" both for the degree of positive or negative reward each represented and also for the extent to which each value was believed to be fostered or defeated through the influence of each of the two attitude objects, respectively. From these judgments it was possible to compute an over-all "index of cognitive structure." By testing the relationship between this index and the independent measure of attitudinal affect it was shown that stable positive affect toward an attitude object is associated with beliefs relating that object to the attainment of positive values and the blocking of negative values, while stable negative affect toward an attitude object is associated with beliefs relating it to the attainment of negative values and the blocking of positive values. It was also confirmed that moderate attitudinal affects, as compared to extreme ones, are associated with beliefs that relate the attitude object to less important values, or if to important values then with less confidence as to the existence of clear-cut instrumental relationships between the attitude object and the values in question. Data from this study also indicated that variation in attitudinal affect is separately correlated with at least two aspects of the person's set of attitudinal cognitions. The first of these is the over-all believed potency of the attitude object for achieving or blocking the realization of his values; the second is the over-all felt importance of those values.

In general terms what emerged from this study was the conclusion that stable patterns of feeling toward social objects are accompanied by, or organized in close relationship with, stable beliefs consistent with those affects. The major key to such consistency appears to be that the individual tends to relate positive attitude objects to goal attainment and negative attitude objects to frustration of his goal orientations.

ATTITUDE CHANGE   The conception of attitude as an affective-cognitive structure has utility not only because it fits correlational findings such as those reported above but also because it suggests a way of theorizing about attitude change. The author's approach to the formulation of a structural theory of attitude change is founded on the following basic propositions:

(1) When the affective and cognitive components of an attitude are mutually consistent, the attitude is in a stable state.

(2) When these components are mutually inconsistent, to a degree that exceeds the individual's "tolerance limit" for such inconsistency, the attitude is in an unstable state.

(3) In such an unstable state the attitude will undergo reorganizing activity until one of three possible outcomes is achieved. These outcomes are: (a) rejection of the communications, or other forces, that engendered the original inconsistency between affect and cognition and thus rendered the attitude unstable, i.e. restoration of the original stable and consistent attitude; (b) "fragmentation" of the attitude through the isolation from each other of the mutually inconsistent affective and cognitive components; (c) accom-

modation to the original inconsistency-producing change so that a new attitude, consistent with that change, is now stabilized, i.e. attitude change.

In broad terms it is possible to specify some of the conditions under which each of these three outcomes is most likely to occur. Thus on the assumption that an individual's attitudes (defined as his consistent and persisting affective-cognitive structures) usually enable effective regulation of his adaptive behavior and are thus of value to him, it would be predicted that he will attempt to preserve them intact. From this it follows that *if possible* an individual will ultimately reject influences which have caused a temporary alteration in either the affective or cognitive component of one of his attitudes.

Frequently, however, the potency of the force leading to the alteration of one of the major components of an attitude is so great, or so persistent, as to make it *impossible* of rejection. When this is the case, fragmentation of the attitude is likely to result if, by virtue of the needs or "objective realities" that maintain it, the component persisting from the original attitude structure is unalterable. However, when this component is capable of alteration, it would be expected to give way, and general reorganization leading to the erection of a new attitude (i.e. attitude change) will result.

Restricting our concern to the case in which attitude change *does* occur, it may be asked: What are the specific lawful relationships between its occurrence and such variables as the content and organization of the change-inducing communication, the individual's level of tolerance for affective-cognitive inconsistency, and the relation of the attitude to other attitudes held by the same individual? No answer to such questions will be attempted here except to indicate that a large part of the available experimental literature on attitude change may be interpreted as indicating some of the parameters and parameter values that are associated with the attitude-change outcome in situations where inconsistency between attitude components has been produced.

The validity of a theoretical perspective, however, is not established by the claim that data collected for other purposes can be fitted to it; rather it is necessary to show that hypotheses derived from it are directly supported by available experimental evidence. For the purposes of this report, then, it seems desirable to elaborate not upon details and extensions of the propositions given above but rather upon the main attitude-change hypothesis resident in that set of propositions. In its simplest form this hypothesis is that *the production of inconsistency between the affective and cognitive portions of an attitude will culminate in a general attitude reorganization (through which the affective-cognitive inconsistency is reduced or eliminated) when (1) the inconsistency exceeds the individual's present tolerance limit and (2) the force producing it cannot be ignored or avoided.* In the remainder of this paper these two qualifying conditions are assumed, though not necessarily restated, whenever this hypothesis or data bearing upon it are discussed.

Two different predictions can be derived from this hypothesis. The first is simply that if a person somehow undergoes an "irreversible" change in his beliefs about an attitude object his affect toward that object will show corresponding change. The second prediction is the converse: if a person somehow undergoes an "irreversible" change in his *affect* toward an object his beliefs about that object will show corresponding change.

At present there is much clearer and stronger evidence available for the former prediction than for the latter one. Some of this evidence is based upon the impression of applied workers in the persuasion professions that if an audience member's beliefs about the value-serving and value-blocking powers of an "object" (such as a consumer product, a social policy, or a political candidate) can be reorganized, his feelings toward that object, and ultimately his behavior toward it, will undergo corresponding change. In addition to this kind of evidence there are scores of experimental studies in which communications designed to change cognitions about attitude objects are directed at subjects. A result found in the majority of these studies is that such communications, if potent enough, do produce further change effects in evaluative (affective) responses. Most of these studies, however, do not provide for a precise check of whether, and to what extent, the communications designed

to alter cognitions actually do so. Recently, however, a number of methods for the measurement of the cognitive aspects of attitude structures have become available. The test of cognitive structure used in the aforementioned correlational study by the author is one of these. It has since been employed in attitude change studies by Carlson and Peak. While neither of these experiments was intended as a test of the present theoretical formulation, both were concerned with the prediction that change in beliefs about an attitude object will generate change in feelings toward that object.

In Carlson's study subjects were tested on two separate occasions for their affective and cognitive responses toward the social object "Negroes being allowed to move into white neighborhoods." Intervening between the two testing sessions was a manipulation designed to produce changes in the "perceived instrumentality" aspect of a number of the subject's beliefs about the attitude object. Thus the typical anti-desegregation subject who at first believed that housing desegregation would *lower* the worth of property (a negative instrumental relation between the attitude object and the value "worth of property") was exposed to a special manipulation intended to transform his belief to one in which desegregation would be seen as *raising* the worth of property.

Comparison of the premanipulation and postmanipulation cognitive structure tests showed that the typical subject *did* alter his beliefs about the separate relationships of the attitude object to each of a number of separate values. Furthermore, it was found that, along with the production of such changes in the cognitive component of the person's attitude, consistent change, of roughly corresponding magnitude, was also obtained in his *affective* response toward the attitude object. Thus these data lend support to the first of the two predictions stated above; they confirm the hypothesis that the production of inconsistency in an attitude structure through modification of its cognitive component does eventuate in correlated consistency-restoring modification of its affective component.

In the study by Peak an attempt was made to produce a temporary alteration in the strength or pertinence of a general value ("making good grades") seen by her subjects to be instrumentally served by such attitude objects as the use of discussion techniques in college courses. It was shown that when attitudinal cognition changes, in the sense that the goal seen as served by the attitude object increases in its importance to the person, the affective response toward that object undergoes corresponding change.

While it does not deal with the sort of large-scale affective-cognitive inconsistency that Carlson is concerned with, this study too seems to demonstrate that change in the cognitive portion of an attitude tends to generate consistent change in its affective portion. A further value is that it shows that affect modification will be fostered not only by changes in the "instrumentality" aspect of cognitions about attitude objects but also by changes in the felt importance of the goals believed to be attained through the attitude object's instrumental powers.

However, to demonstrate, as our basic hypothesis asserts, that affective-cognitive inconsistency (rather than mere cognitive reorganization) is an underlying condition for attitude change, the reverse prediction must also be confirmed: it must be shown that the production of an irreversible change in an attitude's affective component will generate corresponding change in its cognitive component.

This prediction, unlike its opposite, does not receive unequivocal confirmation in the available experimental literature. Nevertheless, some of the attitude change techniques that have been reported, particularly those involving direct approval or disapproval from peer groups or prestigeful figures, might be interpreted as producing direct modification of affective responses. A similar impression is created when nonexperimental examples of "emotional" persuasion techniques are examined. But in either the experimental or nonexperimental case it is likely that such influence procedures also tend to directly modify some attitudinal cognitions.

A specific aim in two recent studies by the author was to develop and investigate the effects of a "pure" experimental manipulation of attitudinal affect, one which did not directly act upon the cognitive content of the attitude being modified. The intention was to test experimentally the second of the two predictions drawn from the main hypothesis given above. The manipulation used in these studies involved posthypnotic suggestion of affect change. The second of these studies will be described in detail both for its bearing upon the main hypothesis and also to provide some idea of the style of experimentation by which the theory is being more fully developed.

AN EXPERIMENT INVOLVING DIRECT AND SUSTAINED ALTERATION OF ATTITUDINAL AFFECT   In the first study involving hypnotic manipulation of attitudinal affect eleven experimental and eleven control subjects were tested on two separate occasions for their affective and cognitive responses toward various attitude objects. Between the two testing sessions the experimental subjects (all of whom were capable of achieving deep hypnosis) were placed in hypnosis and then given the suggestion that upon awakening their affective reactions toward two separate attitude objects would be changed (from positive to negative, or vice versa) and that they would have no memory of the suggestion's having been made until the presentation of an amnesia-removing signal. It was assumed that such posthypnotic suggestion would foster strong and "irreversible" affect change for as long as posthypnotic amnesia was maintained. In a control group which received no affect manipulation the affective and cognitive responses toward attitude objects remained stable from the first to the second test administrations. In the experimental group significant change occurred not only in the subjects' affects toward the attitude objects but also in their *beliefs* about the relationships between each of those objects and various "values" deemed important by the subjects. Additional control data ruled out the possibility that these changes could have been due to any general tendency toward response instability rather than to the effects of the affect manipulation.

By using a second control procedure in which subjects "role-played" the occurrence of affect change, and by interviewing conducted both before and after removal of the experimental subjects' posthypnotic amnesias, it was found that the affect and belief changes achieved by the experimental subjects were experienced by them as legitimate and veridical; the subjects really felt and *believed* differently about the attitude objects on which they had received the posthypnotic suggestions of affect change. Aspects of this study have been reported in a number of publications, and it will not be further described or discussed here except to note that its replication and extension were the main purposes of the study described below.

In this second study the hypnotic manipulation of attitudinal affect was kept in force for a full week rather than for a period of one or two hours, as was the case in the earlier study. Eight new experimental subjects were used in this experiment and were tested for both their affective and cognitive responses to three different attitude objects on six different occasions. The first of these occasions came three days before the delivery of a posthypnotic suggestion of affect change with regard to one of the three attitude objects. In all cases the subject's original affect toward this object ("the abandonment of the United States policy of giving economic aid to foreign nations") was originally negative and was hypnotically manipulated in the positive direction in a way that involved no reference to any of his beliefs about the attitude object's relationships with any of his values. Specifically each subject was told in hypnosis:

After you awake, and continuing until our next meeting, you will feel very strongly opposed to the United States policy of giving economic aid to foreign nations. The mere idea of the United States giving economic aid to foreign nations will make you feel displeased and disgusted. Until your next meeting with me you will continue to feel very strong and thorough opposition to the United States policy of economic aid to foreign nations. You will have no memory whatsoever of this suggestion's having been made . . . until the amnesia is removed by me giving you the signal at our next session.

Following the delivery of the posthypnotic suggestion the subject was awakened from hypnosis and the measures of affect and cognition were readministered. Two days later, and two days after that, these tests were again administered. Exactly one week after the hypnotic session the subject's amnesia for that session was removed and the experiment fully explained to him. Up to this point in the sequence all subjects had been led to believe that the hypnotic session and the testing sessions (the former conducted by the author and the latter by an associate) had no connection with each other, that they represented different and unrelated experiments.

However, toward the end of the first week, two subjects did gradually develop vague and uncertain suspicions that some sort of hypnotic manipulation might have been used. But both insisted that they had no memory of any such event, that they were merely "reasoning" from the fact that they had undergone sudden and intense changes in their feelings and beliefs on the foreign aid issue.

Three days after amnesia removal, and seven days after that, the measures of affect and cognition were again administered to all subjects. Before presenting the data that bear on the prediction that the production of strong affect change generates corresponding change in associated cognitions it will be necessary to describe the separate measures of affect and cognition by which these data were obtained. These measures were similar to those used in the author's two earlier studies described above.

The measure of affect consisted of three scales covering a 16-point range from "extremely in favor" to "extremely opposed." One of these scales dealt with the issue on which the subjects received the hypnotic affect manipulation. The other two scales dealt with issues that were not subjected to any manipulation and thus served as control areas against which changes on the manipulated issue could be compared.

The measure of the cognitive component involved thirty-two so-called "value cards." Sample value items are "all human beings having equal rights," "people being well educated," "making one's own decisions," "attaining economic security." In taking this test the subject first judges each of the thirty-two values in terms of its importance to him, using a scale with a range of 21 points. The scale runs from -10 (which stands for "gives me maximum dissatisfaction") to $+10$ (which stands for "gives me maximum satisfaction"). He then judges each of these same values in terms of whether, and to what extent, he thinks it will be attained or blocked as a consequence of the attitude object. On this task he uses an 11-point scale running from −5 (which stands for "extreme blocking") through −0 (which stands for "neither blocked nor attained") to +5 (which stands for "extreme attainment"). Thus at the end of the testing procedure there are available for each value term the subject's judgment of its importance as a positive or negative state and his judgment of how that value's realization will be affected by the attitude object. These two judgments are algebraically multiplied for each value term respectively. In turn the thirty-two products are algebraically summed. The resulting quantity is taken as an index of the over-all import of the cognitive structure associated with the attitude object. In effect this index expresses, in a single number, the extent to which the subject sees the attitude object as serving the attainment or blocking of his values. This index was separately obtained for each of the three attitude objects (the one subjected to affect manipulation and the two not subjected to such manipulation) from the data collected during each of the six separate testing sessions.

To test the prediction that the production of a large and irreversible affect change will generate comparable changes in beliefs about the attitude object, affect-change scores and cognition-change scores were computed for the three separate attitude objects. These scores referred to the differences between the index obtained from the subject's premanipulation test performance and each of the five postmanipulation test performances respectively. By application of the Randomization Test for Matched Pairs it was possible to determine whether the subject's affect-change and cognition-change scores for the manipulated attitude object were significantly greater than the means of their change scores for the two nonmanipulated attitude objects.

As shown in the accompanying table, until the amnesia removal the subjects showed significant change not only in their affective responses toward "abandoning the United States policy of economic aid to foreign nations" but also in their beliefs about how such abandonment will affect the realization of their values. When the test records are examined it is found that these statistically significant differences are based upon large-scale shifts in both affect and cognition. Thus a typical subject changes his affective evaluation from extreme opposition to abandonment of foreign aid to extreme approval. At the same time he changes many of his related beliefs. For example, whereas before the affect manipulation he believes that abandoning foreign aid would defeat such positive goals (for him) as "the avoidance

PROBABILITIES OF THE DIFFERENCES BETWEEN THE CHANGE SCORES
FOR THE MANIPULATED AND NONMANIPULATED ATTITUDES*

TESTING SESSIONS FROM WHICH CHANGE SCORES ARE COMPUTED†	AFFECT CHANGE	COGNITIVE CHANGE
Session 1–Session 2	.008	.024
Session 1–Session 3	.008	.024
Session 1–Session 4	.008	.008
Session 1–Session 5	N.S.‡	.056
Session 1–Session 6	N.S.‡	.064

* All probabilities are two-tailed and are obtained through application of the Randomization Test for Matched Pairs. All significant differences are in the direction: manipulated attitude > mean of nonmanipulated attitudes.

† The first testing session occurred three days before hypnotic manipulation of affect toward "foreign aid"; the second testing session came immediately after the manipulation; and the third and fourth sessions came three and five days, respectively, after the manipulation. The fifth and sixth sessions came ten days and seventeen days after the manipulation (i.e. three days and ten days after "amnesia removal"). The same tests were used in each of the six sessions—the affective scales dealing with the foreign aid issue and with the two unmanipulated issues, and the cognitive structure measures for each of those issues.

‡ N.S. = not significant.

of economic depression" and would serve such negative goals as "the open expression of disagreement between people" he now sees the abandoment of foreign aid as *fostering* the former goal and *defeating* the latter.

Nor is this the only kind of change observed in the subject's cognitions about the attitude object. He also alters his evaluation of some of the value terms, sometimes even to the extent of changing positive values to negative ones or negative values to positive ones. In the latter case beliefs about the relationship between the attitude object and such transformed values are usually left unaltered, thus reversing their import.

It should not be concluded however that *all* the beliefs expressed by the typical subject are consistent with the altered attitudinal affect. Usually some of his original beliefs persist within the new structure and are inconsistent with its over-all import, though typically the intensity with which these beliefs are held is reduced after the affect manipulation. But in the light of the theoretical propositions advanced above it is not assumed that total and perfect consistency need obtain in a stable attitude structure; all that is assumed is that in such a stable structure affective-cognitive inconsistency, if present at all, is at a level below the individual's tolerance limit. At any rate, examination of the postmanipulation attitude structures of the subjects reveals, in most cases, an impressive degree of cognitive reorganization in the direction consistent with the altered affect.

As in the first study involving affect manipulation, interview procedures revealed that the subjects' changes in affect and cognition were *experienced* by them rather than merely "role-played." Indeed, the findings reported in the last two rows of the table provide a special kind of evidence to this effect in connection with the subjects' cognitive changes. These findings refer to data obtained after the posthypnotic amnesia was removed and the nature of the experiment was fully explained to each subject. While the removal of amnesia for the affect manipulation is followed by a return to the initial affective response, enough of the cognitive changes persist to make for a significant difference between the cognition-change scores on the manipulated issue and the mean of the cognition-change scores on the two non-manipulated issues.

Since after amnesia removal the subjects' affective responses reverted to their original scale positions it might be contended that the significant persistence of some of the cognitive changes calls into question our conception of attitude as an internally consistent affective-cognitive structure. Examination of the subjects' test performances reveals, however, that while a number of altered beliefs do persist, a still larger number are changed back to their original form. Thus, after amnesia removal, in seven out of the eight cases the over-all index of cognitive structure has a negative sign and is thus consistent with the restored negative affect.

Many other aspects of this study, including data drawn from a group of unhypnotized control subjects, have not been covered in this account but will be detailed in a later report. But the data that have been reported or reviewed in this paper seem to provide strong confirmation for the general hypothesis that the production of affective-cognitive inconsistency within a previously stable attitude makes for attitude change. The confirmation of this hypothesis argues for the validity of the more general set of theoretical propositions from which it was derived.

5 *Group Processes*

Not all social behavior occurs in a group setting. An individual may show the influence of other persons when alone with his thoughts; and even when others are present, key influences may come from persons far removed. Nevertheless, most of the continuity in social behavior comes through groups— groups of persons present in face-to-face settings and the larger organizations of which such groups may be part.

In Part 5 the focus is upon processes that are primary ingredients of group behavior. Attention will not be paid so much to particular kinds of groups as to the social psychological dynamics typical of group behavior generally.

A case study of group behavior, "Stoerpenberg Camp," by Gerald Raines, is the opening reading of this part. This report of a prisoner-of-war setting also serves as the initial focus for Project 8, "Discussion Groups." This project provides a vehicle for firsthand group experience to accompany the analyses of the readings.

One way to conceive of groups is as systems of ongoing interaction. The group can be viewed as the product of what individuals say and do to each other. Through such interaction, expectations about future behavior develop, including the roles different members may be expected to play in group activity. Such a focus upon groups as systems of interaction is illustrated by Philip Slater's article, "Role Differentiation in Small Groups."

Another way to conceive of groups is as the product of more elementary relationships between the individuals involved. While not necessarily contradicting a group interaction approach, a "social exchange" approach puts the emphasis upon the smaller units of interaction. In his article, "Social Behavior as Exchange," George C. Homans presents the case for viewing group behavior according to a model of more elementary exchanges between individuals.

The final reading of Part 5 presents a somewhat detailed series of experiments on the apparent increase in risk-taking by persons in a group setting. George Madaras and Daryl Bem in "Risk and Conservatism in Group Decision-Making" attempt to solve the mystery of when and why this effect occurs. The results of their analysis remind us of the way broader cultural values may affect decision processes of groups. In other words, groups are never completely self-contained entities, but they always to some extent reflect the broader organizations of institutionalized ways and cultural values that members bring to the group.

19. *Stoerpenberg Camp (Case Study)*

GERALD RAINES

The following case study of group formation is based upon a report by Gerald Raines, a participant in the events described below. While names of places and persons have been changed, the main events did occur as described.

They moved about the building peering out the windows at the drab winter landscape, or sat around the tables—now and then dropping down on a bunk, hands under head, to lie staring at the ceiling. They were one hundred and sixty American prisoners of war, all having been captured in the Battle of the Bulge two months ago, now the Kreigsarbeiter Kommando unit at Stoerpenberg, somewhere in western Germany.

The first two days they had done little but lie on their bunks and wait to be fed. Slowly drifting about from one man to another, casual conversations brought out what little was known about their situation. All were privates, not N.C.O.'s or officers, all had been in combat units of one kind or another. They represented a fair cross-section of their country, as no regional group dominated. Some of the men had been able to talk to the guards and found out that the camp was at the edge of a large town, and that they were to be used as workers in the fields nearby and in general utility work about the town.

They were housed in a gymnasium that had been part of a group of factory buildings. It evidently had been used as a worker's recreation center. At one end of the building a few tumbling mats and gymnastic bars were all that remained of the building's former utility. Down the center of the building was an aisle formed by two rows of tables. Behind the tables on each side were rows of

This report was originally prepared for use in social science classes at the University of Kansas. It is here used with special acknowledgement to the members of the Department of Sociology, University of Kansas, who have given permission for its present use. All rights reserved by the University of Kansas.

double-decked bunks, while at the far end of the gymnasium three rooms were partitioned off from the central part. The center room was fitted with washing troughs, to the north a storage room, and to the south a lavatory. At this end of the building on the outside was a narrow long plot of ground used as an exercise yard for prisoners.

By the next day the German officer in charge informed the prisoners that it would be necessary for them to choose a group leader. This leader would convey to the group the regulations and orders of the work unit and would be responsible for the carrying out of such living quarters rules as would be found to be necessary for health and sanitation.

After the interpreter told the prisoners of this, they began to discuss it among themselves. They were seated around the tables; either at the tables or lying on their bunks were the only places with enough space for two or three of them to get together. It was the general opinion that an election should be held. Very shortly men at different tables began to move around to other tables advocating their candidate. Finally by action of the group, certain men were proposed as candidates. The votes were taken by show of hands. If a proposed candidate seemed to have a fairly large number of people behind him he was considered in the running, and if not, was immediately dropped. The choice soon narrowed down to a few men. These men were presented to the group by their backers and each candidate had campaign speeches made in his favor. After each candidate had had his case presented, the final vote was taken by a show of hands. The choice was Kent, a man of good physical appearance, who had demonstrated commanding personality and superior social presence during the leader election.

Kent immediately began his office by bringing up the very important question of how the prisoners' food was to be distributed. Under the conditions food was of paramount importance and was without doubt the topic most constantly on every prisoner's mind. Kent suggested that the tables were the logical basis of distribution and therefore each table should choose a table leader and then consider how to share the food ration. The men at the tables responded quickly to this and turned their attention to the choice of table leaders. The choices here were not made as in the election of the group leader. There was no formal "politicking," rather an informal mulling over of those at the tables. Certain aspects of prisoners' backgrounds seemed to have weight, such as education, having acted as a non-commissioned officer, and especially the ability to verbalize easily and fluently. Since at each table there were informal sub-groups of men who had previously had acquaintance, there was more knowledge of individual backgrounds than in the choice of the group leaders.

Shortly after the table leaders were chosen, several of them went to Kent and suggested that they set up a council to govern the unit. Kent agreed and thereafter the council was convened regularly. At the council the table leaders were informed of any developments regarding the German administration of the work unit so that they might inform their tables. After this various problems were discussed as to living arrangements, clean-up details and all the minutiae of their every-day existence. Most of the matters were settled by the council at its meetings, but if at times they felt a matter to be an exception, it was returned to the tables for a referendum among the members before action was taken. If one of the men felt he had a legitimate "gripe" he went to the table leader. If the table leader could not settle it to his satisfaction, then the table leader would bring it before the council at their next meeting. Here a final settlement of the matter would be made except for the rare cases in which it was decided to have a mandate from the group at large.

In a few weeks the formal structure of the group was functioning very effectively. The prisoners were organized into compact units, their economic and social order had been established, the routine necessities of their life were met, with each man having certain duties to perform in a regular rotation for the benefit of all. Behind the formal structure was the code of the group. The code was not a formal thing, no one had written it down or made speeches about it, yet everyone knew what it was, lived by it or knew what to expect if he did not.

The first and most important rule was that of no stealing, with great emphasis on food and tobacco. It was desirable to keep as clean as possible, not to "let go" even though being clean required some effort. As to the work being done for the Germans, it was perfectly justifiable to exert as little as necessary to get by, but in doing so not to get caught. It was also permissible to steal from the Germans, in fact in any way to commit any act that would result in advantage to a prisoner, but he must not get caught. If caught the prisoner's duty was clear, to identify himself as the sole participant and to bear the brunt of German displeasure. There were to be no formal efforts at "crossing" the Germans on the part of the group.

Within two weeks the mass of men who had been thrown together in the gymnasium at Stoerpenberg had evolved from a condition of social chaos into a small but complete society that within the environmental limitations met the pragmatic test—it worked.

In the third week of March, 1945, as the result of an incident among the members of Table Five, the leaders of the work unit suddenly found themselves with a difficult problem. One of the men at the table was accused of stealing food and the uproar over it threatened to break up the work unit's system. One of the members of Table Five was a man named Court. From the very first, Ainslee, the table leader of Number Five, had been aware that Court did not fit into any of the informal groups at the table, nor did he seem to have any friends at any of the other tables. His manner was listless and apathetic, withdrawn from the life about him, his reactions rather slow and confused when any situation arose that required him to participate in some activity. His personal habits were very lax to the point of being filthy, even though some facilities existed for washing and grooming. It was Ainslee's opinion that Court was mentally ill or had suffered some intense experience during his capture that had dulled his perception of his present situation.

Whatever the reasons, Court was one of the very few men who did not actively participate in the life of the group. His sole interest was food, not only the ration issued, but the saving of bread from the daily issue made. This bread he accumulated by not eating all that he was given, each day adding another small portion to his bunk. Court was very suspicious of his fellow prisoners and spent much of his free time in carefully checking over his hoard. By the middle of March much of the bread he had managed to save was stale and unpalatable; indeed he was not seen to eat any of it, but rather derived his satisfaction from handling it and knowing that it was there when he wished to look at it.

An interested observer of Court's behavior was Bartrum, physically the largest man at Table Five. On several occasions Bartrum had watched Court checking his hoard. He had remarked on the futility of Court's actions in casual conversations with others. Many of them agreed with him and as food was the most important aspect of the group life, some felt that it was wrong for one man to waste food that could be well utilized by others. However, these sentiments never became more organized than the opinions expressed in conversation.

Each evening the men of the work units stood in the aisle and were counted by one of the German noncommissioned officers. Late in March Bartrum was late to the head-count formation and, immediately after the men were dismissed, returned quietly to his bunk. A short time later the men around Table Five were startled by hoarse cries. Court was moving around and around his bunk, searching here and there, uttering moans and weeping. Ainslee and several others moved quickly over to Court. Apparently much of his hoard of bread had been stolen.

In a few minutes a large crowd of the men had collected about Court's bunk and the news of his loss passed quickly among them. Soon everywhere men were grouping together, glancing toward Court, who had continued his sorrowful lament. The low hum of many voices began to comment on the fact that Bartrum had been late to head count. Little by little a remark here, a comment there, a growing suspicion began to arise among them. Ainslee had decided to go to Kent and organize a search among the members of the group when a few of the men walked over to Bartrum's bunk and began looking around. Bartrum began to protest this action when suddenly one of the men found a chunk of bread tucked away at one end of the bunk. He shouted aloud his find and turned upon Bartrum. A thick knot of men rapidly swirled about Bartrum, cursing, shouting, and striking at him. Bartrum attempted to fight clear, stammering incoherently, as more and more joined the mass about him. The room was full of the uproar, and the confusion spread until every man in the room was part of the hubbub. Kent, the group leader, had caught the significance of the cries of the outraged men around Bartrum and realized that if he did not act quickly Bartrum would be killed. Throwing himself into the crowd, he fought his way to Bartrum. Seizing Bartrum by the collar, Kent managed to crawl up on top of a table where he could be seen above the mob, still holding Bartrum firmly. At first he could not make himself heard, but as more and more of the men saw who it was that held Bartrum, they became quieter. Taking a deep breath, Kent tried again, "Okay, I hate the bastard as much as you do, but this isn't the way to do it." Howls of protest greeted his statement but Kent kept on talking, holding out that the man must be handled by their regular set-up and not by a mob. Meanwhile several of the table leaders had fought their way to Kent and now began to ring about him.

Slowly the protest began to lessen, and Kent bore down on the fact that the group would have its chance to take action after the council had tried Bartrum. As the crowd became quieter, Kent felt the immediate danger was over, and so calling to the table leaders to come with him, he jumped down from the table and, holding tightly to Bartrum, pushed his way through the men. They let him pass and the leaders walked with Kent and Bartrum to the end of the room. Here on the old tumbling mats they sat down to consider what they must do.

20. *Role Differentiation in Small Groups*

PHILIP E. SLATER

When persons come together in unstructured discussion groups, is there any tendency for certain kinds of roles to emerge out of the interaction between individuals? If so, what kinds of roles are most likely to appear? Slater's work, described in the following excerpts, suggests answers to these questions.

Small group research provides a most fruitful meeting-ground for psychological and sociological thinking. Few fields of study lend themselves so easily to this dual perspective. The concept of "role" holds a potentially strategic position in this rapprochement, but its use in empirical studies has thus far left this potentiality unexploited.

We might define a role as a more or less coherent and unified system of items of behavior. With even this minimal definition it becomes apparent that role performance in this small group situation will have both consequences which are important to the functioning of the group in which the role is performed and personal consequences of importance to the individual who performs it. Similarly, an individual may be motivated to perform a role both by specific inducements offered by the group and by more general needs operating within the individual himself.

The rather general failure to consider simultaneously both of these aspects of role performance has constituted a very real stumbling-block in small group research. This paper will attempt to illustrate the way in which consideration of both psychological and sociological factors may aid in the interpretation of tendencies for members of small experimental groups to behave in systematically differentiated ways.

Our research in this area has been centered around five problems:

(1) To what extent do group members distinguish between different *kinds* of favorable evaluations of their fellow group members, or, conversely, to what degree do they tend to rank fellow members similarly on criteria assumed to be different? A consistent tendency for subjects to rate one man high on one criterion and another man high on a second criterion would constitute prima facie evidence for the existence of a set of differentiated roles, at least in the minds of the subjects themselves.

(2) What effect do repeated interactions have upon such discriminations? Since randomly composed laboratory groups are rather ephemeral organizations, it might be assumed necessary for some time to elapse before even a crude prototype of the elaborate kind of differentiation found in permanent groups would appear.

(3) How do individuals differentiated by their fellow group members differ in their behavior? How can we characterize this behavior, and how do these characterizations relate to the criteria upon which the individuals were rated?

(4) How do such individuals respond to each other? Do differentiated "specialists" cooperate or compete with each other?

(5) What is the relationship of personality factors to role differentiation? Are there factors which predispose an individual to assume a particular role? What is the effect upon the group as a whole of variations in the motivations of various "specialists"?

Procedure

The sample consisted of 20 groups of from three to seven men each, with four groups of each size. Each group met four times, so that

Excerpted from Philip E. Slater, "Role Differentiation in Small Groups," *American Sociological Review*, 1955, **20**, 300–303 and 308–310. Used by permission of the publisher and author.

a total of 80 meetings were studied. The groups were composed of paid male undergraduates at Harvard who knew each other only casually, if at all, prior to the first meeting. They were told that we were engaged in the study of group discussion and decision-making, and that we would observe them through a one-way mirror. Each subject was given a five-page factual summary of an administrative problem which the subjects were asked to solve as a group, assuming the role of administrative staff to the central authority in the case under discussion. They were given 40 minutes to discuss the case and decide (a) why the persons involved in the case were behaving as they did, and (b) what the central authority should do about it. A new case was used for each meeting. The subjects' remarks during the discussion were classified according to Bales' (1951) set of interaction categories. Following each session the subjects filled out a questionnaire which included the following questions:

(a) Who contributed the best ideas for solving the problem? Please rank the members in order. *Include yourself.*

(b) Who did the most to guide the discussion and keep it moving effectively? Please rank the members in order. *Include yourself.*

(c) How well did you personally like each of the other members? Rate each member on a scale from 0 to 7, where zero means, "I feel perfectly neutral toward him," and seven means "I like him very much."

At the end of the fourth session an additional question was asked:

(d) Considering all the sessions, which member of the group would you say stood out most definitely as a leader in the discussion? How would you rank the others? *Include yourself.*

These questions, along with the Bales interaction scores, constituted the major source of data for this study.

Prior to analysis of the data, each of the 20 groups was assigned to one of two classes, according to whether the members showed high or low agreement on their responses to questions (a) and (b) above. This procedure was followed on the basis of findings by Heinicke and Bales (1953) that these two types of groups showed different developmental characteristics. It was felt that role

differentiation might take different forms in groups with varying degrees of agreement on status ratings.

* * *

Specialization as Perceived by Subjects

Subjects in this sample may be ranked in five different ways for each session. From the interaction scores it was possible to assign rank order to the men according to who talked the most and who *received* the most interaction. From the post-meeting questions it was possible to rank the men on the perceived quality of their ideas, their perceived ability to guide the discussion, and their personal popularity. Our interest in role differentiation stemmed from the relationships of these rank orders to each other.

A simple method of seeking out tendencies toward specialization consists of counting the number of times a man with top rank on any one of these five measures holds top rank on none of the other measures. Such a man might be considered a "specialist," and if such "specialists" are found in one characteristic more often than in the others, this characteristic might be considered a specialized one.

Table 1 indicates that there are more cases in which the best-liked man holds top ranking in only that one characteristic than cases of any other sort of isolated prominence. The difference between this characteristic and the other four is significant at the .001 level, using a chi-square test. Popularity is apparently a relatively specialized achievement.

Further information may be obtained by

TABLE 1. NUMBER OF SESSIONS*
OUT OF A POSSIBLE 80 IN WHICH A
GIVEN PERSON HOLDS TOP POSITION
IN ONE AND ONLY ONE RANK ORDER
OUT OF FIVE POSSIBLE RANK ORDERS

Talking	11.0
Receiving	10.5
Ideas	12.0
Guidance	11.6
Liking	30.4
Total	75.5

*The decimals arise from ties in rankings.

proceeding in the reverse manner and asking rather, how often does the same person in a particular group hold top position on two characteristics? Table 2 shows, for each pair of characteristics, the percentage of cases in which such coincidence occurs.

Table 2 indicates that for both High and Low status-consensus groups, popularity is least often associated with other characteristics. The difference is significant at the .01 level in both cases, using a chi-square test. Marked differences between High and Low groups appear, however, when we examine the table further. The two participation measures, Talking and Receiving, are significantly less often associated with Ideas in the Low groups than in the High (.01 level), and Ideas and Guidance are significantly less often associated with Liking (.01 level). In other words, in the High groups high participation (Talking and Receiving) is associated with high rated task ability (Ideas and Guidance), but neither is strongly associated with popularity. In the Low groups the association of high rated task ability with popularity is even lower (less in fact than chance expectancy), while the association of high participation with high rated task ability tends to break down.

Note that Talking and Receiving are strongly associated in both High and Low groups, as are Ideas and Guidance. This fact perhaps justifies the groupings made above, which will be used throughout this section wherever they seem to be appropriate.

These techniques for determining the amount of specialization among these various characteristics are not entirely satisfactory, since they deal only with the top man on each rank order. To meet this problem, mean rank order correlations between all pairs of characteristics were computed, and are shown in Table 3.

First, as we might expect from Tables 1 and 2, the correlations between Liking and the other four characteristics are the lowest correlations in both the High and Low group matrices. Second, the tendency for amount of participation and rated task ability to be highly correlated in the High groups and poorly correlated in the Low groups is even more sharply outlined in Table 3 than in Table 2.

Differences between the correlations in Table 3 were tested in the following manner: the 10 correlations in each matrix were divided into three sets, with the Talking-Receiving and Ideas-Guidance correlations in the first set, the four correlations between

TABLE 2. PERCENTAGE OF TOTAL NUMBER OF SESSIONS (80) IN WHICH THE SAME PERSON HOLDS TOP POSITION IN TWO RANK ORDERS AT THE SAME TIME

| HIGH STATUS-CONSENSUS GROUPS | | | | |
	T	R	I	G	L
Talking		51.3	63.3	36.5	20.5
Receiving			53.3	39.0	34.3
Ideas				56.3	32.0
Guidance					45.5
Liking					

| LOW STATUS-CONSENSUS GROUPS | | | | |
	T	R	I	G	L
Talking		52.5	43.7	40.0	32.0
Receiving			28.7	42.5	37.0
Ideas				50.0	16.5
Guidance					20.0
Liking					

TABLE 3. INTERCORRELATIONS BETWEEN TALKING, RECEIVING, AND RATINGS ON IDEAS, GUIDANCE, AND LIKING. MEAN RANK ORDER CORRELATIONS OF 64 SESSIONS (SIZE 3 EXCLUDED)

| HIGH STATUS-CONSENSUS GROUPS | | | | |
	T	R	I	G	L
Talking		.88	.80	.75	.38
Receiving			.74	.74	.46
Ideas				.83	.41
Guidance					.49
Liking					

| LOW STATUS-CONSENSUS GROUPS | | | | |
	T	R	I	G	L
Talking		.69	.48	.51	.10
Receiving			.44	.52	.16
Ideas				.71	.14
Guidance					.27
Liking					

the participation measures and the rated task ability measures in the second set, and the four correlations between Liking and the other measures in the third set. The three sets were then tested against each other by means of sign tests. Note that in the first set the correlations are high in both High and Low groups, in the second set they are high in the High groups and relatively low in the Low groups, while in the third set they are relatively low in both.

In the High groups there was no significant difference between the first two sets. The first set was significantly higher than the third set, at the .01 level, and the second set was significantly higher than the third at the .05 level. In the Low groups the first set was significantly higher than the second and the second significantly higher than the third, both at the .01 level.

Popularity, then, again appears to be the most specialized characteristic, regardless of the degree of status-consensus in the group. In Low status-consensus groups, however, the tendency for Liking to separate itself from other characteristics is stronger, and seconded by the dissociation of rated task ability from amount of participation.

In summary, role differentiation in the High groups seems to be bipartite, with an active "task specialist" and a best-liked man. In the Low groups, it tends to be tripartite (as well as more extreme), with an active participator who is neither well-liked nor highly rated on task ability, a more passive task specialist who is not well-liked, and a popular individual who is neither active nor highly rated on task ability.

*   *   *

Discussion

According to Barnard (1938), the survival of any organization depends upon its ability to solve two problems: the achievement of the purposes for which the organization was formed, and the satisfaction of the more immediate needs of the members of the organization. On the small group level, Bales (1951) makes a related distinction between the problems of the group involving goal achievement and adaptation to external demands, and problems involving internal integration and the expression of emotional ten-

sions. The first group of problems he calls Adaptive-Instrumental problems, the solution of which demands activity in the Task area. The second he calls Integrative-Expressive problems, the solution of which demands activity in the social-emotional area. Bales goes on to emphasize the difficulties inherent in attempting to solve both groups of problems at the same time.

Similar difficulties arise when the same *individual* attempts to take an active lead in solving these problems simultaneously. In large organizations the solution of Integrative-Expressive problems is in large part left to the leaders of informal groups, the importance of which Barnard and others have emphasized.

We have found that the most fundamental type of role differentiation in small experimental groups is the divorcing of task functions from social-emotional functions. Presumably, the ideal leader of a small group would be sufficiently skillful and flexible to alternate these types of behavior in such a way as to handle both problems, and maximize his status on all possible dimensions. He would be able to make both an active, striving response to the task and a sympathetic response to the individual needs of group members. He would be a high participator, well-liked, rated high on task ability, and eventually chosen leader.

Such individuals are rare. They appear occasionally in High status-consensus groups, almost never in Low. It is possible that the absence in the Low groups of anyone approaching this ideal type is responsible for their low status-consensus. Where a group must choose between individuals who are in different ways one-sided and limited in their capabilities, agreement on ratings will be difficult to attain.

There are at least two kinds of reasons for the rarity of such men. First, there are sociological factors, revolving around the non-compatibility of the task and social-emotional roles. Adaptation to pressures from outside the group, such as are created by a task which must be performed, involves, by definition, change. The individual who presses toward solution of a task inadvertently forces those around him to make continual minor adjustments in their behavior, and to reexamine continually their ideas and values in the light of these external demands. The individual who concerns himself with internal social-emotional problems, on the other hand, is supportive in his responses to the ideas and behavior of those around him and continually reaffirms their dominant values. The orientation of the task specialist is thus more technological, that of the social-emotional specialist more traditionalistic. It is presumably the latter type of behavior which seems more appealing to members called upon to indicate whom they personally like best.

This is not to say that the task specialist will actually be disliked, but rather that his task emphasis will tend to arouse some negative feelings—feelings which may not be expressed, and which will never outweigh his value to the group in the minds of its members. Such feelings merely neutralize any strong positive feelings other members may hold toward him. Only in the Low groups are task specialists actually *un*popular, and this phenomenon is perhaps expressive of the rigidity with which Low group task specialists perform their role.

The second set of reasons may be called psychological. These have to do with the individual's predisposition to assume a particular role. Men who are best-liked may "have to be liked" and may achieve prominence in this role because of the ingratiating skills they have acquired during their lives in bringing this desired situation about. Avoidance of conflict and controversy may be a felt necessity for this type of person—hence, his behavior will show nothing that could be a source of disharmony. He will avoid even the thought that he might like some of his fellow members better than others. His rate of interaction will be average—not too high, not too low. He will in fact retire into the conventional safety of the "average Joe." He may even avoid the performance of task functions altogether, because of the personal threats which task activity might hold for him. Instead, he will express the group's feelings and questions and place its stamp of approval upon what has already come to pass.

The task specialist, on the other hand, may assume this role only because of an unwillingness or inability to respond to the needs of others. A compulsive concentration on an abstract problem will serve as an intellectual shield against the ambiguity of human feelings. Needs to express hostility may be channeled into aggressive and dogmatic problem-solving attempts.

When these motives determine the assumption of a specialized role in a group, the outlook for this group would seem to be poor. The F-score data suggest that such motives may in fact determine the behavior of specialists in Low status-consensus groups.

It is even possible that the presence in a group of individuals with motives of this sort *creates* low status-consensus. The difficulty of choosing between inadequate specialists has already been mentioned. Furthermore, it seems reasonable to expect that rigidity in the personality structure will be associated with rigidity in the value structure of the individual concerned. The F-scale is in fact founded on this assumption. Such absolutistic value systems, rigidly held and zealously defended, will impede the formation of any kind of consensus, particularly consensus on the relative emphasis the group should place upon task and social-emotional activities.

The way in which this kind of consensus in turn determines the degree of consensus on a particular rating may be illustrated by considering again the process of choosing a leader. It was suggested above that the man chosen as leader is that individual who is felt to possess those qualities which best serve to satisfy *both* the task and social-emotional problems of the group. Since different groups emphasize task and social-emotional problems in varying proportions, the attribution of leadership will depend not only upon the choice of one person over another but also upon the differential stress placed upon these group problems by the group. The group problems might thus be conceived as factors, with weights assigned to them by the group according to some elementary kind of value consensus. One group, e.g., might attribute leadership on the basis say, of .7 task ability, .3 likeability; another might reverse the weights. The fact that Liking coincides so seldom with Leadership suggests that in our sample social-emotional skills are not highly valued and are given a low weight. This may be due to the heavy task demands placed upon the group by the experimental situation or to the emphasis placed upon task ability and achievement by our culture.

In any case, Leadership will be attributed to that member who has the highest combined rating on these and perhaps other factors. But if implicit agreement on weights is lacking, each rater will be making a qualitatively different evaluation, and Leadership consensus becomes almost impossible.

Similarly, in making more specialized evaluations, a rater must decide what a specialist is supposed to do before deciding how well he does it. If there is no agreement in a group about what a given role should include, then roles will be performed in accordance with individual norms and will be evaluated in terms of personal criteria. Agreement on role definitions is thus hindered by rigid value systems at the very time when the inflexibility characteristic of specialists operating under these conditions makes this agreement all the more imperative.

In this discussion we have isolated three types of role structure.

(1) The rare case in which a single leader performs all functions and differentiation does not occur. This is a High group phenomenon.

(2) The case in which moderate specialization arises simply because the specialists lack the exceptional talent necessary to counteract the sociological pressures toward differentiation. Choice of role is undoubtedly determined by personality factors as well as situational factors. Such preferences will not, however, be immutable. This is the more common case in High groups.

(3) The case in which extreme specialization is brought about by psychological as well as sociological pressures. Specialization is sharp and disruptive, due to the fact that it springs from an overdetermined response to inner needs rather than a flexible response to the needs of others, or to the demands of an ever-changing task situation. Specialists perform in a particular role because they "have to" rather than because it is useful or desirable. This is a Low group phenomenon.

Thus while differentiation occurs in both High and Low status-consensus groups, it seems to occur for different reasons. It is only the depth and breadth of the differentiation which will supply an immediate clue to which kinds of reasons are operating. One final example of this duality of meaning is the highest participator, who has not been considered in much of the foregoing analysis.

It will be recalled that in High groups, the highest participator usually receives the highest rating on task ability. Approval and acceptance of his ideas perhaps encourages him to participate more heavily and also generates his high rating. In Low groups, the highest participator is far less often rated highly. He apparently does not adjust his amount of participation to the approval and acceptance he receives, but persists in interacting despite their absence. His participation time is determined by his own aggressiveness, by insensitivity rather than responsiveness to feedback from others. In keeping with the motivations of other Low group specialists, he talks, not because it is helpful to the group for him to do so, but because he has to.

In short, Low group specialists are going through many of the same motions as High group specialists, but their needs and purposes differ. It would seem likely that *double entendres* of this sort constitute a major factor in obscuring the complexity of small group relationships.

21. *Social Behavior as Exchange*

GEORGE C. HOMANS

According to George Homans, the study of small groups is essentially the study of "elementary" social behavior—the behavior that goes on in direct person-to-person exchanges. Furthermore, larger groups and organizations can also be seen as resting ultimately upon such elementary behavior. In the following article Homans argues that elementary behavior may be seen as taking place through "exchanges of goods."

As I survey small-group research today, I feel that, apart from just keeping on with it, three sorts of things need to be done. The first is to show the relation between the results of experimental work done under laboratory conditions and the results of quasi-anthropological field research on what those of us who do it are pleased to call "real-life" groups in industry and elsewhere. If the experimental work has anything to do with real life—and I am persuaded that it has everything to do—its propositions cannot be inconsistent with those discovered through the field work. But the consistency has not yet been demonstrated in any systematic way.

The second job is to pull together in some set of general propositions the actual results, from the laboratory and from the field, of work on small groups—propositions that at least sum up, to an approximation, what happens in elementary social behavior, even though we may not be able to explain why the propositions should take the form they do. A great amount of work has been done, and more appears every day, but what it all amounts to in the shape of a set of propositions from which, under specified conditions, many of the observational results might be derived, is not at all clear—and yet to state such a set is the first aim of science.

The third job is to begin to show how the propositions that empirically hold good in small groups may be derived from some set

Reprinted, with slight adaptation, from an article by George C. Homans in *American Journal of Sociology*, 1958, **LXII**, 597–606, by permission of the publisher, The University of Chicago Press. Copyright © 1958 by The University of Chicago.

of still more general propositions. "Still more general" means only that empirical propositions other than ours may also be derived from the set. This derivation would constitute the explanatory stage in the science of elementary social behavior, for explanation *is* derivation. (I myself suspect that the more general set will turn out to contain the propositions of behavioral psychology. I hold myself to be an "ultimate psychological reductionist," but I cannot know that I am right so long as the reduction has not been carried out.)

I have come to think that all three of these jobs would be furthered by our adopting the view that interaction between persons is an exchange of goods, material and non-material. This is one of the oldest theories of social behavior, and one that we still use every day to interpret our own behavior, as when we say, "I found so-and-so rewarding"; or "I got a great deal out of him"; or, even, "Talking with him took a great deal out of me." But, perhaps just because it is so obvious, this view has been much neglected by social scientists. So far as I know, the only theoretical work that makes explicit use of it is Marcel Mauss's *Essai sur le don*, published in 1925, which is ancient as social science goes. It may be that the tradition of neglect is now changing and that, for instance, the psychologists who interpret behavior in terms of transactions may be coming back to something of the sort I have in mind.

An incidental advantage of an exchange theory is that it might bring sociology closer to economics—that science of man most advanced, most capable of application, and, intellectually, most isolated. Economics studies exchange carried out under special circumstances and with a most useful built-in numerical measure of value. What are the laws of the general phenomenon of which economic behavior is one class?

In what follows I shall suggest some reasons for the usefulness of a theory of social behavior as exchange and suggest the nature of the propositions such a theory might contain.

An Exchange Paradigm

I start with the link to behavioral psychology and the kind of statement it makes about the behavior of an experimental animal such as the pigeon (Skinner, 1953). As a pigeon explores its cage in the laboratory, it happens to peck a target, whereupon the psychologist feeds it corn. The evidence is that it will peck the target again; it has learned the behavior, or, as my friend Skinner says, the behavior has been reinforced, and the pigeon has undergone *operant conditioning*. This kind of psychologist is not interested in how the behavior was learned: "learning theory" is a poor name for his field. Instead, he is interested in what determines changes in the rate of emission of learned behavior, whether pecks at a target or something else.

The more hungry the pigeon, the less corn or other food it has gotten in the recent past, the more often it will peck. By the same token, if the behavior is often reinforced, if the pigeon is given much corn every times it pecks, the rate of emission will fall off as the pigeon gets *satiated*. If, on the other hand, the behavior is not reinforced at all, then, too, its rate of emission will tend to fall off, though a long time may pass before it stops altogether, before it is *extinguished*. In the emission of many kinds of behavior the pigeon incurs *aversive stimulation*, or what I shall call "cost" for short, and this, too, will lead in time to a decrease in the emission rate. Fatigue is an example of a "cost." Extinction, satiation, and cost, by decreasing the rate of emission of a particular kind of behavior, render more probable the emission of some other kind of behavior, including doing nothing. I shall only add that even a hard-boiled psychologist puts "emotional" behavior, as well as such things

as pecking, among the unconditioned responses that may be reinforced in operant conditioning. As a statement of the propositions of behavioral psychology, the foregoing is, of course, inadequate for any purpose except my present one.

We may look on the pigeon as engaged in an exchange—pecks for corn—with the psychologist, but let us not dwell upon that, for the behavior of the pigeon hardly determines the behavior of the psychologist at all. Let us turn to a situation where the exchange is real, that is, where the determination is mutual. Suppose we are dealing with two men. Each is emitting behavior reinforced to some degree by the behavior of the other. How it was in the past that each learned the behavior he emits and how he learned to find the other's behavior reinforcing we are not concerned with. It is enough that each does find the other's behavior reinforcing, and I shall call the reinforcers—the equivalent of the pigeon's corn—*values*, for this, I think, is what we mean by this term. As he emits behavior each man may incur costs, and each man has more than one course of behavior open to him.

This seems to me the paradigm of elementary social behavior, and the problem of the elementary sociologist is to state propositions relating the variations in the values and costs of each man to his frequency distribution of behavior among alternatives, where the values (in the mathematical sense) taken by these variables for one man determine in part their values for the other.

I see no reason to believe that the propositions of behavioral psychology do not apply to this situation, though the complexity of their implications in the concrete case may be great indeed. In particular, we must suppose that, with men as with pigeons, an increase in extinction, satiation, or aversive stimulation of any one kind of behavior will increase the probability of emission of some other kind. The problem is not, as it is often stated, merely, what a man's values are, what he has learned in the past to find reinforcing, but how much of any one value his behavior is getting him now. The more he gets, the less valuable any further unit of that value is to him, and the less often he will emit behavior reinforced by it.

The Influence Process

We do not, I think, possess the kind of studies of two-person interaction that would either bear out these propositions or fail to do so. But we do have studies of larger numbers of persons that suggest that they may apply, notably the studies by Festinger, Schachter, Back, and their associates on the dynamics of influence. One of the variables they work with they call *cohesiveness*, defined as anything that attracts people to take part in a group. Cohesiveness is a value variable; it refers to the degree of reinforcement people find in the activities of the group. Festinger and his colleagues consider two kinds of reinforcing activity: the symbolic behavior we call "social approval" (sentiment) and activity valuable in other ways, such as doing something interesting.

The other variable they work with they call *communication* and others call *interaction*. This is a frequency variable; it is a measure of the frequency of emission of valuable and costly verbal behavior. We must bear in mind that, in general, the one kind of variable is a function of the other.

Festinger and his co-workers (1950) show that the more cohesive a group is, that is, the more valuable the sentiment or activity the members exchange with one another, the greater the average frequency of interaction of the members. With men, as with pigeons, the greater the reinforcement, the more often is the reinforced behavior emitted. The more cohesive a group, too, the greater the change that members can produce in the behavior of other members in the direction of rendering these activities more valuable. That is, the more valuable the activities that members get, the more valuable those that they must give. For if a person is emitting behavior of a certain kind, and other people do not find it particularly rewarding, these others will suffer their own production of sentiment and activity, in time, to fall off. But perhaps the first person has found their sentiment and activity rewarding, and, if he is to keep on getting them, he must make his own behavior more valuable to the others. In short, the propositions of behavioral psychology imply a tendency toward a certain proportionality between the value to others of the behavior a man gives them and the value to him of the behavior they give him.

Schachter (1951) also studied the behavior of members of a group toward two kinds of other members, "conformers" and "deviates." I assume that conformers are people whose activity the other members find valuable. For conformity is behavior that coincides to a degree with some group standard or norm, and the only meaning I can assign to *norm* is "a verbal description of behavior that many members find it valuable for the actual behavior of themselves and others to conform to." By the same token, a deviate is a member whose behavior is not particularly valuable. Now Schachter shows that, as the members of a group come to see another member as a deviate, their interaction with him—communication addressed to getting him to change his behavior—goes up, the faster the more cohesive the group. The members need not talk to the other conformers so much; they are relatively satiated by the conformers' behavior: they have gotten what they want out of them. But if the deviate, by failing to change his behavior, fails to reinforce the members, they start to withhold social approval from him: the deviate gets low sociometric choice at the end of the experiment. And in the most cohesive groups—those Schachter calls "high cohesive-relevant"—interaction with the deviate also falls off in the end and is lowest among those members that rejected him most strongly, as if they had given him up as a bad job. But how plonking can we get? These findings are utterly in line with everyday experience.

Practical Equilibrium

At the beginning of this paper I suggested that one of the tasks of small-group research was to show the relation between the results of experimental work done under laboratory conditions and the results of filed research on real-life small groups. Now the latter often appear to be in practical equilibrium, and by this I mean nothing fancy. I do not mean that all real-life groups are in equilibrium. I certainly do not mean that all groups must tend to equilibrium. I do not mean that groups have built-in antidotes to change: there is no homeostasis here. I do not mean that we assume equilibrium. I mean only that we sometimes *observe* it, that for the time we are with a group—and it is often short—there is no great change in the values of the variables we choose to measure. If, for instance, person A is interacting with B more than with C both at the beginning and at the end of the study, then at least by this crude measure the group is in equilibrium.

Many of the Festinger-Schachter studies are experimental, and their propositions about the process of influence seem to me to imply the kind of proposition that empirically holds good of real-life groups in practical equilibrium. For instance, Festinger *et al.* (1950) find that, the more cohesive a group is, the greater the change that members can produce in the behavior of other members. If the influence is exerted in the direction of conformity to group norms, then, when the process of influence has accomplished all the change of which it is capable, the proposition should hold good that, the more cohesive a group is, the larger the number of members that conform to its norms. And it does hold good.

Again, Schachter found, in the experiment I summarized above, that in the most cohesive groups and at the end, when the effort to influence the deviate had failed, members interacted little with the deviate and gave him little in the way of sociometric choice. Now two of the propositions that hold good most often of real-life groups in practical equilibrium are precisely that the more closely a member's activity conforms to the norms the more interaction he receives from other members and the more liking choices he gets from them too. From these main propositions a number of others may be derived that also hold good.

Yet we must ever remember that the truth of the proposition linking conformity to liking may on occasion be masked by the truth of other propositions. If, for instance, the man that conforms to the norms most closely also exerts some authority over the group, this may render liking for him somewhat less than it might otherwise have been.

Be that is it may, I suggest that the laboratory experiments on influence imply propositions about the behavior of members of small groups, when the process of influence has worked itself out, that are identical with propositions that hold good of real-life groups in equilibrium. This is hardly surprising if all we mean by equilibrium is that all the change of which the system is, under present conditions, capable has been effected, so that no further change occurs. Nor would this be the first time that statics has turned out to be a special case of dynamics.

Profit and Social Control

Though I have treated equilibrium as an observed fact, it is a fact that cries for explanation. I shall not, as structural-functional sociologists do, use an assumed equilibrium as a means of explaining, or trying to explain, why the other features of a social system should be what they are. Rather, I shall take practical equilibrium as something that is itself to be explained by the other features of the system.

If every member of a group emits at the end of, and during, a period of time much the same kinds of behavior and in much the same frequencies as he did at the beginning, the group is for that period in equilibrium. Let us then ask why any one member's behavior should persist. Suppose he is emitting behavior of value A_1. Why does he not let his behavior get worse (less valuable or reinforcing to the others) until it stands at $A_1 - \Delta A$? True, the sentiments expressed by others toward him are apt to decline in value (become less reinforcing to him), so that what he gets from them may be $S_1 - \Delta S$. But it is conceivable that, since most activity carries cost, a decline in the value of what he emits will mean a reduction in cost to him that more than offsets his losses in sentiment. Where does he stabilize his behavior? This is the problem of social control.

Mankind has always assumed that a person stabilizes his behavior, at least in the short run, at the point where he is doing the best he can for himself under the circumstances, though his best may not be a "rational" best, and what he can do may not be at all easy to specify, except that he is not apt to think like one of the theoretical antagonists in the *Theory of Games*. Before a sociologist rejects this answer out of hand for its horrid profit-seeking implications, he will do well to ask himself if he can offer any other answer to the question posed. I think he will find that he cannot. Yet experiments designed to test the truth of the answer are extraordinarily rare.

I shall review one that seems to me to provide a little support for the theory, though it was not meant to do so. The experiment is reported by H. B. Gerard, a member of the Festinger-Schachter team, under the title "The Anchorage of Opinions in Face-to-Face Groups" (1954). The experimenter formed artificial groups whose members met to discuss a case in industrial relations and to express their opinions about its probable outcome. The groups were of two kinds: high-attraction groups, whose members were told that they would like one another very much, and low-attraction groups, whose members were told that they would not find one another particularly likable.

At a later time the experimenter called the members in separately, asked them again to express their opinions on the outcome of the case, and counted the number that had changed their opinions to bring them into accord with those of other members of their groups. At the same time, a paid participant entered into a further discussion of the case with each member, always taking, on the probable outcome of the case, a position opposed to that taken by the bulk of the other members of the group to which the person belonged. The experimenter counted the number of persons shifting toward the opinion of the paid participant.

The experiment had many interesting results, from which I choose only those summed up in Tables 1 and 2. The three different agreement classes are made up of people who, at the original sessions, expressed different degrees of agreement with the opinions of other members of their groups. And the figure 44, for instance, means that, of all members of high-attraction groups whose initial opinions were strongly in disagreement with those of other members, 44 per cent shifted their opinion later toward that of others.

In these results the experimenter seems to have been interested only in the differences in the sums of the rows, which show that there is more shifting toward the group, and less shifting toward the paid participant,

TABLE 1. PERCENTAGE OF SUBJECTS CHANGING TOWARD SOMEONE IN THE GROUP

	Agreement	Mild Disagreement	Strong Disagreement
High attraction	0	12	44
Low attraction	0	15	9

TABLE 2. PERCENTAGE OF SUBJECTS CHANGING TOWARD THE PAID PARTICIPANT

	Agreement	Mild Disagreement	Strong Disagreement
High attraction	7	13	25
Low attraction	20	38	8

in the high-attraction than in the low-attraction condition. This is in line with a proposition suggested earlier. If you think that the members of a group can give you much—in this case, liking—you are apt to give them much—in this case, a change to an opinion in accordance with their views—or you will not get the liking. And, by the same token, if the group can give you little of value, you will not be ready to give it much of value. Indeed, you may change your opinion so as to depart from agreement even further, to move, that is, toward the view held by the paid participant.

So far so good, but, when I first scanned these tables, I was less struck by the difference between them than by their similarity. The same classes of people in both tables showed much the same relative propensities to change their opinions, no matter whether the change was toward the group or toward the paid participant. We see, for instance, that those who change least are the high-attraction, agreement people and the low-attraction, strong-disagreement ones. And those who change most are the high-attraction, strong-disagreement people and the low-attraction, mild-disagreement ones.

How am I to interpret these particular results? Since the experimenter did not discuss them, I am free to offer my own explanation. The behavior emitted by the subjects is opinion and changes in opinion. For this behavior they have learned to expect two possible kinds of reinforcement. Agreement with the group gets the subject favorable sentiment (acceptance) from it, and the experiment was designed to give this reinforcement a higher value in the high-attraction condition than in the low-attraction one. The second kind of possible reinforcement is what I shall call the "maintenance of one's personal integrity," which a subject gets by sticking to his own opinion in the face of disagreement with the group. The experimenter does not mention this reward, but I cannot make sense of the results without something much like it. In different degrees for different subjects, depending on their initial positions, these rewards are in competition with one another: they are alternatives. They are not absolutely scarce goods, but some persons cannot get both at once.

Since the rewards are alternatives, let me introduce a familiar assumption from economics—that the cost of a particular course of action is the equivalent of the foregone value of an alternative—and then add the definition: Profit = Reward − Cost.

Now consider the persons in the corresponding cells of the two tables. The behavior of the high-attraction, agreement people gets them much in the way of acceptance by the group, and for it they must give up little in the way of personal integrity, for their views are from the start in accord with those of the group. Their profit is high, and they are not prone to change their behavior. The low-attraction, strong-disagreement people are getting much in integrity, and they are not giving up for it much in valuable acceptance, for they are members of low-attraction groups. Reward less cost is high for them, too, and they change little. The high-attraction, strong-disagreement people are getting much in the way of integrity, but their costs in doing so are high, too, for they are in high-attraction groups and thus foregoing much valuable acceptance by the group. Their profit is low, and they are very apt to change, either toward the group or toward the paid participant, from whom they think, perhaps, they will get some acceptance while maintaining some integrity. The low-attraction, mild-disagreement people do not get much in the way of integrity, for they are only in mild disagreement with the group, but neither are they giving up much in acceptance, for they are members of low-attraction groups. Their rewards are low; their costs are low too, and their profit—the difference between the two—is also low. In their low profit they resemble the high-attraction, strong-disagreement people, and, like them, they are prone to change their opinions, in this case, more toward the paid participant. The subjects in the other two cells, who have medium profits, display medium propensities to change.

If we define profit as reward less cost, and if cost is value foregone, I suggest that we have here some evidence for the proposition that change in behavior is greatest when perceived profit is least. This constitutes no direct demonstration that change in behavior is least when profit is greatest, but if, whenever a man's behavior brought him a balance of reward and cost, he changed his behavior away from what got him, under the circumstances, the less profit, there might well come a time when his behavior would not change further. That is, his behavior would be stabilized, at least for the time being. And, so far as this were true for every member of a group, the group would have a social organization in equilibrium.

I do not say that a member would stabilize his behavior at the point of greatest conceivable profit to himself, because his profit is partly at the mercy of the behavior of others. It is a commonplace that the short-run pursuit of profit by several persons often lands them in positions where all are worse off than they might conceivably be. I do not say that the paths of behavioral change in which a member pursues his profit under the condition that others are pursuing theirs too are easy to describe or predict; and we can readily conceive that in jockeying for position they might never arrive at any equilibrium at all.

Distributive Justice

Yet practical equilibrium is often observed, and thus some further condition may make its attainment, under some circumstance, more probable than would the individual pursuit of profit left to itself. I can offer evidence for this further condition only in the behavior of subgroups and not in that of individuals. Suppose that there are two subgroups, working close together in a factory, the job of one being somewhat different from that of the other. And suppose that the members of the first complain and say: "We are getting the same pay as they are. We ought to get just a couple of dollars a week more to show that our work is more responsible." When you ask them what they mean by "more responsible," they say that, if they do their work wrong, more damage can result, and so they are under more pressure to take care. Something like this is a common feature of industrial behavior. It is at the heart of disputes not over absolute wages but over wage differentials—indeed, at the heart of disputes over rewards other than wages.

In what kind of proposition may we express observations like these? We may say that wages and responsibility give status in the group, in the sense that a man who takes high responsibility and gets high wages is admired, other things equal. Then, if the members of one group score higher on responsibility than do the members of another, there is a felt need on the part of the first to score higher on pay too. There is a pressure, which shows itself in complaints, to bring the *status factors*, as I have called them, into line with one another. If they are in line, a condition of *status congruence* is said to exist. In this condition the workers may find their jobs dull or irksome, but they will not complain about the relative position of groups.

But there may be a more illuminating way of looking at the matter. In my example I have considered only responsibility and pay, but these may be enough, for they represent the two kinds of thing that come into the problem. Pay is clearly a reward; responsibility may be looked on, less clearly, as a cost. It means constraint and worry—or peace of mind foregone. Then the proposition about status congruence becomes this: If the costs of the members of one group are higher than those of another, distributive justice requires that their rewards should be higher too. But the thing works both ways: If the rewards are higher, the costs should be higher too. This last is the theory of *noblesse oblige*, which we all subscribe to, though we all laugh at it, perhaps because

the *noblesse* often fails to *oblige*. To put the matter in terms of profit: though the rewards and costs of two persons or the members of two groups may be different, yet the profits of the two—the excess of reward over cost—should tend to equality. And more than "should." The less-advantaged group will at least try to attain greater equality, as, in the example I have used, the first group tried to increase its profit by increasing its pay.

I have talked of distributive justice. Clearly, this is not the only condition determining the actual distribution of rewards and costs. At the same time, never tell me that notions of justice are not a strong influence on behavior, though we sociologists often neglect them. Distributive justice may be one of the conditions of group equilibrium.

Exchange and Social Structure

I shall end by reviewing almost the only study I am aware of that begins to show in detail how a stable and differentiated social structure in a real-life group might arise out of a process of exchange between members. This is Peter Blau's description of the behavior of sixteen agents in a federal law-enforcement agency. (Blau, 1955, pp. 99–116.)

The agents had the duty of investigating firms and preparing reports on the firms' compliance with the law. Since the reports might lead to legal action against the firms, the agents had to prepare them carefully, in the proper form, and take strict account of the many regulations that might apply. The agents were often in doubt what they should do, and then they were supposed to take the question to their supervisor. This they were reluctant to do, for they naturally believed that thus confessing to him their inability to solve a problem would reflect on their competence, affect the official ratings he made of their work, and so hurt their chances for promotion. So agents often asked other agents for help and advice, and, though this was nominally forbidden, the supervisor usually let it pass.

Blau ascertained the ratings the supervisor made of the agents, and he also asked the agents to rate one another. The two opinions agreed closely. Fewer agents were regarded as highly competent than were regarded as middle or low competence; competence, or the ability to solve technical problems, was a fairly scarce good. One or two of the more competent agents would not give help and advice when asked, and so received few interactions and little liking. A man that will not exchange, that will not give you what he has when you need it, will not get from you the only thing you are, in this case, able to give him in return, your regard.

But most of the more competent agents were willing to give help, and of them Blau says:

A consultation can be considered an exchange of values: both participants gain something, and both have to pay a price. The questioning agent is enabled to perform better than he could otherwise have done, without exposing his difficulties to his supervisor. By asking for advice, he implicitly pays his respect to the superior proficiency of his colleague. This acknowledgement of inferiority is the cost of receiving assistance. The consultant gains prestige, in return for which he is willing to devote some time to the consultation and permit it to disrupt his own work. The following remark of an agent illustrates this: "I like giving advice. It's flattering, I suppose, if you feel that others come to you for advice."

Blau goes on to say: "All agents liked being consulted, but the value of any one of very many consultations became deflated for experts, and the price they paid in frequent interruptions became inflated." This implies that, the more prestige an agent received, the less was the increment of value of that prestige; the more advice an agent gave, the greater was the increment of cost of that advice, the cost lying precisely in the foregone value of time to do his own work. Blau suggests that something of the same sort was true of an agent who went to a more competent colleague for advice: the more often he went, the more costly to him, in feelings of inferiority, became any further request. "The repeated admission of his inability to solve his own problems . . . undermined the self-confidence of the worker and his standing in the group."

The result was that the less competent agents went to the more competent ones for help less often than they might have done if the costs of repeated admissions of inferiority had been less high and that, while many agents sought out the few highly competent ones, no single agent sought out the latter much. Had they done so (to look at the exchange from the other side), the costs to the highly competent in interruptions to their own work would have become exorbitant. Yet the need of the less competent for help was still not fully satisfied. Under these circumstances they tended to turn for help to agents more nearly like themselves in competence. Though the help they got was not the most valuable, it was of a kind they could themselves return on occasion. With such agents they could exchange help and liking, without the exchange becoming on either side too great a confession of inferiority.

The highly competent agents tended to enter into exchanges, that is, to interact with many others. But, in the more equal exchanges I have just spoken of, less competent agents tended to pair off as partners. That is, they interacted with a smaller number of people, but interacted often with these few. I think I could show why pair relations in these more equal exchanges would be more economical for an agent than a wider distribution of favors. But perhaps I have gone far enough. The final pattern of this social structure was one in which a small number of highly competent agents exchanged advice for prestige with a large number of others less competent and in which the less competent agents exchanged, in pairs and in trios, both help and liking on more nearly equal terms.

Blau shows, then, that a social structure in equilibrium might be the result of a process of exchanging behavior rewarding and costly in different degrees, in which the increment of reward and cost varied with the frequency of the behavior, that is, with the frequency of interaction. Note that the behavior of the agents seems also to have satisfied my second condition of equilibrium: the more competent agents took more responsibility for the work, either their own or others', than did the less competent ones, but they also got more for it in the way of prestige. I suspect that the same kind of explanation could be given for the structure of many "informal" groups.

Summary

The current job of theory in small-group research is to make the connection between experimental and real-life studies, to consolidate the propositions that empirically hold good in the two fields, and to show how these propositions might be derived from a still more general set. One way of doing this job would be to revive and make more rigorous the oldest of theories of social behavior —social behavior as exchange.

Some of the statements of such a theory might be the following. Social behavior is an exchange of goods, material goods but also non-material ones, such as the symbols of approval or prestige. Persons that give much to others try to get much from them, and persons that get much from others are under pressure to give much to them. This process of influence tends to work out at equilibrium to a balance in the exchanges. For a person engaged in exchange, what he gives may be a cost to him, just as what he gets may be a reward, and his behavior changes less as profit, that is, reward less cost, tends to a maximum. Not only does he seek a maximum for himself, but he tries to see to it that no one in his group makes more profit than he does. The cost and the value of what he gives and of what he gets vary with the quantity of what he gives and gets. It is surprising how familiar these propositions are; it is surprising, too, how propositions about the dynamics of exchange can begin to generate the static thing we call "group structure" and, in so doing, generate also some of the propositions about group structure that students of real-life groups have stated.

In our unguarded moments we sociologists find words like "reward" and "cost" slipping into what we say. Human nature will break in upon even our most elaborate theories. But we seldom let it have its way with us and follow up systematically what these words imply. Of all our many "approaches" to social behavior, the one that sees it as an economy is the most neglected, and yet it is the one we use every moment of our lives— except when we write sociology.

22. *Risk and Conservatism in Group Decision-Making*

GEORGE R. MADARAS AND DARYL J. BEM

The following article presents a good example of the scientific method in action. Starting with an unexpected phenomenon, greater risks reported for groups than for individuals, the authors take us in step-by-step fashion to consider various explanations. Alternative hypotheses are gradually eliminated and the explanation becomes more clear. Finally, limitations of risky behavior of groups are pointed out by certain counter-influences toward conservatism.

Several recent studies have indicated that groups are willing to take higher levels of risk than are the individuals who make up the groups. The experiment by Stoner (1961), who first reported this phenomenon,

From the *Journal of Experimental Social Psychology*, 1968, **4**, 350–364, by permission of the authors and the publisher, Academic Press, Inc.

is paradigmatic of these studies. Stoner had male graduate students of industrial management indicate the lowest odds they would accept for selecting a risky, but desirable, alternative when given the choice of a more certain, but less desirable, alternative. Stoner's problems covered a wide range of topics, entailing possible losses of life, money, preslige, and self-satisfaction. An illustrative example is Item 10:

. . . Mr. K is a successful businessman who has participated in a number of civic activities of considerable value to the community. Mr. K has been approached by the leaders of his political party as a possible congressional candidate in the next election. Mr. K's party is a minority party in the district, though the party has won occasional elections in the past. Mr. K would like to hold political office, but to do so would involve a serious financial sacrifice, since the party has insufficient campaign funds. He would also have to endure the attacks of his political opponents in a hot campaign.

Imagine that you are advising Mr. K. Listed below are several probabilities or odds of Mr. K's winning the election in his district. PLEASE CHECK THE LOWEST PROBABILITY THAT YOU WOULD CONSIDER ACCEPTABLE TO MAKE IT WORTHWHILE FOR MR. K TO RUN FOR POLITICAL OFFICE.

The subject could elect not to take the risky alternative at all, or to indicate his willingness to take it with 1, 3, 5, 7, or 9 chances in 10 that Mr. K would win the election. The lower the minimum acceptable odds selected by the subject, the riskier his choice is said to be.

Working alone, each individual made twelve such decisions. Stoner's subjects were then brought together into groups of six and required to select a level of risk unanimously acceptable to all members of the group for each problem. When the group discussions were completed, the subjects were again separated and asked to indicate their personal risk preferences on each problem.

Using this procedure, Stoner found that the groups' decisions, as well as the private risk preferences of the individuals, had shifted toward greater riskiness, i.e., toward an acceptance of lowered guaranteed odds of success for attempting the risky alternative. This "risk shift" was not found in Stoner's control sample, which simply reconsidered the problems after a period of weeks, with no group discussion intervening.

This finding contradicted the general belief that groups are more reserved and conservative in behavior than individuals (Whyte, 1956). For example, when Bateson (1966) asked students to predict the outcome of such an experiment, about 90% predicted a decrease in riskiness following the group discussion.

The possibility that the unique attributes of Stoner's business-school sample might have accounted for the risk shift has been discounted by Wallach, Kogan, and Bem (1962) and Wallach and Kogan (1965), who have replicated Stoner's finding with male and female groups of undergraduate students. In addition, the risk shift has also been replicated in tasks other than hypothetical discussions of risk. For example, Wallach, Kogan, and Bem (1964) offered monetary rewards for correct solutions to College Board questions and found that group discussions of problem difficulty led individuals to attempt higher-risk (i.e., more difficult) problems than they had chosen previously. Bem, Wallach, and Kogan (1965) have also replicated the risk shift offering monetary reward under threat of aversive consequences for failure. These extensions of the original Stoner study have supported the generalizability of the risk-shift phenomenon across subject populations and in both hypothetical and real-life situations.

A number of explanations have been offered for the risk-shift phenomenon. Of these, four have received the most attention: leadership, diffusion of responsibility, rationality, and a cultural value for risk. We shall briefly review the support for each.

The leadership hypothesis was derived from correlational evidence that riskier members of the group, as defined by their initial questionnaires, are also perceived as more self-assured (Clausen, 1965) and as more influential members of the group (Wallach et al., 1962; Rim, 1963, 1964a, 1964b). Nordhøy (1962) has also found that the acknowledged "leader" on each problem was the individual who was initially the most extreme in the direction in which the group eventually shifted. However, the recent failure of Kogan and Wallach (1966) to replicate their previously reported significant relationship between initial levels of risk and perceived influence, has led Kogan and Wallach (1967) to conclude that "while the leadership hypothesis may prove to be a partial explanation, it can hardly qualify as the sole cause of group-induced shifts toward enhanced risk-taking."

The diffusion-of-responsibility hypothesis contends that the "affective bonds formed in discussion . . . may enable the individual to feel less than proportionally to blame when he entertains the possible failure of risky decision" (Wallach and Kogan, 1965), thus leading a group to accept greater risk than an individual decision-maker who is presumably deterred by his greater feeling of responsibility for possible failure.

Although this hypothesis is favored by Wallach and Kogan themselves, it receives support only from indirect kinds of evidence designed primarily to rule out other explanations. (For a review, see Brown, 1965, pp. 656–708.) The hypothesis that there is some sort of a diffusion of responsibility also relies heavily on evidence that group discussion is a necessary and sufficient condition for eliciting the group shift toward risk (Marquis, 1962; Wallach, Kogan, and Burt, 1965), a conclusion which now appears to be false. Recent studies by Bateson (1966) and Flanders and Thistlethwaite (1967) have demonstrated that a risk shift as strong as that obtained from groups may be elicited from individual subjects who are given the task of preparing additional arguments for group debate. That is, a shift toward risk was obtained from individual decision-makers in the absence of *any* kind of group discussion. It is unlikely, therefore, that the diffusion of responsibility is an adequate explanation of the shift.

The rationality hypothesis of the shift toward risk assumes that group discussion tends to eliminate errors and to increase the average level of information in the group (Clausen, 1965). This assumption is consistent with the findings of Bateson (1966) and Flanders and Thistlethwaite (1967), mentioned above, who were able to elicit a risk shift from individuals asked to restudy the risk situations in preparation for group debate. These investigators concluded that improved comprehension of the situations might account for the shift toward risk that is found in group decisions.

Presumably, improved comprehension means a more adequate understanding of the expected returns for the risk and non-risk alternatives. The rationality argument would thus seem to imply that the expected value of the riskier alternatives is higher than that of the conservative alternatives and, accordingly, the shift toward risk represents a "rational" shift toward higher expected return. This hypothesis, however, has been weakened in a study by Wallach *et. al.* (1964) in which groups chose to attempt more difficult and, therefore, more risky aptitude problems even though the expected monetary return for correct responses was equal for all items. In another study, subjects have risked physical discomfort when in groups even though riskier alternatives yielded *decreased* expected returns (Bem *et al.*, 1965). Thus, the shift toward risk cannot be explained by a higher expected return for the risky alternative unless one is willing to postulate that there is some added value in being perceived as a risktaker. This, in fact, is what Brown (1965) has proposed in his "cultural value for risk" hypothesis.

Brown presumes that our culture values and rewards the individual who appears to be slightly more daring than his peers. Hinds' (1962) finding that subjects consistently rate themselves as very similar to, but more risky than, fellow discussants may reflect the implicit social desirability of that risk position. Brown further suggests that group discussion may serve to provide information to the individual about the risk levels of his fellow discussants. Upon discovering that his initial position was not so daring as he had thought, he readjusts his risk level to maintain his image as a risktaker, leading a group of such subjects to shift their joint decisions in the risky direction. This image-maintenance process might, then, account for the group-induced risk shift.

The studies by Bateson (1966) and Flanders and Thistlethwaite (1967), cited earlier, can also be assimilated into the cultural-value-for-risk explanation. In both of these experiments, subjects were asked to assemble additional arguments in preparation for a group debate of the problems. Even though no group interaction actually took place, a risk shift was obtained which was as large as that typically elicited by group discussion. The individual shifts obtained in these studies could be due to a culturally-induced predisposition to consider and favor risk arguments when anticipating group discussion. (Although a very similar control condition in Bem *et al.* [1965] did not produce a risk shift, their subjects were not required to write down actual arguments but merely to "reconsider" their initial decisions.)

Thus, much of the evidence is congruent with the value-for-risk hypothesis. But, there is still no direct evidence that a high-risk taker is viewed more favorably than his more conservative counterpart in these situations. The following experiment was designed to see if such evidence would be obtained.

If a risky action is more desirable to members of our culture than a conservative one, their evaluations of a high-risk taker should differ from their evaluations of a more conservative decision maker. If clear differences in such evaluations favored the risk-taker, we might argue that a cultural value for risk could account, at least in part, for the shift toward risk.

Method

Fifty male undergraduates from the Carnegie Institute of Technology participated in this study. Each subject was given a set of items identical to those on the Stoner questionnaire, except that the subject was told that the central figure of the problem had accepted (or rejected) the riskier alternative at a certain level of odds. To illustrate with our previous example (Item 10), the subject might be told that Mr. K had a three-in-ten chance of winning the election and, knowing this, had chosen to run for office.

The subject was told that the experimenter was interested in learning how individuals come to perceive one another, and was asked to rate ten central figures on the following Semantic Differential scales: calm-excitable, hard-soft, feminine-masculine, unsuccessful-successful, cruel-kind, sociable-unsociable, fast-slow, weak-strong, active-passive, and good-bad. The problems used were those ten which had elicited the risk shifts in the Wallach *et al.* (1962) study. They were split into two sets of five problems matched for similarity (e.g., one life-and-death matter, one occupational choice,

etc.) and for the size of the risk shifts reported in earlier work (Wallach *et al.*, 1962).

Each subject rated each of the ten central figures. On five of the risk problems, the central figure was described as having been given one of five levels of risk for the more desirable alternative (1, 3, 5, 7, or 9 chances in 10), and having chosen to accept the risk. On each of the remaining problems, he was described as having been given one of these levels of risk and having chosen to reject the risk.

Thus, each subject judged each central figure only once, but judged a given level of risk twice—once for an "accept," and once for a "reject" decision. Each problem was represented at all levels of risk in both the "accept" and "reject" conditions across the fifty subjects.

After all subjects had completed the questionnaire, they were informed of the nature of the study and dismissed.

Results and Discussion

All ratings were scored on a seven-point scale, with the socially desirable end of the scale (italicized in Table 1) scored as seven. Each subject earned a preference score for risk by having the total of his five risk-rejector ratings subtracted from the total of his five risk-acceptor ratings. The larger this difference in the positive direction, the more favorably the subject viewed the risk-acceptors over those who chose not to take the risk. This difference score was computed for each of the ten scales for each subject.

A standardized difference (t) score was then computed for each scale, representing all problems at each level of risk and in the accept and reject conditions. As can be seen in Table 1, subjects rated risk-acceptors as being more strong, active, successful, fast, hard, and masculine, and somewhat more good and sociable, but less calm and kind than risk-rejectors. (A t score greater than 2.01 is beyond the 97.5% level on the Student Distribution using 49 df.)

These results provide support for the hypothesis, favored by Brown (1965), that risk is a socially desirable characteristic, and group-discussion effects could thus be due to the desirability of being perceived as

TABLE 1. DIFFERENCE BETWEEN
SUBJECTS' RATINGS OF RISK-
ACCEPTORS AND RISK-
REJECTORS
$(N = 50)$

RATING SCALE	MEAN DIFFERENCE	T SCORE
Weak-*Strong*:	2.160	15.22
Passive-*Active*:	2.324	14.82
Unsuccessful-*Successful*:	1.540	11.95
Slow-*Fast*:	1.548	11.37
Soft-*Hard*:	1.788	10.75
Feminine-*Masculine*:	1.424	10.50
Bad-*Good*:	0.600	4.31
Unsociable-*Sociable*:	0.432	3.27
Excitable-*Calm*:	−0.468	−2.17
Cruel-*Kind*:	−0.368	−3.03

a risk-taker. This finding is also consistent with the hypothesis that the individual shifts toward risk found by Bateson (1966) and Flanders and Thistlethwaite (1967) are due to a culturally-induced predisposition to consider and favor risk arguments when considering risk situations in detail.

*   *   *

A Mechanism for the Value-Induced Shift Toward Risk

The manner in which the cultural value for risk induces the shift toward risk remains unclear. Brown (1965) has suggested that the risk shift is based upon an image-maintenance phenomenon: As a subject enters the group, he considers himself to be a high-risk taker. But with discussion of the problems, he learns that his risk levels are not the lowest in the group, and alters his risk preferences to maintain his image as a risk taker. The crucial information transmitted in the group, therefore, concerns the levels of risk which are acceptable to other members of the group, and not information specific to the risk items.

The studies of Bateson (1966) and Flanders and Thistlethwaite (1967), however, suggest an alternative hypothesis. With group interaction (or with more detailed individual study), each subject is likely to consider a larger number of arguments relevant to each problem. Since the culture values risk, each subject may be predisposed to give greater consideration to risk arguments, a suggestion consistent with Nordhøy's (1962) observation that risk-supportive arguments appeared to predominate in group discussion. This bias of information flow may, itself, mediate the risk shift. Thus, the crucial information transmitted in the group is not about the risk levels of others, according to this hypothesis, but about specific information regarding the situation being discussed.

Suppose a group were permitted to discuss only some of the problems, but not others which were highly similar. These two mechanisms of a value-induced risk shift suggest different effects upon the undiscussed problems. If the crucial information transmitted in the group is the risk level of others, a hypothetical subject would be cognizant of his relative conservatism on the undiscussed problems after group discussion of other problems, and would alter his risk preferences on the undiscussed problems as well. If the crucial information transmitted in the group is specific to the items discussed, however, our hypothetical subject would not alter his risk preferences on these undiscussed items.

In the following test of the relative adequacy of these two models, the ten-item Stoner questionnaire was again divided into two closely matched sets of five items each. The groups were asked to discuss one of the five-item sets after they had completed the entire questionnaire as individuals. If individual reconsideration of the undiscussed items displayed the shift toward risk, it would imply that the crucial information transmitted in group discussion concerns the risk levels of other members of the group, and the image-maintenance hypothesis would be favored. If ratings of the undiscussed items were unaffected by such reconsideration, it would imply that the crucial information is item-specific, and the biased-information hypothesis would be favored.

Method

Twelve groups of three and twelve groups of four undergraduate males from Carnegie Institute of Technology were recruited to participate in this study from introductory psychology classes in partial fulfillment of their experimental requirements. The procedure followed was identical with that used in the individual administration of the original Stoner questionnaire. That is, each subject was instructed to rate the minimally acceptable odds for attempting the risky—but desirable—course of action in each of ten risk situations.

When all individual subjects had completed their task, their books were collected and new books distributed. These booklets had only five of the problems which each subject had just completed. Each problem in the set had a matching item in the other set whose content was highly similar, whose initial risk level was comparable, and which, in previous research, had elicited a shift toward risk of approximately equal magnitude. Six three-man and six four-man groups discussed the odd items from the ten-item questionnaire to group consensus. The remaining twelve groups discussed the matched even items. The groups were told that they had filled out the questionnaire so that they would become familiar with all of the situations, but that they would "only discuss half of the items today because of time constraints." In all other respects, the instructions for the group condition were identical with those found in Wallach *et al.* (1962).

When the group had made its decisions for all five situations, the experimenter collected the group's decisions and again requested individual decisions on all ten problems. These instructions were again identical to those used in the postindividual condition by Wallach *et al.* (1962). When their work was done, the subjects were informed of the nature of the experiment and dismissed.

Results and Discussion

Probability preferences were scored on a one-to-ten basis; that is, a 5/10 choice was scored as 5. The total mean shifts were calculated separately for the five discussed and the five nondiscussed items by taking the differences between pre- and postgroup ratings. Since no significant differences were obtained between the three- and four-man groups, their data were combined for analysis. A significant shift toward a willingness to

take greater risk was found for the discussed items, replicating the usual risk-shift finding ($\mu_{diff} = 1.87$, $p < .002$; all ts reported here are two-tailed with 23 df). No such shift in willingness to take risk was found for the matched nondiscussed items ($\mu_{diff} = -0.16$, n.s.). The significant difference between the discussed and the nondiscussed items ($t = 3.49$, $p < .002$) argues that the crucial information transmitted in group discussion is not the risk levels of others, but information relevant to the specific items discussed.

Such a conclusion follows from the fact that as each subject decides upon an undiscussed item following the group discussion, he possesses knowledge about the risk level of others on such an item, but has not heard arguments specific to the particular item under consideration. This finding is thus consistent with a model of the risk shift that maintains that individuals are culturally predisposed to generate and to favor risk arguments when considering risk dilemmas in detail. It is not consistent with a model of the risk shift that proposes that individuals seek out, and adjust their risk levels to, the risk levels of others.

Generality of the Phenomenon

How general is the risk-shift phenomenon? Wallach *et al.* (1962) have obviously felt that it is general enough to warn us of its dangers in the risk considerations of chiefs-of-staff and large organizations, when increased risk-taking might work against our best interests. Yet our intuitions tells us that such groups are more conservative—not riskier—than are their individual members. The reason for this discrepancy is not clear.

Perhaps the risk studies have centered their attention on too small a subset of group decisions. It is true, of course, that the phenomenon has been demonstrated with a number of populations and in both hypothetical and real-life situations. But attention in the risk studies has been focused primarily upon the desirability of the risk alternatives, rather than upon the actual probabilities of their success or failure. That is, subjects have typically been told that they are *not* to consider what the risks might actually be, but only what minimal odds they would consider acceptable for attempting the risky alternative. But "conservatism" in real life may well reside in the assessment of probabilities, as well as in the assessment of the relative utilities of the alternatives.

Some indication that this might be the case has been observed by Vroom (private communication), who has found that group ratings of administrative problem-solutions are more pessimistic than individual ratings of the same solutions. That is, his subjects indicated that problem-solutions were less likely to succeed after group discussion than they had indicated in their pregroup ratings. If the group discussion of real-world probabilities indicated that there was less likelihood of success for the risk alternative, the group might be less likely to suggest that the central figure attempt the risk.

To examine this possibility, the entire risk-shift experiment was repeated, using the usual paradigm (Wallach *et al.*, 1962), except that each item also required the subject to estimate the probabilities of success for the Stoner problem, and to indicate how strongly he would suggest that the central figure take the risk. His lowest acceptable odds for taking the risk alternative were also assessed, as usual.

Method

Fourteen groups of three male undergraduates were recruited from their introductory psychology classes at Carnegie Institute of Technology as part of their required participation in psychological studies. Upon arrival each subject was asked to examine the

Stoner questionnaire, and received instructions like those in the Wallach *et al.* (1962) study except that he was instructed to make three judgments for each Stoner item rather than one.

In addition to asking for the lowest acceptable odds for the risk alternative—as is usually done—these instructions asked for an estimate of the likelihood of success of the risk alternative, and how strongly the subject would suggest that the risk alternative be chosen. Thus he was instructed to: ". . . Imagine that you are advising Mr. K. Listed below are several probabilities or odds of Mr. K's winning the election in his district." [See further instructions in the accompanying chart.]

These initial individual decisions served as a baseline from which to assess the shifts occurring in the group and in the final individual conditions.

Instructions for the group and final administrations were essentially identical to those used in Wallach *et al.* (1962), except that full consensus was not required in the group condition. (Consensus has been shown to be unnecessary for eliciting the risk shift [Wallach and Kogan, 1965].) When the final individual responses were completed, the subjects were informed of the nature of the experimentation and dismissed.

Results and Discussion

All probability estimates were scored on a one-to-ten (in ten) basis, and the seven-point rating scale was scored with "definitely

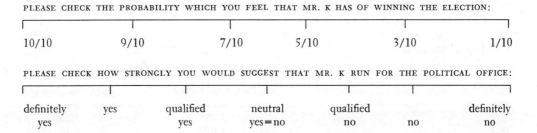

PLEASE CHECK THE PROBABILITY WHICH YOU FEEL THAT MR. K HAS OF WINNING THE ELECTION:

| 10/10 | 9/10 | 7/10 | 5/10 | 3/10 | 1/10 |

PLEASE CHECK HOW STRONGLY YOU WOULD SUGGEST THAT MR. K RUN FOR THE POLITICAL OFFICE:

| definitely yes | yes | qualified yes | neutral yes = no | qualified no | no | definitely no |

PLEASE CHECK THE *LOWEST* PROBABILITY THAT YOU WOULD CONSIDER ACCEPTABLE TO MAKE IT WORTHWHILE FOR MR. K TO RUN FOR POLITICAL OFFICE:

| 1/10 | 3/10 | 5/10 | 7/10 | 9/10 | 10/10 |

yes" as seven. A group mean was calculated for each of the three questions in each condition, over all 12 items. A two-tailed *t* test was employed to assess the shifts in judgments from the pretest to group, and from the pretest to post-test decisions.

It is seen in Table 2 that the results replicate the pessimistic shift demonstrated by Vroom's administrative decision-makers. That is, these subjects rated the probabilities of success for the risk alternatives as being significantly lower in both the group and the final individual ratings than in their initial estimates (row A, Table 2). But despite the perceived greater risk for the desirable course of action, these groups were still willing to suggest more strongly that the risk alternative be chosen (row B), and still replicated the now-familiar willingness to take lower probabilities of success (row C). (The latter two shifts returned to a nonsignificant difference in the individual post-test condition, a reversion to original risk preferences similar to that reported by Wallach and Kogan [1965].)

The shift toward greater pessimism found here may reflect a reduction of misinformation in the group discussion, an effect observed in early small-group research by Shaw (1932) and Thorndike (1938). Thorndike has concluded that this increase in group accuracy is due to the greater influence of more accurate and more confident group members. Although this shift toward pessimism did not eliminate the risk-shift effect in this study, it might conceivably act as a force toward conservatism in real-life administrative decisions.

Another force toward conservatism might be a decision-maker's feeling of responsibility for the possible failure of the chosen alternative if the consequences of such failure would impinge on others. In the Wallach *et al.* (1964) study, subjects who were told that their personal risk levels would be applied to fellow subjects became more conservative in their risk ratings. This force is logically distinct from . . . morality questions, in which the selection of the risk alternative is itself regarded as immoral (or otherwise too costly) regardless of success or failure.

It may well be that in the context of real-life decision-making, these three forces toward conservatism—the group pessimism shift, the responsibility to others for failure, and questions of morality—may counteract the culturally-induced shift toward risk. Their effects may thus account for the discrepancy between our intuitions about the nature of group decisions and the results of the risk-shift studies. Clearly more direct investigation of the relative contributions of these opposing forces to administrative decision-making would be desirable before extending the findings of the narrowly focused risk studies to such decision-making contexts.

TABLE 2. PESSIMISM AND RISK RATINGS AS A FUNCTION OF GROUP DISCUSSION

QUESTION	MEAN OF PRETESTS	MEAN OF GROUPS	MEAN OF POST-TESTS
(A) Probability of success?	5.76	5.19	5.15
(B) Would you suggest it?	5.31	5.64	5.44
(C) Your lowest probability	6.22	5.86	6.01

	T SCORES	
	Pretest vs. Group	*Pretest vs. Post-test*
(A	6.19‡	6.05‡
(B)	3.26*	1.24
(C)	3.67†	2.12

* $p < .01$.
† $p < .005$.
‡ $p < .0005$, using 13 *df*; all *t*s are two-tailed.

6 *Social Structure and Personality*

Personality may be generally defined as the organization of behavior characteristic of an individual. Since behavioral organization occurs at different levels, it is important to recognize that some aspects of personality are more observable than others, more central than others, or more permanent than others. Something of the nature of the different levels of behavioral organization may be suggested by the following classification:

(1) The organism—the organization of physiological, including neurological, activity

(2) The private identity—the self-concept, the set of definitions a person has of himself and of the meaning of his behavior

(3) The public identity—the combination of roles a person plays in his various groups, organizations, and interpersonal relationships.

For most social psychologists, the center of interest in personality lies in the interrelationship between the private identity and the public identity. This does not imply that the biological organism is unimportant but rather that it usually does not relate directly to the concerns of social psychologists.

The questions social psychologists ask regarding personality often deal especially with the relationship of social structure to personality. The selections that follow are concerned with this general topic.

The idea that culture sets the stage for personality organization is suggested by Ralph Linton's discussion, "Basic Personality Types." He here reviews the development of a framework for viewing culture-personality relationships that was led particularly by the psychoanalyst Abram Kardiner. The selection following Linton's presents a study by E. Adamson Hoebel of culture-personality relationships in a particular society, that of the Cheyenne Indians.

In complex societies of the modern world it is more difficult to see culture-personality relationships than is the case with simpler societies. In the modern world we can often see culture-personality relationships most clearly if we reduce our scope to a subcultural level.

Personality is not shaped just by a generalized impact of culture or subculture. Much more specifically, personality is shaped by the accumulation of particular experiences in a variety of social settings. Sometimes the cumulative impact of social experiences may foster mental illness, as the selection by Lloyd Rogler and August Hollingshead, "Escape into Schizophrenia," suggests. These authors suggest what social factors may distinguish a sample of families with schizophrenia from a similar sample without schizophrenia.

Project 9, "Personality Profiles," which gives the student a chance to check his own view of himself with the way he is seen by someone else, serves as an introduction to the personality variables used in "Resistance to Change in the Self-Concept," by Carl Backman, Paul Secord, and Jerry Peirce. Project 10, "Analysis of Change in the Self-Concept," focuses upon some of the findings of this article. Together the article by Backman and associates and Project 10 emphasize interpersonal roots of the stability of self-concepts.

23. *Basic Personality Types*

RALPH LINTON

Abram Kardiner, psychoanalyst, and Ralph Linton, anthropologist, were leaders in the study of interrelationships between culture and personality. Together they developed a general theory of culture-personality integration and led others to do research to test central ideas of this theory. Kardiner's The Psychological Frontiers of Society *(1945) is an excellent example of this work, and the following selection is from Linton's foreword to this book.*

The key concept discussed here is that of the "basic personality type"—a kind of common denominator of personality for persons of the same culture (which some other writers have termed "modal personality"). Note that this is not at all the same thing as the aspects of personality that give uniqueness to the individual. Note also that Linton acknowledges that the culture-and-personality analysis suggested by this concept has been applied more often to simple primitive societies than to more complex or modern societies.

It is an axiom of science that each new advance springs from a certain platform of knowledge and ideas without which it would have been impossible. The concept of basic personality is no exception to this rule. Its ultimate origins can be traced to certain trends in both cultural anthropology and psychology which had been apparent since the early nineteen hundreds. During this period workers in both disciplines had become increasingly aware of the importance of configuration phenomena and of the necessity for studying both cultures and personalities as wholes. Among anthropologists, the great exponent of this approach was the late Dr. Malinowski, but both he and his followers tended to confine their investigations to the structural and operational rela-

tions between elements within culture. While Dr. Malinowski in particular was fully aware of the importance of the individual in relation to culture, the necessary techniques for dealing with this relationship were lacking. In psychology during the same period, the rapid advance of psychoanalysis resulted in an increased interest in the integrative aspects of the personality and a realization that personalities had to be dealt with as continuums. The Gestalt school of psychology has, of course, laid even greater stress on configurational phenomena, but since its concepts have not been successfully applied to problems of personality and culture, it need be mentioned only as an example of *Zeitgeist.* Unfortunately, the earlier psychoanalysts carried on their investigations entirely within the frame of European culture and largely within that of a single class in European society. Lacking comparative materials, they took many environmental factors for granted and built up an elaborate

From "Foreword" by Ralph Linton to Abram Kardiner, *The Psychological Frontiers of Society,* New York: Columbia University Press, 1945, pp. vi–ix, reprinted by permission of the publisher.

theory of universal human instinct. The various attempts which were made by Freud and others to apply this instinctual approach to the explanation of cultural phenomena and even to the reconstruction of cultural history struck the average anthropologist as fantastic and led him to minimize the very real contributions which psychoanalytic techniques might make to the solution of many of his own problems.

In spite of these difficulties, the period under discussion witnessed the emergence of a new area of concentration on problems of personality and culture. There was a considerable exchange of ideas and techniques between anthropology and psychology, and a series of new concepts began to emerge. Anyone who reviews the literature must feel that the idea of basic personality type was "in the wind" some time before Dr. Kardiner and I began our collaboration. However, so far as I can discover, the first concrete statement of the concept was that embodied in *The Individual and His Society*, published in 1939. Since that time the concept has been employed by several other writers, with minor variations in content and especially in terminology, but I still prefer the original.

The concept of basic personality types as developed and used by Dr. Kardiner and myself is in itself a configuration involving several different elements. It rests upon the following postulates:

(1) That the individual's early experiences exert a lasting effect upon his personality, especially upon the development of his projective systems.

(2) That similar experiences will tend to produce similar personality configurations in the individuals who are subjected to them.

(3) That the techniques which the members of any society employ in the care and rearing of children are culturally patterned and will tend to be similar, although never identical, for various families within the society.

(4) That the culturally patterned techniques for the care and rearing of children differ from one society to another.

If these postulates are correct, and they seem to be supported by a wealth of evidence, it follows:

(1) That the members of any given society will have many elements of early experience in common.

(2) That as a result of this they will have many elements of personality in common.

(3) That since the early experience of individuals differs from one society to another, the personality norms for various societies will also differ.

The *basic personality type* for any society is that personality configuration which is shared by the bulk of the society's members as a result of the early experiences which they have in common. It does not correspond to the total personality of the individual but rather to the projective systems or, in different phraseology, the value-attitude systems which are basic to the individual's personality configuration. Thus the same basic personality type may be reflected in many different forms of behavior and may enter into many different total personality configurations.

Although the delimitation of the basic personality types of different societies has been one important aspect of our investigations, we have been equally concerned with the functional relations between these types and the cultures of the societies investigated. In other words, we have tried to discover not only what the basic personality types were but also how they were produced and what influence they exerted upon the culture itself. These dynamic features must be regarded as an integral part of the concept as we have developed and employed it. In the course of their therapeutic work, psychoanalysts have discovered that certain configurations of early experience tend to produce certain personality configurations in the adult. Transferring these findings to the investigation of societies as wholes, it becomes possible to make tentative predictions as to what sort of people the child-rearing techniques of a particular society would be likely to produce. The culture of the society can then be investigated to see how far this culture as a whole might prove congenial to individuals of this particular sort. In all the societies which have been investigated so far the compatibility has been of a high order. It seems safe to conclude that in relatively stable cultures, such as those of "primitive" societies, there is a close interrelation between the basic personality type and the culture as a whole. For the individual, this means that the projective systems formed in early childhood will be constantly reinforced by later experience. Conversely, the average individual in such a society will find that most of the culture patterns which he is called on to assume in later life are congenial and can be readily accepted. In other words, in stable societies the basic personality type and the culture configuration tend to reinforce and perpetuate each other. Unfortunately, we have had few opportunities so far to investigate the interrelations of basic personality and culture in changed situations, but there can be little doubt that the basic personality type plays an important part in determining a society's reaction to innovations. Innovations which are congenial to the personality type probably are accepted and incorporated into the society's culture much more readily than those which are uncongenial.

24. *Cheyenne Culture and Personality*

E. ADAMSON HOEBEL

The Cheyennes are an Indian tribe that, after the introduction of the horse, lived a nomadic life on the Great Plains. In the following excerpts from The Cheyennes: Indians of the Great Plains, *E. Adamson Hoebel describes the interrelationships between Cheyenne culture, patterns of socialization, and typical characteristics of adult personality. This description gives a clear picture of culture-personality relationships in a particular tribal society.*

Reserved and dignified, the adult Cheyenne male moves with a quiet sense of self-assurance. He speaks fluently, but never carelessly. He is careful of the sensibilities of others and is kindly and generous. He is slow to anger and strives to suppress his feelings, if aggravated. Vigorous on the hunt and in war, he prizes the active life. Towards enemies he feels no merciful compunctions, and the more aggressive he is, the better. He is well versed in ritual knowledge. He is neither flighty nor dour. Usually quiet, he has a lightly displayed sense of humor. He is sexually repressed and masochistic, but that masochism is expressed in culturally approved rites. He does not show much creative imagination in artistic expression, but

he has a firm grip on reality. He deals with the problems of life in set ways while at the same time showing a notable capacity to readjust to new circumstances. His thinking is rationalistic to a high degree and yet colored with mysticism. His ego is strong and not easily threatened. His superego, as manifest in his strong social conscience and mastery of his basic impulses, is powerful and dominating. He is "mature"—serene and composed, secure in his social position, capable of warm social relations. He has powerful anxieties, but these are channeled into institutionalized modes of collective expression with satisfactory results. He exhibits few neurotic tendencies.

The typical grown-up Cheyenne woman exhibits much the same constellation of traits. Not having the direct outlet for aggressive impulses that men find in war, she is touchier in domestic relations and apt to be a bit willful within her family. Grinnell calls her "masterful." She is more artistically creative that the male, but still within pre-scribed limits. She is equally repressed sexually but manifests less compensatory behavior in masochism and aggression against enemies—although both these traits are discernible in her.

The molding of the adult, of course, begins in infancy. Cheyenne children are highly valued by their parents and by the tribe. From the outset, their lives are made as comfortable as is possible. They are strictly taught and steadily but gently molded toward the Cheyenne ideal in an atmosphere of love and interest. The Cheyenne child is rarely physically punished, and we have seen how daughters may react in suicide if their mothers are overly harsh or vindictive after they have grown up.

*   *   *

Newborn babies are gently greased, powdered, and wrapped in soft robes. If the weather is cold, they are carried in the mother's arms for warmth and comfort. Cheyenne mothers use the cradleboard—a wooden frame carried on the mother's back and on which is a laced-up animal-skin "cocoon" in which the infant is tightly bound like a mummy. The baby is ordinarily not put on the cradleboard until some weeks after its birth. The advantage of its use is that the mother may go about her work with an assurance that her baby will not get into trouble. If traveling, or watching a dance or ceremony, she carries the board like a knapsack; when working in the lodge, she hangs it upright from one of the lodge poles; when working outside the lodge, she leans it against the lodge covering. Although the infant is tightly confined when tied in the cradleboard, this does not retard its development in learning to walk or in other phases of growth. It must early learn quiet patience, however. Crying is not tolerated. The Cheyennes say this is because a squalling baby might give away the camp position at night when enemy raiders are seeking it for an attack. On a deeper level, however, the Cheyennes abhor anyone forcing his will upon others by self-display, and this behavior principle must be learned from the outset. Crying babies are not scolded, slapped, or threatened. They are simply taken out on the cradleboard away from the camp and into the brush where they are hung on a bush. There the squalling infant is left alone until it cries itself out. A few such experiences indelibly teach it that bawling brings not reward but complete and total rejection and the loss of all social contacts. On the other hand, the good baby is cuddled and constantly loved. When not on the board it is rocked in the arms of its mother or grandmother and soothed with lullabies. It is nursed whenever it shows a desire (self-demand feeding).

As the infant gets a little older, it is more often carried about on its mother's back in a blanket sling rather than on the cradleboard. Its head projects about her shoulders; it hears and sees all she does; it shares the warmth of her body and feels the movements of her muscles; it receives food passed over the mother's shoulder; it even sleeps on her back as she goes about her household tasks. It is enveloped in warmth, movement, and affectionate attention. Its body is gently soothed with medicated ointments and soft vegetable ointments. Its early years are full of adult-given gratification. Its frustrations must, however, be quickly internalized, for the alternative is isolation in the brush. This is the first lesson learned, and it must be remembered at all times; it pervades Cheyenne life. Children are to be quiet and respectful in the presence of elders. The learned have much to offer, and what one acquires in wisdom about the Cheyenne way one acquires through learning taught by those who know the way. Cheyenne relations between younger and elder are thus the relations of pupils and teachers—and pupils must be deferential.

On the basis of this well-established relationship, Cheyenne children are continuously exhorted by their elders: "Be brave, be honest, be virtuous, be industrious, be generous, do not quarrel! If you do not do these things, people will talk about you in the camp; they will not respect you; you will be shamed. If you listen to this advice you will grow up to be a good man or woman, and you will amount to something." The values of the Cheyennes are made explicit in a steady stream of sermonizing that expostulates what is deeply woven into everyday life. The values are reinforced by many explicit mechanisms of public and family approval.

A child does not have to wait until he is grown up to be able to practice what is preached and to experience the satisfaction of performance. Cheyenne children are little replicas of their elders in interests and deed. Children begin to learn adult activities and practice them in play at incredibly early ages. Boys learn to ride almost as soon as they learn to walk, girls soon after. At two or three, they ride with their mothers, and by the time they are five or six, little boys are riding bareback on their own colts and mastering the use of the lasso. By seven or eight, they help with the herding of the camp's horses. Little girls, as soon as they can toddle, follow their mothers to gather wood and bring in water, the mothers patiently helping them with their pint-sized burdens. Boys get small, but good quality, bows and arrows as soon as they can effectively learn to use them.

*　　*　　*

A boy's first real hunt and war party comes early in life—at twelve or thirteen. His first buffalo kill is rewarded with great public recognition, if his family can afford it. His father calls out the news for all in the camp to hear, and he announces that he is giving a good horse—even his best one—to some poor man, in honor of the event. This man gets on the horse to ride all around the camp, singing a song in praise of the boy. The youngster's mother may get up a feast, to which the father publicly invites a number of poor people to share in the family's good fortune. Gifts of blankets and other valuables may be distributed at the end of the feast. The same thing is done when a boy comes home from his first war party.

It is easy to imagine the sense of glowing pride of the young teen-ager who gets such attention on his first manly successes. Cheyenne youths have little reason to be rebels-without-cause. They slip early into manhood, knowing their contributions are immediately wanted, valued, and ostentatiously rewarded. In the family response we see also the signalizing of Cheyenne social consciousness. Some families do better than others, winning more goods and more prestige, but what they have is shared with those who are less able and more luckless. The boy and his parents get tremendous ego-gratification; at the same time, however, they must

think of others. Here, too, we see revealed the Cheyenne attitude toward wealth. It is not to be hoarded or to be self-consumed. Stinginess and miserliness are un-Cheyenne. Its value derives from its being given away. Chiefs, who are the greatest exemplars of Cheyenne virtues, are the greatest givers. Note also, that the Cheyennes do not expect an equal return in gifts, except in marriage exchanges; nor is there anything comparable to the Northwest Coast Indian potlatch with its competitive rivalries. Cheyenne boys learn to become highly competitive in the skills of hunt and war. They are rewarded with great individual prestige for successful performance, but the fact is also impressed upon them that they fight for the benefit of the tribe, "to protect the people," and that the fruits of the hunt are to be widely shared.

It is also important to observe that there are no initiation or puberty rites for boys in Cheyenne culture. Cheyenne children acquire full adult status by performance, without the necessity of undergoing hazing by the old men or any other form of *rite de passage*.

*　　*　　*

For the Cheyenne girl, on the other hand, there is a clear-cut transition rite. . . .

The first menstruation of a girl is a great event. She has entered womanhood, and her father calls the news to the entire camp from beside his lodge door. If wealthy in horses, he gives one away to signalize the occasion. Like other Indians, the Cheyennes nonetheless consider menstrual blood to be defiling and inimical to the virility of males and to their supernatural powers. The girl therefore retires to an isolation, or moon, hut so that there will be no danger of her polluting her father's or brothers' sacred paraphernalia. Before going, however, she lets down her hair, bathes, and has her body painted all over in red by her older woman relatives. She takes a ceremonial incense purification just before she goes into the hut, where she remains four days with her grandmother, who looks after her and advises her on womanly conduct. At the end of the period, she is again smudged completely to purify her for reentry into social life. Until menarche, all Cheyenne women leave their tipis for the moon lodge, but only unmarried girls must go through the purification each time.

After her first menses, each girl receives her chastity belt from her mother. She wears it constantly until married. Even after marriage she wears it whenever her husband is away at war or on the hunt. She wears it whenever she goes away from her lodge to gather wood or water. For any man other than her husband to touch it is a private delict of the first magnitude.

*   *   *

In summing up this study of the Cheyennes, the following points must be mentioned. The Cheyennes stand out among the nomadic Indians of the Plains for their dignity, chastity, steadfast courage, and tightly structured, yet flexible, social organization. Never a large tribe, they have held their own with outstanding success. They have come to terms with their environment and with themselves. They are exceedingly rational and skilled in cultural adaptation through felicitous social inventiveness and manipulation. Although deep down they are beset with anxieties, their anxieties are institutionally controlled.

25. *Escape into Schizophrenia*

LLOYD H. ROGLER AND AUGUST B. HOLLINGSHEAD

Most culture-personality writings have emphasized the impact of the culture as a whole upon personality formation and have called attention especially to the early years of life. However, both of these emphases may be misleading. An individual's personality is shaped not so much by the culture as a whole as it is by the particular social environment in which he lives. Furthermore, early experience may be important in personality formation without necessarily giving permanent shape to the personality. Later events may well change behavior sufficiently that personality change can be said to have occurred.

Consider, for example, the development of schizophrenia. Some have suggested that schizophrenia is rooted in the pattern of personality based on early experiences with parents. This may be true in some cases, but a study by Rogler and Hollingshead suggests that the crucial factors in the development of most cases of schizophrenia may arise in later stages of the life cycle. Their research with lower-class families of San Juan, Puerto Rico, indicates that schizophrenics are distinguished from nonpsychotic individuals not so much by early experience as by the particular problems associated with meeting responsibilities of adult social roles. Furthermore, it is the cumulative effect of such problems that Rogler and Hollingshead emphasize—suggesting that it is not any one kind of problem particularly, but rather the overpowering effect of facing a combination of difficult circumstances that sets the stage for schizophrenia. The following excerpts are from Rogler and Hollingshead's conclusions.

We began this study with three basic questions to be answered: Do the life histories

Reprinted from Lloyd H. Rogler and August B. Hollingshead, *Trapped: Families and Schizophrenia*, New York: John Wiley & Sons, Inc., 1965, pp. 401–416, by permission of the publisher.

of persons who develop schizophrenia differ from those of persons who are not schizophrenic? When and under what circumstances do persons who become schizophrenic exhibit the symptoms characteristic of this affliction? What effect does schizophrenia in a husband or a wife have on the family?

The theoretical frame of reference we used to answer each of these questions postulates that a person's experiences in his effective social environment influence the development, onset, and consequences of schizophrenia. The effective environment is encompassed by the social groups, particularly the families of orientation and procreation, which enmesh the person throughout his lifetime. Other relevant social groups are composed of work associates, friends, and neighbors. Interpersonal relations in the effective environment are organized according to expectations of role performance, and the behavior of a person is analyzed according to the adequacy with which he performs or fulfills the expectations of his social roles.

To apply the frame of reference to the basic questions of the research, we made an exploratory study of families living in the urbanized area of San Juan, Puerto Rico. For our data we went to the sources: the men and women who lived through the experiences they related to us. Their responses, in repeated interviews stretching over several months, to our systematic, searching questions were supplemented by observations in the homes and neighborhoods in which they live. Repeated interviews of husbands and wives, combined with direct observations, enable us to study these families as they face the problems of everyday living in their natural setting.

To gather the data needed to answer our questions, we limited the study to families in which the husband and wife are between 20 and 39 years of age, are in the lowest socioeconomic class, and have never been treated for mental illness. To attain the objectives of the study, however, we had to be able to make comparisons between two groups of families: there had to be a schizophrenic husband or wife in each family of one group, whereas the other group had to be free of schizophrenia.

*   *   *

The families of orientation into which the husbands and wives were born shared the culture of lower-status persons in Puerto Rico a generation ago. The parents were illiterate or semiliterate. The fathers were predominantly agricultural laborers employed in the sugar cane fields or on small hillside farms. Few mothers were employed outside of the home as they were occupied with the many chores of the housework, childbearing, and child care. The parental families were large; all were burdened with poverty. One-half of the families were broken by the death or desertion of one parent before our respondents were 15 years of age. Adulterous behavior by the father is reported to have occurred in some two homes out of three; excessive drinking of rum was often combined with adultery. Economic and interpersonal problems existed in approximately 95 per cent of the parental homes. Mental illness is ascribed to some member of one-half of the families of orientation. The basic conclusion we have reached is that the parental families of persons who are mentally healthy do not differ socially or culturally from the families of persons who suffer from schizophrenia.

The husbands or wives who are schizophrenic present no evidence that they were exposed to greater hardships, more economic deprivation, more physical illnesses, or personal dilemmas from birth until they entered their present marriage than do the mentally healthy men and women. Before the onset of their illness, the schizophrenic men and women took part in the same activities as the well men and women. They had as many friends as the well persons; they viewed their friends and think they were viewed by their friends in the same terms as the well persons think of their early peer relationships. The leisure time activities of the two groups were similar. There is no evidence that the sick persons were more prone to solitary activities than the well ones.

In sum, systematic comparisons between the mentally healthy and the sick persons indicate that they are remarkably similar in their assumption of the appropriate social roles for each sex at the customary age. The life histories demonstrate that in childhood, youth, and early adult life there are only a few significant differences between the behavior of those who are now mentally healthy and those who are suffering from schizophrenia. One notable difference is the more frequent occurrence of nightmares during childhood among the sick than among the well persons. The occupational histories are almost identical in the two groups, with the exception that the schizophrenic women were gainfully employed at an earlier age than the well women.

The effective social environment that enmeshed these young men and women during the years that have elapsed between the time they were under the control of parental family and the present, confronted all of them with a series of social and personal problems. They have either solved these issues successfully, or they have become victims of them.

*   *   *

The effective social environment creates a series of common and repetitive difficulties with which a person must cope. It often prevents a smooth transition from one stage of the life cycle to the next. It imposes competing and contradictory demands on a person at specifiable periods in the life arc. It creates aspirations without providing the means for their achievement. It generates social processes which lead to conflict, mutual withdrawal, and alienation between neighbors. All together, the problems and tension points confronted by the typical husband and wife form a maze which they have entered but from which they have not emerged.

Over and above such problems, the trajectory of the life arc of each person who now suffers from schizophrenia is broken at a discernible point in time. Our second question focuses on the circumstances under which the break occurs. The break in the life arc coincides with a complex of interrelated crises the schizophrenic person experienced during the 12 months preceding the perceived onset of his illness. He views these critical experiences as personal dilemmas with which he has to wrestle and, in some way, solve. His competence is called into question by the crises he faces. His adequacy in the performance of his basic social roles as a man and a husband, or a woman and a wife, is on trial. Coping with the difficulties that encompass him becomes the central issue in his life.

Systematic comparisons of the six types of perceived personal problems reported by the sick persons (and families) with those of the well persons (and families) demonstrate that each of the diagnostic family types in the sick group encountered many more problems than the well families during the problematic year. There are more economic difficulties and more severe physical deprivation in the sick than in the well families. There are far more interspouse conflicts among the sick families than the control families; difficulties with members of the extended family are more frequent and more severe. The sick families report more quarrels and fights with their neighbors. There are more physical illnesses in the schizophrenic families. Finally, more sick persons than well persons, male as well as female, note a disparity between their own perception of the difficulties they encountered and the ways they think their spouses viewed these same problems. Stated otherwise, the schizophrenic men and women think their spouses do not understand the personal difficulties they face, as well as the men and women in the control group do. In general, the person who is diagnosed as suffering from schizophrenia perceives himself as bombarded by a multiplicity of personal and family problems he is not able to handle. The behavioral evidence shows, however, that he struggles to solve them by every means available to him.

*   *   *

The acceleration of problems in the life of the vulnerable persons and in the family, combined with the self-awareness of role failure, appears to be a factor in the development of the illness. A husband who inadequately fulfills the role demands required of him has this fact brought to his attention by his wife, relatives, or other persons outside the immediate family. As a consequence, his failure creates interpersonal difficulties in the home, on the job, and, often, in the neighborhood. The sense of inadequacy which results from a failure to fulfill normal role requirements becomes an intrinsic part of his very being. Relentless social pressures are converted internally into emotional stress. The besieged person, unable to cope with his external and internal crises, becomes physically and mentally distraught. He becomes the victim of his failure.

External stresses and internal strains in one area of role performance tend to give rise to role failure in other areas of a person's life space. A heightened sense of personal inadequacy on the job or in child care creates more difficulties in the family, as other persons react to the social and psychological conflict engendered by the distraught person. He, in turn, reacts to others in ways that exacerbate the pressures and stresses he feels, giving rise to additional interpersonal difficulties. Failure to cope with the dilemmas which beset him becomes manifest in his behavior as a concomitant of the decompensation that is occurring in his personality structure. The way the anxiety-ridden and fearful person, as well as others in his life space, interprets his behavior is another aspect of the problem that engulfs him.

*   *   *

The etiological processes culminating in the development of schizophrenia may be of relatively recent origin. Childhood and adolescent experiences provide meager clues for an understanding of the way the illness develops. In contrast, at a recent and discernible period in the life arc prior to the eruption of overt symptomatology, a rash of insoluble, mutually reinforcing problems emerges to trap the person. We suggest that further research focus on this critical period. To arrive at a more precise understanding of the experiences and events which transpire during this period, field studies must develop research techniques to identify and measure interactional processes which bind the person into intolerable dilemmas. We suggest further that the analysis of role performance in sick and well persons and families is a promising approach to understanding the development of schizophrenia.

The third question of this research focuses on the effect of schizophrenia on the family. Affinal and consanguineal relatives in the extended families of the persons who are free of schizophrenia are bound together by a norm of mutual help. The economic help exchanged ranges from token to total support. Persons are advised by relatives on how to solve problems. A crisis such as illness or death brings relatives together with offers to serve and to help. The women more than the men keep the bonds of kinship active and intact by identifying problems and marshaling resources to solve problems. Through a process of collecting and disseminating information, the women preserve the social visibility of even those relatives who do not live nearby.

Whereas the well families give more help than they receive, the sick families receive more help than they give. . . .

Role performances in the families free of schizophrenia are in accord with expectations common in the culture. The division of labor requires that the husband be the breadwinner, the wife the homemaker. At home the husband can be aloof from household details and problems, yet he maintains final control over the major decisions which affect the family. The wife accepts his authority, defers to him, and endeavors to serve him by keeping an orderly and tranquil home. With the perceived onset of the illness, a drastic change ensues in the husband-schizophrenic families. As the husband withdraws from social relations with colleagues, associates, and friends, the wife endeavors to cope with the economic problems created by his inability to work. Soon, the wife seeks full-time employment in a factory or as a servant. At home, she nurtures and protects the husband; she takes him to *curanderas*, spiritualistic mediums, and psychiatrists. An unplanned result of this process is that the wife gains increments of control over her husband who is relegated to a dependent role. The work roles are reversed as the family reorganizes itself to cope with the illness. By this method, many tensions in the family are alleviated.

The onset of the wife's illness has an opposite effect on the family, irrespective of the husband's mental status: tension points are exacerbated, and the family is disorganized. The sick wife repeatedly denies her husband sexual intercourse. She criticizes him for his meager earnings. She defies his authority, exchanges insults with him, and engages him in physical brawls. The well husband married to a sick women often philanders, spending his free time away from home. If he also is sick, he withdraws into his home only to be confronted by a belligerent wife with whom he now has a greater opportunity to fight. The discord, confusion, and chaos of the families with a sick mother envelop the children, who are more often psychiatrically disturbed and retarded in their educational development than are the children of well mothers. These findings clearly demonstrate that there is a relationship between the sex role of the afflicted person and the solidarity, harmony, and stability of the nuclear and extended family.

The most striking and pervasive characteristic of the sick man's relationship to his wife and to other members of the extended family is his dependence on them. This is incongruous with the cultural definition of the *macho*, which emphasizes strength of character, independence, and freedom. The theme of the sick women is rebellion against both her husband and other figures of authority. Such a rebellious attitude is inconsistent with the ideals of feminine behavior; a woman is expected to be humble, deferential, and conforming. The disparity between behavior and the ideals embodied in social roles gives rise to problems for the sick wife which do not emerge when only the husband is sick. Irrespective of the mental status of the husband, a male is not attuned by attitude, temperament, or skill to cope with the problems created by a sick wife. He is indifferent to her complaints, strives to coerce her into behaving more appropriately, or escapes from the house to participate in street-corner activities with his peers. His behavior does not compensate for her lack of normal role performance as does

that of the well wife married to a sick husband. In point of fact, the husband's responses are not only inflexible and unadaptive, given the requirements of the family situation, but also serve to provoke the sick wife into greater rebellion, irritation, and despair.

* * *

Here we have shown that schizophrenia is associated with inadequate role performance of the person who is afflicted. A disparity emerges between what the person does and what he ought to do according to the expectations embodied in his roles. As a result of this change, the role performance of his spouse is also changed. The sick or well husband married to a schizophrenic wife alters his behavior in such a way as to intensify and perpetuate the problems created by the wife's illness, but the well wife copes with the problems created by her husband's illness. Fundamentally, her ability to cope derives from the general role of women in the culture. Women more than men specialize in matters of illness, and it is the women who bear the burden of socio-emotional support in time of illness and distress.

26. Resistance to Change in the Self-Concept

CARL W. BACKMAN, PAUL F. SECORD, AND JERRY R. PEIRCE

Personality may in a general way reflect the culture as a whole or the characteristics of a more limited subcultural environment. But a crucial aspect of personality, the self-concept, may be seen as rooted even more specifically in the particular interpersonal relationships that tie an individual to other persons.

Carl W. Backman and Paul F. Secord have developed an "interpersonal congruency theory" which holds that a person seeks maximum congruency among the following elements: (1) his self-concept, (2) his perception of his own behavior toward other persons, and (3) his perception of the behavior of others toward him.

Sometimes a person's behavior may be adjusted to fit with the self-concept. At other times the self-concept may be adjusted to be congruent with the cues of other persons. It is this last possibility that is explored in the following article by Backman, Secord, and Peirce. The specific research hypothesis is that a feature of the self-concept will be more resistant to change if there is high consensus among others that this feature is indeed characteristic than if such consensus is lacking. In the following selections we are introduced to this study and given a summary of findings. These findings will then be analyzed in Project 10.

The self-concept has been the focus of considerable research and theorizing since the early work of James, Cooley, and Mead. All too often, however, research has not been guided except in a loose fashion by theory. Consequently the total accumulation of substantive findings has been disappointing. At the same time, self-theory has remained vague and rudimentary. More recently the development of a number of cognitive theories closely integrated with programs of systematic research has given promise of a greater articulation between research and theory in this area. While these theories in general have been concerned with the broader problem of stability and change of attitudes, their work has implications for attitudes pertaining to the self. One of these approaches, in particular, interpersonal congruency theory, while not focusing exclu-

Excerpts are reprinted from "Resistance to Change in the Self-Concept as a Function of Consensus Among Significant Others," *Sociometry*, 1963, **26**, 102–109, with permission of the publisher, the American Sociological Association, and the authors.

sively on the self, affords it a central place, and outlines the conditions under which the self remains stable or changes.

Basic to interpersonal congruency theory is the assumption that there exists within the cognitive organization of the individual a tendency to achieve a state of congruency between three components of what has been termed the interpersonal matrix. These components include an aspect of self of an individual (S), S's interpretation of his behavior relevant to that aspect, and S's perception of the related aspects of the other person (O) with whom he is interacting. Thus an interpersonal matrix is a recurring functional relation among these three components. S strives to achieve congruency among the components of the matrix. Congruency is a cognitive phenomenon; i.e., each component enters into a state of congruency only as a perceptual–cognitive experience on the part of S. All three components of the matrix are in a *state of congruency when S perceives his behavior and that of O as implying definitions of self congruent with relevant aspects of his self-concept.*

Forces that stabilize or bring about changes in either of the other two components of the matrix will, by virtue of this principle, affect the stability of the self. Sources of stability in S's behavior as well as that of O include the residues of previous experience—learned responses—as well as constancies in the stimulus environment. These constancies in turn result not only from the expectations that constitute the social system and guide the behavior of S and O, but also from the operation of a number of interpersonal processes that stem ultimately from the tendency to achieve congruency. While the role of the social system is recognized by most theories that regard the self as a reflection of the views of other persons toward S, these interpersonal processes require further comment. Interpersonal congruency theory, while recognizing the importance of the social structure in fashioning the self, does not view S as passive in the process. Rather S is seen as actively structuring his relations with others so as to achieve and maintain congruency. He does this in the following ways.

In the first place, he selectively interacts with other persons, preferring those who treat him in a manner congruent with his self-concept, and avoiding those who do not. Similarly, he selectively evaluates others, depending upon their attitudes toward him. He does this by liking those who treat him in a congruent fashion, and disliking those who do not. Thus he maximizes the effect of congruent actions and minimizes the effect of incongruent actions on the self-concept. He may also misperceive the actions of others toward him in the belief that they see him as he sees himself, when in actuality, their views of him are somewhat discrepant with his own. Finally, he develops certain behavior patterns that elicit from others reactions that are congruent with his self-definitions. These include not only manipulative behaviors calculated to evoke certain congruent responses, but also less self-conscious, more enduring actions that lead others to treat S in a manner congruent with his self-concept.

A final source of stability and change stems from the manner in which matrices are related to each other. A given matrix may be considered *relevant* to those matrices that contain one or more of the same or similar components as the given matrix. For example, an S who considers himself intelligent may exhibit behaviors in a variety of situations that are interpreted by him as congruent or incongruent with his belief concerning his intelligence. Thus he may obtain high grades in school, play expert chess, but may be a poor bridge player. With respect to the matrix component involving other persons, people may ask him for help in solving problems, he may generally win debates, but his father may criticize his intellectual accomplishments. Matrices having no components in common are considered irrelevant, and as having no effect upon each other.

Matrices vary with respect to *centrality*. The centrality of a matrix is a function of the number of relevant other matrices that stand in a supportive relation to it, and the value of the O-components in these matrices. The term *centrality* is chosen in preference to salience or centrality, since the latter terms already have several other established meanings in this field. The greater the centrality of a matrix, the more resistant it is to change, and should it change, the greater the resultant shifts in other matrices. The present study is concerned with one aspect of centrality, namely, the relative number of *O-components* having congruent relations with a given aspect of self. The contribution of S's *behavior-components* to centrality is ignored for the purposes of the present paper. Put simply, the thesis of the present paper is as follows: If a variety of significant other persons are perceived by S to agree in defining an aspect of S's self-concept congruently, their views support each other and his self-concept. If this condition were to prevail, the particular aspect of self involved would be expected to be more resistant to change than if S were to perceive less consensus among significant others. Thus, the main hypothesis of the present study may be stated as follows:

The greater the number of significant other persons who are perceived to define an aspect of an individual's self-concept congruently, the more resistant to change is that aspect of self.

The hypothesis was tested by choosing

for comparison, for each S, a self-ascribed trait on which S perceived high consensus to exist among five significant other persons, and a self-ascribed trait on which perceived consensus was low. Individuals were then subjected to strong pressure to change their perception of these traits, created by means of a highly credible, but false personality assessment. The degree of change in the high consensus trait was compared with change in the low consensus trait.

* * *

The main hypothesis of the study, as stated previously, is that an aspect of self will be more resistant to change when S believes that there is consensus among significant other persons concerning that aspect. A need high in consensus and one low in consensus for each individual were manipulated downward in an attempt to secure movement of these needs on a second self-ranking form. In general several forces could be expected to be generated by this manipulation. One is a tendency to lower one's self-ratings on these two traits. Another is the arousal of resistance to change, and some individuals in whom resistance is aroused might even rank themselves higher than they did initially on the need. Resistance of this sort would be expected because the acceptance of an incongruent self-definition not only requires a change in the matrix containing that aspect but in all related matrices in which that aspect is imbedded. Thus the threat of widespread incongruence could easily create resistance to acceptance. More frequently, of course, this resistance effect might be expected for the high consensus trait. While these two forces are represented by downward and upward movement in self-

ranks, respectively, a certain amount of random movement in both directions due to error of measurement will be superimposed upon these other movements. In order to examine the movement due to acceptance or resistance to manipulation uncontaminated by random movement, the best test of the hypothesis is a comparison of the movement of the high consensus trait with the movement for the low consensus trait.

Table 1 lists in the first two columns the number of steps that the high and low consensus need was moved by each individual. Downward movements are positively labeled; upward movements are given a negative sign. Relative movement, shown in the last column of Table 1, was determined by subtracting the movement of the high consensus trait from the low. If the relative movement represented by the difference score is positive, the hypothesis is supported for that subject. This analysis allows for random effects operating to move a need upward and still permits a test of the relative effects of the degree of consensus. For example, as indicated in the first row of Table 1, deference was chosen as the low consensus need for subject 1 and autonomy as the high consensus need. From the initial self-ranking to the post-manipulation self-ranking he moved deference 8 rank steps downward and autonomy 2 rank steps upward. This yields a net change of 10 steps in the direction of the hypothesis. As may be seen by inspection of the difference column, 26 individuals produced a net difference in the direction of the hypothesis, 2 showed no change, and 12 changed in an opposite direction.

TABLE 1. CHANGES IN HIGH AND LOW CONSENSUS MANIPULATED TRAITS FOR EACH SUBJECT

SUBJECT	TRAITS MANIPULATED LOW, HIGH	MOVEMENT OF		Difference
		Low Consensus Trait	High Consensus Trait	
1	Def, Aut	8	−2	10
2	Aut, Aff	8	0	8
3	Def, Aba	8	1	7
4	Chg, Nur	7	0	7
5	Aba, Nur	7	0	7
6	Def, Nur	6	−1	7
7	Agg, End	8	1	7
8	Int, Nur	5	0	5
9	Suc, Aff	5	0	5
10	Exh, Chg	5	0	5
11	Def, Chg	4	−1	5
12	Def, Aba	9	5	4
13	Chg, Suc	4	1	3
14	Aff, Int	3	0	3
15	Ord, Ach	5	2	3
16	Chg, Ach	6	3	3
17	Aba, Int	2	−1	3
18	Het, Def	5	2	3
19	Int, Chg	3	1	2
20	Het, End	5	3	2
21	Chg, Aba	5	3	2
22	Het, Chg	4	2	2
23	Het, Int	−1	−3	2
24	Exh, Ach	3	1	2
25	Ord, Ach	5	4	1
26	Aba, Het	1	0	1
27	Chg, Int	0	0	0
28	Chg, Aut	3	3	0
29	Int, Aut	0	1	−1
30	Aff, End	1	2	−1
31	Ach, Nur	0	1	−1
32	Het, Chg	0	2	−2
33	Exh, Ach	7	9	−2
34	Ach, Aba	−2	0	−2
35	Suc, Ach	−2	1	−3
36	Aba, Suc	1	5	−4
37	Dom, Ord	4	8	−4
38	Het, Dom	−3	4	−7
39	End, Nur	0	7	−7
40	Int, Aff	−2	6	−8

[Variables of this table are further discussed in Project 9, especially pp. 203–4.]

Projects

PROJECT 1
The College Student Role

In Selection 3 Levinson points to problems associated with a unitary assumption concerning a role. The organizationally acceptable definition of a particular role may not be fully congruent with the interpretations of the role made by a participant. Thus it becomes an empirical question as to the degree of congruence between the role definitions of organizations and those of individual participants.

This project affords the student an opportunity to assess the degree of congruence between these two dimensions of a role. In this project we will attempt to assess the degree of congruence between students' conceptions of what is appropriate behavior for them and their perceptions of how the college or university defines their role.

One modification regarding Levinson's conceptualization has been made. Rather than assessing how the university administrator *actually* defines the student role, we will deal only with the student's perceptions of the administrator's definition. This will be compared to the respondent's own orientation to that social role.

In addition to measuring the congruence between the perception of the organization's definition of the student role and the participant's interpretation, we shall be interested in seeing how the amount of congruity relates to the authoritarianism* of the respondent as measured by the F-scale.

HYPOTHESIS: *The students scoring high on authoritarianism will be more likely to register high congruence than students scoring low on authoritarianism.*

The rationale for the hypothesis is the assumption that students with a high authoritarianism are more likely to bring their role conceptions in line with their perceptions of how authorities define these roles.

For this exercise each student is to ask another college student outside of this course to answer the following scales. Scales 1 and 2 measure the respondent's definition of the student role and his perception of how the typical administrator would define that same role. Scale 3 is the F-scale measuring authoritarianism. After the respondent has given his responses to Scales 1, 2, and 3, you are to summarize them on Worksheet 1d. Your instructor will provide directions for filling out the tables and analyzing your data.

Be sure to put your name and class on Worksheet 1d so that you can obtain credit for this project.

---

* Authoritarianism refers to certain personality characteristics. Included are a dependence on authority, ethnocentrism, high conformity, overcontrol of emotions, and rigidity of thinking.

PROJECT 1

Worksheet 1a

Scale 1

Directions to Respondent

(1) Respond to the following ten items as you believe a *typical administrator at your university* would respond.

(2) Consider each item carefully and simply respond in terms of the amount of agreement or disagreement you believe the typical administrator would indicate for each item.

SA (Strongly Agree)
 A (Agree)
 I (Indifferent)
 D (Disagree)
SD (Strongly Disagree)

(3) Mark beside each item the choice you think the *typical administrator* would make.

Items

_____ 1. The university administration should make decisions regarding student conduct because students lack the maturity to make such decisions themselves.

_____ 2. Although students are often legitimately concerned with society, they lack realistic experience and therefore are unlikely to supply useful solutions to societal problems.

_____ 3. Students should have more power regarding the hiring and firing of faculty.

_____ 4. Student sexual behavior should not be under the jurisdiction of the university. Sexual behavior is a private matter and the business of the student only.

_____ 5. The university has an obligation to restrict student behavior in a manner consistent with parental demands.

_____ 6. Students who commit a crime outside the university community must still be held subject to university discipline.

_____ 7. Students should have more power to decide what courses should be offered at a college or university.

_____ 8. Because of the increasing size of college enrollments, students should be satisfied with impersonal relationships with their teachers.

_____ 9. It is outside the student's role to question what material a particular teacher considers important and chooses to present.

_____10. Students should spend more time with their class assignments and less with activities not sponsored by the university.

PROJECT 1

Worksheet 1b

Scale 2

Directions to Respondent

(1) Respond to the following ten items in terms of *your own personal feelings*.

(2) Consider each item carefully and simply respond in terms of the amount of agreement or disagreement you feel regarding that item.

SA (Strongly Agree)
A (Agree)
I (Indifferent)
D (Disagree)
SD (Strongly Disagree)

(3) Mark *your choice* beside each item.

Items

_____ 1. The university administration should make decisions regarding student conduct because students lack the maturity to make such decisions themselves.

_____ 2. Although students are often legitimately concerned with society, they lack realistic experience and therefore are unlikely to supply useful solutions to societal problems.

_____ 3. Students should have more power regarding the hiring and firing of faculty.

_____ 4. Student sexual behavior should not be under the jurisdiction of the university. Sexual behavior is a private matter and the business of the student only.

_____ 5. The university has an obligation to restrict student behavior in a manner consistent with parental demands.

_____ 6. Students who commit a crime outside the university community must still be held subject to university discipline.

_____ 7. Students should have more power to decide what courses should be offered at a college or university.

_____ 8. Because of the increasing size of college enrollments, students should be satisfied with impersonal relationships with their teachers.

_____ 9. It is outside the student's role to question what material a particular teacher considers important and chooses to present.

_____10. Students should spend more time with their class assignments and less with activities not sponsored by the university.

PROJECT 1

Worksheet 1c

Scale 3

Directions to Respondent

Read carefully each item below. On the blank space next to each item indicate your agreement or disagreement with that item. Use the following code for your responses.

SA (Strongly Agree)
 A (Agree)
 I (Indifferent)
 D (Disagree)
SD (Strongly Disagree)

Items

_____ 1. Obedience and respect for authority are the most important virtues children should learn.

_____ 2. A person who has bad manners, habits, and breeding can hardly expect to get along with decent people.

_____ 3. If people would talk less and work more, everybody would be better off.

_____ 4. The businessman and the manufacturer are much more important to society than the artist and the professor.

_____ 5. Science has its place, but there are many important things that can never possibly be understood by the human mind.

_____ 6. Young people sometimes get rebellious ideas, but as they grow up, they ought to get over them and settle down.

_____ 7. What this country needs most, more than laws and political programs, is a few courageous, tireless, devoted leaders in whom the people can put their faith.

_____ 8. No sane, normal, decent person could ever think of hurting a close friend or relative.

_____ 9. Nobody ever learned anything important except through suffering.

_____10. What youth needs is strict discipline, rugged determination, and the will to work and fight for family and country.

_____11. An insult to our honor should always be punished.

_____12. People who commit sex crimes, such as rape and attacks on children, deserve more than mere imprisonment; such criminals ought to be publicly whipped, or worse.

_____13. There is hardly anything lower than a person who does not feel great love, gratitude, and respect for his parents.

_____14. Most of our social problems would be solved if we could somehow get rid of the immoral, crooked, and feeble-minded people.

_____15. Homosexuals are hardly better than criminals and ought to be severely punished.

_____16. When a person has a problem or worry, it is best for him not to think about it but to keep busy with more cheerful things.

_____17. Every person should have complete faith in some supernatural power whose decisions he obeys without question.

_____18. Some people are born with an urge to jump from high places.

_____19. People can be divided into two distinct classes: the weak and the strong.

_____20. Someday it will probably be shown that astrology can explain a lot of things.

_____21. Wars and social troubles may someday be ended by an earthquake or a flood that will destroy the whole world.

_____22. No weakness or difficulty can hold us back if we have enough willpower.

_____23. It is best to use some prewar authorities in Germany to keep order and prevent chaos.

_____24. Most people don't realize how much our lives are controlled by plots hatched in secret places.

_____25. Human nature being what it is, there will always be war and conflict.

_____26. Familiarity breeds contempt.

_____27. Nowadays when so many different kinds of people move around and mix together so much, a person has to protect himself especially carefully against catching an infection or a disease from them.

_____28. Nowadays more and more people are prying into matters that should remain personal and private.

_____29. The wild sex life of the old Greeks and Romans was tame compared to some of the goings-on in this country, even in places where people might least expect it.

PROJECT 1

Worksheet 1d

Data Report

Student's Name:_____

Class:_____

Date:_____

Record the responses to Scales 1, 2, and 3 in the appropriate parts below. The respondent's name is not to be given. Indicate only your name and class on each scale so that you receive credit for participating in this project.

Scale 1

For each item, fill in the responses (SA, A, I, D, SD) to Scale 1.

1_____ 2_____ 3_____ 4_____ 5_____ 6_____ 7_____
8_____ 9_____ 10_____

Scale 2

For each item, fill in the responses (SA, A, I, D, SD) to Scale 2.

1_____ 2_____ 3_____ 4_____ 5_____ 6_____ 7_____
8_____ 9_____ 10_____

Scale 3

1_____ 2_____ 3_____ 4_____ 5_____ 6_____ 7_____
8_____ 9_____ 10_____ 11_____ 12_____ 13_____ 14_____
15_____ 16_____ 17_____ 18_____ 19_____ 20_____
21_____ 22_____ 23_____ 24_____ 25_____ 26_____
27_____ 28_____ 29_____

Summary

After completing Analyses I and II, fill out the following. Use the cutoff points suggested by your instructor, for both congruity and authoritarianism dimensions.

Congruity (check one)
_____High
_____Low
Authoritarianism (check one)
_____High
_____Medium
_____Low

ANALYSIS I: *Obtaining Ranks: Scales 1 and 2*

Each student should look at the responses for Scales 1 and 2 as recorded on Worksheet 1d. Your task is first to enter the raw responses from the worksheet in Table 1. Be careful to list responses under the appropriate scale. The raw responses will be *SA, A, I, D,* or *SD.*

TABLE 1

SCALE 1—STUDENT'S PERCEPTION OF ADMINISTRATOR'S DEFINITION			SCALE 2—STUDENT'S DEFINITION		
Item	*Response*	*Rank**	*Item*	*Response*	*Rank**
1			1		
2			2		
3			3		
4			4		
5			5		
6			6		
7			7		
8			8		
9			9		
10			10		

* These ranks must be adjusted for ties. See instructions below.

After you have entered the raw scores, you may rank-order each item. Begin by looking for all items scored *SA* on Scale 1. If there is only one, assign it the number *1*. If there are several *SAs*, you must adjust the ranks. Since the *SAs* would be tied for first place (rank), you average their ranks. Thus if there are three *SAs*, you add their positions, 1, 2, and 3, and divide by 3. The result, which is 2, would be the rank for the three items scored *SA*. Since three ranks have been taken, the next rank to be assigned would be 4, and so forth. Remember that any time items are tied at a rank, add the ranks they would occupy (for example, 5 and 6) and divide by the number of items tied (2). Then assign the result (in this case, 5.5) to all the tied items.

Repeat this ranking procedure for Scale 2.

The next step is to compute the Spearman rank-order correlation. (See appendix for further clarification of Spearman rank-order correlation.) In a table like Table 2, enter the rank-orders for each scale, as computed in Table 1. Then indicate the difference in ranks between Item 1 on both scales, Item 2 on both scales, and so forth. Square each of the differences you find and enter the answer in the last column of Table 2. Total this column to obtain Σd^2—the sum of the differences that have each been squared. Your instructor will provide directions for computing the Spearman rank-order correlation from Σd^2. This is read as the summation of differences that have each been squared.

TABLE 2. RANK-ORDER DIFFERENCES

	SCALE 1	SCALE 2		
Item	Rank	Rank	Differences (d)	(d^2)
1				
2				
3				
4				
5				
6				
7				
8				
9				
10				
				$\Sigma d^2 =$

ANALYSIS II: *Comparing With Authoritarianism*

You should by now have a correlation from the previous section. Now you must score Scale 3. The following procedure may be used.

(1) Assign the following numerical values to responses to Scale 3 on Worksheet 1c: SA–5, A–4, I–3, D–2, SD–1.

(2) Add all the numerical values.

(3) Using cutoff points indicated by your instructor, determine whether the Scale 3 responses indicate high, medium, or low authoritarianism. If your instructor does not give cutoff points, use the following:

> 130 points and over   —high authoritarianism
> 45-129 points   —medium authoritarianism
> 44 points and below—low authoritarianism

Your instructor will also help you decide cutoff points for high and low congruity. After this is done, complete Worksheet 1d.

Expect something like the following table for a tabulation of the data by the instructor. Your instructor will probably have plans for a statistical analysis of this data.

AUTHORITARIANISM

		Low	Medium	High
	Low			
CONGRUITY	High			

PROJECT 2
Social Status: Auxiliary Characteristics

In Selection 4 Hughes takes the position that even though an individual may possess the technical qualifications to perform the functions associated with a particular occupational status, he may have additional characteristics not typically associated with that status. These auxiliary characteristics can prevent him from gaining access to that status. Futhermore, even if he gains access to the status, certain auxiliary characteristics may influence who will seek his services.

This project is designed to investigate which auxiliary characteristics respondents believe affect a person's chances of success in certain selected occupations. It should be carefully understood that this project deals with respondents' perceptions and not necessarily with factors actually operative in the occupational marketplace. However, occupational mobility is influenced not only by actual discriminatory barriers but also by perceptions of what barriers are believed to exist.

The auxiliary characteristics used here fall under three headings, sex, religion, and race. The study is set up so that you may assess the relationship between the *respondent's own characteristics* regarding these dimensions and his *perceptions of discriminatory barriers.* Your class may decide to study the relationship between all the characteristics listed or a partial list, such as the relationship between being Catholic and perceiving Catholicism as increasing or decreasing the probabilities of occupational success.

Each student is to administer the questions in Sections A and B to another person not taking this course. Do not tell the respondent the purpose of the study. If a special sample is to be used, your instructor will provide the appropriate instructions. Each respondent is to record his responses on Worksheet 2a. You are to fill in your name on the worksheet so that you may obtain credit for the study. Do not ask the respondent to identify himself. After you have collected your data, turn to the section entitled "Summary of Data."

Worksheet 2a

Student's Name:_____

Class:_____

Date:_____

Section A

In the chart on page 154, eight column headings represent eight auxiliary characteristics that are often associated with various occupations. Your task is to indicate
which of these characteristics in your opinion would increase or decrease a person's
chances of being successful in each of the twenty occupations listed. Each occupation listed has eight columns associated with it. Mark an *I* in the column if you
think that particular characteristic *increases* a person's chances of success in that
occupation. Mark a *D* in the column if you think that particular characteristic
decreases a person's chances of success in that occupation. Mark an *NR* if you
think that that particular characteristic is *not relevant* to probabilities of success
in that occupation. Answer in terms of the occupational structure as it exists
presently in the United States.

Auxiliary Characteristics

Code: *I*—Increases a person's chances of success
       D—Decreases a person's chances of success
       NR—Not relevant to a person's chances of success

Section B

Indicate your sex, religion, and race by checking the appropriate characteristic in
each of the columns below.

SEX		RELIGION		RACE	
Male	_____	Catholic	_____	Caucasian	_____
Female	_____	Jewish	_____	Negro	_____
		Protestant	_____	Oriental	_____
		Other	_____	Other	_____
		None	_____		

OCCUPATIONAL STATUS

	MALE	FEMALE	CATHOLIC	JEWISH	PROTESTANT	CAUCASIAN	NEGRO	ORIENTAL
Astronaut								
Automobile Mechanic								
Banker								
Business Executive								
Computer Specialist								
Electrician								
Elementary School Teacher								
Encyclopedia Salesman								
Farm Laborer								
Fireman								
Garbage Collector								
Lawyer								
Laundry Operator								
Medical Doctor								
Registered Nurse								
Plumber								
Policeman								
Secretary								
Sociologist								
Train Porter								

Summary of Data

The main part of the analysis will be to determine the relationship between the respondent's characteristics and his perceptions regarding how certain auxiliary characteristics influence occupational success. This· is accomplished by totaling the number of times a respondent sees a particular characteristic, for example, Catholicism, as increasing or decreasing a person's chances of occupational success across all the occupational categories. To obtain this information, simply look at Worksheet 2a, and since in this example Catholicism is column 3, count the number of Is, Ds, or NRs registered in that column for all occupational categories.

Since there are a very large number of combinations between a respondent's characteristics and his perceptions of auxiliary characteristics and occupational success, your instructor will probably want to be selective. However, any combination can be placed into the following two-by-two design. (See appendix for explanation of design.)

Example

RESPONDENT'S CHARACTERISTIC

		Catholic	Protestant
CHARACTERISTIC: CATHOLICISM	Increase *I*	*a*	*b*
	Decrease *D*	*c*	*d*

Remember that the specific respondent characteristic and auxiliary characteristic will be chosen by your instructor. You are to indicate how your data reflect the particular relationship chosen for study. Use Worksheet 2b to report your results.

Your instructor, upon receiving your data, will be able to group them and run a test for statistical significance.

PROJECT 2

Worksheet 2b
Data Report

Student's Name:_____

Class:_____

Date:_____

The purpose of this sheet is to tabulate your results in terms of the auxiliary characteristic chosen by your instructor. It is important to realize that if, for example, the auxiliary characteristic is being female we will be comparing males and females in their responses. In other words, we are interested in finding out if males and females differ in the degree to which they see being a female as increasing or decreasing the chances for occupational success. Your task is to count the number of times your respondent saw being female as increasing or decreasing a person's chances of occupational success. You will gain this information by looking at Worksheet 2a. In the example where "female" is the auxiliary characteristic you would simply count the number of times "I" or "D" was marked in the column headed "Female" across the twenty occupational categories. Record your data in the following table.* All data collected by students will be grouped by the instructor.

RESPONDENT'S CHARACTERISTIC

AUXILIARY CHARACTERISTIC	*Increase*	_____
	Decrease	_____

*It is easy to construct as many tables of this sort as are needed. Simply use the table above as a model. Of course don't forget to put your name and class on any tables you want to hand in for class credit.

PROJECT 3
Cross-Cultural Evidence on Effects of Early Socialization

Fixation and Its Consequences

According to psychoanalytic theory, severe frustration in a child's early development may lead to "fixation"—that is, an arrested state of emotional development. The child is unable to move beyond preoccupation with an emotional problem and the things he consciously or unconsciously associates with it. Even as an adult, the personality may bear the imprint of such early frustration in the way an individual processes thoughts and feelings that had once been linked with his early frustrations.

Take, for example, severe frustrations concerned with feeding or weaning during the first year of life. During this "oral stage" of development (as psychoanalysts call the early period), the mouth may be an especially important organ for experiencing the world. Frustrations with feeding or weaning may strike at the heart of a child's earliest personality development. Such frustrations may leave their imprint in a general way of relating to people, as well as in a way of relating to food. So, at least, we are led to expect by writings of psychoanalysts.

Or take the somewhat later problems of toilet training; these too might involve severe frustrations. If training during this "anal stage" is too rigidly received, the person may develop a compulsive quality in dealing with things in general—as well as perhaps a more specific preoccupation with bathroom activities.

Such ideas from psychoanalysis have found an important place in culture-and-personality writings, especially those dealing with early socialization. Recognizing that different infant training practices tend to be found in different cultures, social scientists have looked for the impact of such practices upon typical patterns of adult personality. Kardiner and Linton's work on "basic personality" (presented in the last part of this book) provides a notable example. It is assumed that the early training practices show a similarity within a given culture and that these practices tend to set a particular direction for the development of adult personality.

Still another implication of such culture-and-personality theories is that similar patterns of personality (in turn largely shaped by early child-rearing practices) will find expression in cultural themes. For example, in a society's religion and art we might expect to find reexpressed some of the themes emphasized by early personality formation in that culture.

Putting together these ideas from psychoanalysts and culture-and-personality students, we may drive the following generalizations:

(1) Especially severe and repeated frustrations in early child development create fixations that shape later patterns of adult personality.

(2) When most children in the same society experience similar patterns of early frustration (due to culturally patterned forms of early child training), this leaves its mark in typical patterns of adult personality in that society.

(3) Typical, widely shared patterns of adult personality in a given society in turn foster the selection of cultural patterns most congruent with such personality patterns.

Some Evidence

A study based broadly upon the kind of thinking outlined above has been done by John W. M. Whiting and Irvin L. Child. They studied patterns of early socialization in many different cultures and related such socialization to other features of culture. In reporting their results in *Child Training and Personality* (1953), Whiting and Child include several chapters on the relationship of early socialization practices to explanations of illness.

Whiting and Child theorized that frustration experienced concerning early weaning or feeding may create a more generalized "oral socialization anxiety," which expresses itself in adult personality and in broader cultural themes. For example, it may predispose persons to explain unknown illness as caused by the effects of eating or drinking.

Likewise, particularly severe frustrations associated with rigid toilet training may yield a generalized "anal socialization anxiety," which may express itself in adult compulsions with things of all sorts. For example, preoccupation with rituals and charms for the prevention and cure of disease might be considered an expression of such "anal socialization anxiety."*

Out of 75 cultures from all over the world for which Whiting and Child examined anthropological records, 39 had sufficient information to allow a classification of cultures in terms of both (1) the extent of severity of "oral socialization anxiety" and (2) the extent of oral explanations of illness. The results may be summarized in Table 1.

*We have not here adequately represented the full theory contained in *Child Training and Personality*. We have intended only to present enough of the ideas to introduce the data that follows. Students may find a much fuller discussion of the above ideas in the book (Whiting and Child, 1953).

TABLE 1. ORAL SOCIALIZATION ANXIETY AND ILLNESS EXPLANATIONS

	NUMBER OF SOCIETIES WITH PRESENCE OR ABSENCE OF DISTINCTIVELY ORAL EXPLANATIONS OF ILLNESS	
	Present	*Absent*
Societies above the median rating on "oral socialization anxiety"	17	3
Societies below the median rating on "oral socialization anxiety"	6	13

Source: Whiting and Child (1953), p. 156.

Of the 75 cultures examined, only 20 had sufficient information to allow a classification in terms of both (1) the extent of severity of "anal socialization anxiety" and (2) the presence or absence of anal explanations of illness. The results may be summarized in Table 2.

Assuming that the data of these tables adequately summarize the evidence on early socialization and on illness explanations of many different cultures, do they offer convincing evidence for a child-training interpretation of cultural forms? Specifically, do they support the idea that explanations of illness in a culture will tend to reflect common fixations of early socialization?

We shall not go into all the lines of interpretation that would be required by a full answer to these questions. We will instead focus on the rather simple question of whether the evidence presented shows any patterns at all. Is the evidence sufficiently definite that we can say that cultures with high oral socialization anxiety also tend to be cultures with oral explanations of illness? Is the evidence sufficiently definite that we can say that cultures with high anal socialization also tend to be cultures with anal explanations of illness?

The Chi-Square Test

We may ask whether the pattern of frequencies of Table 1 (or Table 2) is significantly different from what would be expected by a chance arrangement. If not, we would not be much impressed by the evidence. However, if the pattern does depart significantly from chance, we should be more impressed by the evidence of a relationship between variables. Of course, any particular distribution of frequencies might *sometime* occur by chance, but extreme distributions are so unlikely that we can point out how improbable such a distribution would be.

A test of statistical significance is a means of pointing to how improbable a given arrangement would be by the laws of chance. The chi-square (χ^2) test is a technique for measuring statistical significance when data are in the form of frequencies (numbers of cases). It is a measure of the extent to which a distribution of frequencies departs from what would be expected by chance.

TABLE 2. ANAL SOCIALIZATION ANXIETY AND ILLNESS EXPLANATIONS

	NUMBER OF SOCIETIES WITH PRESENCE OR ABSENCE OF DISTINCTIVELY ANAL EXPLANATIONS OF ILLNESS	
	Present	*Absent*
Societies at or above the median rating on "anal socialization anxiety"	6	5
Societies below the median rating on "anal socialization anxiety"	4	5

Source: Whiting and Child (1953), p. 158.

Directions for computing the value of χ^2 are given in the appendix of this book.

After studying the discussion of statistical inference in the appendix, the reader should be prepared to evaluate the statistical significance of the data in Table 1. Is there a strong relationship between oral socialization anxiety and oral explanations of illness? That is, do societies high on one of these variables also tend to be high on the other? If so, it would be at least indirect evidence for interpreting certain cultural patterns as reflecting typical oral fixations of early childhood.

Remember that the data of Table 1 had the following form:

$a=17$	$b=3$
$c=6$	$d=13$

$a+b=20$
$c+d=19$

$a+c=23 \quad b+d=16 \qquad a+b+c+d=39$

Figure the expected frequencies for each of the cells (a, b, c, and d). Then compute the chi-square value and report your results on Worksheet 3. What is the chi-square value? Is this statistically significant? What does this "prove" about early socialization or culture-and-personality relationships?

A similar test of the data in Table 2 should also be made. Results of this should likewise be reported on Worksheet 3. What conclusions can be drawn from this exercise?

PROJECT 3

*Cross-Cultural Evidence on
Effects of Early Socialization*

Table 1 (Oral Socialization Anxiety and Illness Explanations) has the following frequencies:

$a = 17$	$b = 3$	$a + b = 20$
$c = 6$	$d = 13$	$c + d = 19$

$$a + c = 23 \quad b + d = 16 \quad N = 39.$$

Use the following formula for deriving the value of chi square:

$$\chi^2 = \frac{N\left(\mid ad - bc \mid - \dfrac{N}{2}\right)^2}{(a + b)(c + d)(a + c)(b + d)} \; .$$

What is the value of χ^2 obtained? _____

Check whichever of the following most precisely expresses the obtained measure of statistical significance:

_____ $p > .05$ (probability greater than .05 that such a pattern could be attributed to chance)

_____ $p < .05$ (probability less than .05 that such a pattern could be attributed to chance)

_____ $p < .01$

_____ $p < .001$

Table 2 (Anal Socialization and Illness Explanations) has the following frequencies:

$a = 6$	$b = 5$	$a + b = 11$
$c = 4$	$d = 5$	$c + d = 9$

$$a + c = 10 \quad b + d = 10 \quad N = 20$$

What is the value of χ^2 obtained in this case? _____

What statement about statistical significance can be made about this case $(p > .05, p < .05, \text{etc.})$? _____

PROJECT 4
Twenty Statements

The instructor will indicate when Worksheet 4 is to be filled out. He will also later give instructions for collecting and tabulating the answers of the exercise.*

Worksheet 4

Twenty Statements

Student's Name:_____

Class:_____

Date:_____

Below are spaces to write twenty answers to the simple question "Who am I?" Just give twenty different answers to this question. Answer as if you were giving the answers to yourself, not to somebody else. Proceed fairly rapidly, writing the answers in the order that they occur to you. Don't worry about the logic or importance of your answers.

1

2

3

4

5

6

7

8

9

10

11

12

13

14

15

16

17

18

19

20

* This exercise is based on procedures of Manford H. Kuhn and Thomas S. McPartland (1954).

PROJECT 5
Measuring Self-Esteem

Literature dealing with self-concept typically makes a basic distinction between an individual's actual and ideal self. His actual self refers to how he perceives himself at a given time, while his ideal self refers to what he wishes he were at that point in time. Self-esteem is viewed in terms of the discrepancy between an individual's perceived actual self and his ideal self. The greater the discrepancy between the actual and ideal self, the lower one's self-esteem.

This project is designed to acquaint the student with one way in which self-esteem can be estimated. No attempt is made to relate self-esteem to other variables. There is no reason, however, that the instructor cannot design a study that incorporates other variables along with this measure of self-esteem.

The student is free to administer this research to anyone, including himself. The name required on the Worksheet is only to indicate that the student has completed the project. It does not refer necessarily to the respondent.

The project is designed to measure (1) actual self, (2) ideal self, and (3) self-esteem. The latter is computed in terms of the respondent's replies regarding his actual and ideal self.

Your responsibilities on this project can be divided into five major steps:

(1) Have your respondent fill out Sections A and B (Worksheets 5a and 5b), recording his response to each item on the blank alongside each item.

(2) Take the raw scores for both the Actual and Ideal Self scales and enter them in Table 1 on Worksheet 5c.

(3) Working from Table 1, you must now rank-order these raw scores for both the Actual and Ideal ratings. Taking each scale *separately*, begin by assigning the rank of 1 to the item with the highest score. Then find the next highest score and assign that item the rank of 2 and so forth. If you come across ties among your raw scores, you must take special care in assigning them ranks. Suppose that 3 items have the raw score of 6 and that they are tied for Ranks 2, 3, and 4. You simply add the values of these ranks and divide by the number of ranks; in this case, 9 divided by 3 yields 3. Then those items with the raw score of 6 would be assigned the rank value of 3. All ties must be dealt with in this fashion. Enter the rank orders for each scale in Table 2.

(4) To complete Table 2, you must first obtain the rank-order differences on the two scales for each item. If item 4 had a rank value of 3 on the Actual Self scale and 5 on the Ideal Self scale, the difference would be 2. Enter the difference for each item in the appropriate column in Table 2. After this is done for all the items, you must square each difference. Finally, you must add up all these squared differences and enter the answer as Σd^2.

(5) Your instructor will provide directions for statistical analysis of your results. You will want to look at the statistical appendix in this book to help you understand his directions.

PROJECT 5

Worksheet 5a

Section A. Actual Self

Directions to Respondent

Use the nine-point scale below to rate *yourself* on each of the thirty self-referent items. Rate the items most descriptive of yourself at the high end of the scale, those least descriptive of yourself at the opposite end, and those about which you are not sure or undecided in the middle. For each item record your response on the blank next to that item.

	"Least like me"	"Most like me"
Items*	Scale: 0 1 2 3 4 5	6 7 8

_____ 1. I am intelligent.
_____ 2. I have warm emotional relationships with others.
_____ 3. I am a responsible person.
_____ 4. I understand myself.
_____ 5. I am a hostile person.
_____ 6. I respect myself.
_____ 7. I am afraid of sex.
_____ 8. I am a submissive person.
_____ 9. I have an attractive personality.
_____10. I am self-centered.
_____11. I am liked by most people who know me.
_____12. I am concerned with what other people think of me.
_____13. I am impulsive.
_____14. I feel apathetic.
_____15. I don't trust my emotions.
_____16. I feel insecure.
_____17. I am an optimist.
_____18. I am satisfied with myself.
_____19. I am assertive.
_____20. I express my emotions freely.
_____21. I put on a false front.
_____22. I am ambitious.
_____23. I am a hard worker.
_____24. I usually like people.
_____25. I face a crisis or difficulty with confidence.
_____26. I am unreliable.
_____27. My personality is attractive to the opposite sex.
_____28. I have a horror of failing in things I want to do.
_____29. I have to protect myself with excuses, with rationalizing.
_____30. I can communicate my thoughts easily to others.

* These items are adopted from those developed by J. M. Butler and G. V. Haigh. They appear in *Psychotherapy and Personality Change,* edited by Carl Rogers and Rosaland Dymond.

PROJECT 5

Worksheet 5b
Section B. Ideal Self

Directions to Respondent

Use the nine-point scale below to indicate *how you would respond to the self-referent items if you were the type of person you would most like to be.* For each item record your response on the blank next to that item.

	"Most Unlike What I Want to Be"	"Most Like What I Want to Be"
Items	Scale: 0 1 2 3	4 5 6 7 8

_____ 1. I am intelligent.

_____ 2. I have warm emotional relationships with others.

_____ 3. I am a responsible person.

_____ 4. I understand myself.

_____ 5. I am a hostile person.

_____ 6. I respect myself.

_____ 7. I am afraid of sex.

_____ 8. I am a submissive person.

_____ 9. I have an attractive personality.

_____10. I am self-centered.

_____11. I am liked by most people who know me.

_____12. I am concerned with what other people think of me.

_____13. I am impulsive.

_____14. I feel apathetic.

_____15. I don't trust my emotions.

_____16. I feel insecure.

_____17. I am an optimist.

_____18. I am satisfied with myself.

_____19. I am assertive.

_____20. I express my emotions freely.

_____21. I put on a false front.

_____22. I am ambitious.

_____23. I am a hard worker.

_____24. I usually like people.

_____25. I face a crisis or difficulty with confidence.

_____26. I am unreliable.

_____27. My personality is attractive to the opposite sex.

_____28. I have a horror of failing in things I want to do.

_____29. I have to protect myself with excuses, with rationalizing.

_____30. I can communicate my thoughts easily to others.

PROJECT 5

Worksheet 5c

Section C. Raw Scores

Student's Name:_____

Class:_____

Date:_____

TABLE 1. RAW SCORES

ITEM	ACTUAL SELF	IDEAL SELF	ITEM	ACTUAL SELF	IDEAL SELF
1			16		
2			17		
3			18		
4			19		
5			20		
6			21		
7			22		
8			23		
9			24		
10			25		
11			26		
12			27		
13			28		
14			29		
15			30		

PROJECT 5

Worksheet 5d
Section D. Ranks

Student's Name:_____

Class:_____

Date:_____

TABLE 2. RANKS ADJUSTED FOR TIES

ITEMS	RANK ACTUAL SELF	RANK IDEAL SELF	DIFFERENCE (d)	d^2
1				
2				
3				
4				
5				
6				
7				
8				
9				
10				
11				
12				
13				
14				
15				
16				
17				
18				
19				
20				
21				
22				
23				
24				
25				
26				
27				
28				
29				
30				

$$\Sigma d^2 =$$

PROJECT 6
Self-Concept of Ability and Academic Performance

For many years social psychologists have held that evaluations of others, as perceived by an individual, form the basis for his self-concept. An individual's self-concept in turn is assumed to direct his behavior.

If this assumption is correct, then if one were to examine a sample of college students concerning (1) their self-concept of ability, and (2) their perceptions of how others evaluate their ability, and (3) performance as indicated by grades, certain expectations should hold. Basically, one would expect congruence between these three dimensions. However, it is reasonable to assume that under certain circumstances this congruence might not obtain for persons with high self-concepts of ability. For instance, a person may have a high self-concept of ability and perceive that others evaluate his ability in a similar manner; yet for reasons of motivation the individual may not perform accordingly.

For this reason, the following project will test the assumption concerning congruence between the three dimensions just discussed only for subjects recording a low self-concept of ability. The above congruity assumption would be disconfirmed under the condition in which a person with a low self-concept of ability perceives that others evaluate him more highly and/or his actual grade performances are in fact high. Accordingly, the following hypotheses will be tested.

> HYPOTHESIS 1: *Individuals with low self-concepts of ability will also perceive that other people judge them to be of low academic ability.*
> HYPOTHESIS 2: *Individuals with low self-concepts of ability will manifest low levels of academic performance.*

The following questions are to be answered by a college student other than one taking this course. *Do not* have the respondent record his responses on the questionnaire. Use Worksheet 6a for this purpose. Working from Worksheet 6a, carefully complete Worksheet 6b.

You should hand in both worksheets. Your instructor will then be able to run the statistical analysis.

Scales used in Sections A, B, and C are modified versions of scales used by Lee M. Joiner and Edsel Erickson.*

---

* Lee Joiner and E. Erickson. Scales and procedures for assessing social psychological characteristics of visually impaired and hearing impaired student. Project No. 6–8720, Contract No. OEG–3–6–068720.

Original form of these scales copyright 1962, Bureau of Educational Research, Michigan State University. Adapted with permission.

Section A: Self-Report

Directions

Answer the following seven questions by placing a circle around the appropriate letter on Worksheet 6a.

1. How do you rate yourself in school ability compared with your close friends?
   a. I am the best.
   b. I am above average.
   c. I am average.
   d. I am below average.
   e. I am the poorest.

2. How do you rate yourself in school ability compared with those in your college class?
   a. I am among the best.
   b. I am above average.
   c. I am average.
   d. I am below average.
   e. I am the poorest.

3. Where do you think you would rank in your class if you were in graduate school?
   a. Among the best.
   b. Above average.
   c. Average.
   d. Below average.
   e. Among the poorest.

4. Do you think you have the ability to complete college?
   a. Yes, definitely.
   b. Yes, probably.
   c. Not sure either way.
   d. Probably not.
   e. No.

5. In order to become a doctor, lawyer, or university professor, you would need to work beyond four years of college. How likely do you think it is that you could complete such advanced work, assuming financing could be arranged?
   a. Very likely.
   b. Somewhat likely.
   c. Not sure either way.
   d. Unlikely.
   e. Most unlikely.

6. Forget for the moment how others grade your work. In your opinion how good do you think your work is?
   a. My work is excellent.
   b. My work is good.
   c. My work is average.
   d. My work is below average.
   e. My work is much below average.

7. What kind of grades do you think you are capable of getting?
   a. Mostly As

b. Mostly Bs
c. Mostly Cs
d. Mostly Ds
e. Mostly Es

Section B: Parental Perspective

Directions

Pretend you are your mother or father. Answer as they would. On Worksheet 6a circle the letter of your answer for each of the following five items.

1. Do your mother and father say that you can do school work better than, as well as, or more poorly than your friends?
   a. Better.
   b. As well.
   c. More poorly.
2. Do they think you could graduate from college?
   a. Yes.
   b. Maybe.
   c. No.
3. Would your mother and father say you would rank with the best, with average, or with below-average students if you graduate from college?
   a. The best.
   b. Average.
   c. Below average.
4. You would need more than four years of college to become a college teacher or doctor. Do your mother and father think you could do that?
   a. Yes.
   b. Maybe.
   c. No.
5. What grades do your mother and father think you can get?
   a. As and Bs.
   b. Bs and Cs.
   c. Ds and Es.

Section C: Best Friend's Perspective

Directions

Think for a moment about your friends. Answer as they would. On Worksheet 6a circle the letter of your answer for each of the following five items.

1. Would your best friend say that you can do school work better than, as well as, or more poorly than other people your age?
   a. Better.
   b. As well.
   c. More poorly.

2. Would your best friend say that you would rank with the best, with average, or with below-average students if you graduate from college?
   a. Best.
   b. Average.
   c. Below average.
3. Does your best friend think that you could graduate from college?
   a. Yes.
   b. Maybe.
   c. No.
4. You would need more than four years of college to become a college teacher or doctor. Does your best friend think you could do that?
   a. Yes.
   b. Maybe.
   c. No.
5. What grades does your best friend think you are capable of getting?
   a. As and Bs.
   b. Bs and Cs.
   c. Ds and Es.

Section D: Grades

Directions

Now consider your total grade point average since you have been in college. What does it average out to be? On Worksheet 6a circle the letter of the most accurate figure.

a. A.
b. A minus.
c. B plus.
d. B.
e. B minus.
f. C plus.
g. C.
h. C minus.
i. D plus.
j. D.
k. D minus.
l. Below D.

PROJECT 6

Worksheet 6a

Data Report

Student's Name*:_____

Class:_____

Date:_____

Section A: Self-Report. Circle the appropriate letter to indicate your response.
1. a b c d e   2. a b c d e   3. a b c d e   4. a b c d e
5. a b c d e   6. a b c d e   7. a b c d e

Section B: Parental Perspective. Circle the appropriate letter for each item.
1. a b c   2. a b c   3. a b c   4. a b c   5. a b c

Section C: Perspective of Friends. Circle the appropriate letter for each item.
1. a b c   2. a b c   3. a b c   4. a b c   5. a b c

Section D: Grades. Circle the appropriate letter for each item.
a b c d e f g h i j k l

*It is understood that the student here named is not the same person who actually answers the questions of this project.

PROJECT 6

Worksheet 6b

Student's Name:_____

Class:_____

Date:_____

Summary

Worksheet 6a should include the raw scores registered by the person you inter-viewed. With help from your instructor, you must now complete this summary statement of the data given in Worksheet 6a.

The purpose of this worksheet is to determine whether or not your respondent should be classified as high or low on the various scales. If you examine the hypotheses being tested, you will see that this is absolutely necessary for the analysis.

Section A: Self-Report. Use the following number code: a—5
b—4
c—3
d—2
e—1

Using the number code, add up the scores for your respondent on Section A. If he or she scored 28 or more, check *High*. If he scored 14 or less, mark *Low*.
High _____   Low _____

Sections B–C: Perceived Judgments of Others (Parents and Friends). Use the following number code: a—3
b—2
c—1

Using this number code, add up the scores for your respondent on Sections B and C. If the total of both scales together is 25 or above, check *High*. If the total is 15 or less, mark *Low*.
High _____   Low _____

Section D: Academic Performance. Use the following number code: a—12
b—11
c—10
d— 9
e— 8
f— 7
g— 6
h— 5
i— 4
j— 3
k— 2
l— 1

If your respondent's response is coded 9 or above, mark *High*. If your respon-dent's response is 4 or below, mark *Low*._____
High _____   Low _____

PROJECT 7
Selected Attitudes

This project is designed to study one implication from Selection 18, in which Rosenberg suggests that people tend to like those things which facilitate what they value and tend to dislike things which facilitate what they negatively value.

Bearing this in mind, we would expect that if we wanted to predict the negative affect (disliking) regarding any attitude object, we would be aided by knowing (1) what a person values, and (2) whether or not that person sees the attitude object under consideration as facilitating what he positively values or facilitating what he negatively values.

Therefore, we shall test the prediction that if a person expresses a strong or very strong negative value *and* sees the attitude object as facilitating that negative value area, then that person will be most likely to dislike that specific attitude object. Doubt would be cast upon Rosenberg's theory if we found that negative affect toward an attitude object is not directly correlated with the belief that the attitude object facilitates things negatively valued by the individual. Or conversely, that positive affect is not directly correlated with the belief that the attitude object in question facilitates things positively valued by the individual.

Your task is to have another person outside of this class answer the following questions. It would probably improve your study if you go out into the community and get someone other than a student to interview. In any case, record all answers on Worksheet 7a. After completing the interview, you must complete Worksheet 7b. Hand in *both* Worksheets (with your name and class indicated) to your instructor. He will proceed with the statistical analysis or give directions to you for your participation in the analysis.

Interview Schedule

1. One problem facing any nation involves deciding how much money to spend on the military when such expenditure means spending less on programs for the internal needs of that country. How strongly do you feel that an increase in expenditures on the military is *undesirable* when it cuts into domestic programs?
   a. Very strongly.
   b. Strongly.
   c. Indifferent.
   d. Disagree.
   e. Completely disagree.
2. Do you see the current President of the United States as advocating a policy that favors military over domestic expenditures?
   a. Most definitely.
   b. Yes, in general.
   c. I am not sure.
   d. No, not in general.
   e. Definitely not.
3. Much has been said about the increase of crime here in the United States. How strongly do you feel that this increase directly affects your personal security?
   a. I very strongly feel that a person is no longer secure even in his own home.
   b. I strongly feel that we as citizens are less secure because of this increase in crime.
   c. I am not really sure.
   d. While crime may be increasing, I don't feel it affects my personal security.
   e. While crime may be increasing, I would strongly argue that I am as secure today as at any time in the past.
4. Many individuals believe that the Supreme Court has seriously tied the hands of law enforcement agencies and therefore has contributed to the increase in crime. How do you feel about this position?
   a. Strongly agree.
   b. Agree.
   c. Not sure either way.
   d. Disagree.
   e. Strongly disagree.
5. Do you feel that increased sexual freedom is a threat to a society and must be curbed?
   a. Most definitely.
   b. Yes.
   c. I am not sure.
   d. No.
   e. Most definitely not.
6. In your opinion do you believe that current motion picture producers are exploiting sexual themes and thereby contributing to an increase in sexual freedom?
   a. Most definitely.
   b. Yes.
   c. I am not sure.

    d. No.

    e. Most definitely not.

7. Take a few moments and consider your feelings about the current President of the United States. What are your own personal feelings about this man?

    a. I like him very much.

    b. Favorable.

    c. Indifferent.

    d. Unfavorable.

    e. I dislike him very much.

8. What are your own personal feelings about the Supreme Court, especially those members directly responsible for decisions that could be seen as restricting operations of law enforcement?

    a. I strongly dislike them.

    b. Unfavorable.

    c. I neither like nor dislike them.

    d. Favorable.

    e. I like them very much.

9. In general, what are your personal feelings about the present generation of motion picture producers?

    a. I find myself strongly disliking them.

    b. Unfavorable.

    c. I neither like nor dislike them.

    d. Favorable.

    e. I like them very much.

PROJECT 7

Worksheet 7a

Selected Attitudes

Student's Name:_____

Class:_____

Date:_____

Give below the answers to the nine questions by circling the letter of the answer that best represents your attitude.

1. a b c d e

2. a b c d e

3. a b c d e

4. a b c d e

5. a b c d e

6. a b c d e

7. a b c d e

8. a b c d e

9. a b c d e

PROJECT 7

Worksheet 7b

Data Report

Student's Name:_____

Class:_____

Date:_____

Directions

Working from Worksheet 7a, you are to summarize the results of your interview as indicated below. Do this by placing a check in the appropriate place for each question. If any set (I, II, or III) contains one or more neutral responses (c), *record no data for that set.*

Set I: Questions 1, 2, and 7.

Question 1
  Value Area: _____Negative (*a* or *b*)
  Military Expenditures   _____Positive (*d* or *e*)
Question 2
  Cognition   _____Facilitates (*a* or *b*)
                                 _____Blocks (*d* or *e*)

Question 7
  Affect   _____Negative (*d* or *e*)
                                 _____Positive (*a* or *b*)

Set II: Questions 3, 4, and 8.

Question 3
  Value Area: _____Negative (*a* or *b*)
  Crime Increase   _____Positive (*d* or *e*)
Question 4
  Cognition   _____Facilitates (*a* or *b*)
                                 _____Blocks (*d* or *e*)

Question 8
  Affect   _____Negative (*a* or *b*)
                                 _____Positive (*d* or *e*)

Set III: Questions 5, 6, and 9

Question 5
  Value Area: _____Negative (*a* or *b*)
  Sexual Freedom   _____Positive (*d* or *e*)
Question 6
  Cognition   _____Facilitates (*d* or *e*)
                                 _____Blocks (*a* or *b*)

Question 9
  Affect   _____Negative (*a* or *b*)
                                 _____Positive (*d* or *e*)

PROJECT 8

Discussion Groups

The instructor will present lists of students assigned to each of several discussion groups. He may designate one person as "convener" and another as "reporter" for each group. Either the instructor or the convener will select places and times for meetings, and the reporter will report any information required by the instructor. It is suggested that each group be given a simple label and that individuals within groups be identified by initials or by imaginary nicknames (used consistently for all materials), which will not require full identification of individuals to the instructor.

Before meeting in groups, each student should complete and turn in to the instructor Worksheet 8a. This project is based upon the following description of five dilemmas. Worksheet 8a must be turned in to the instructor before the first meeting.

Five Dilemmas

In each of the following dilemmas, you are presented with a situation for which you are asked to indicate the minimum odds of success you would demand before recommending that the more attractive of two alternatives be followed. Read each situation carefully; and before giving your judgment, try to put yourself in the place of the central person in the situation. Then record the answer (*a, b, c, d, e,* or *f*) that comes nearest to indicating the level of risk you would recommend.*

1. Mr. A, an electrical engineer who is married and has one child, has been working for a large electronics corporation since graduating from college five years ago. He is assured of a lifetime job with a modest, although adequate, salary, and liberal pension benefits upon retirement. On the other hand, it is very unlikely that his salary will increase much before he retires. While attending a convention, Mr. A is offered a job with a small, newly founded company that has a highly uncertain future. The new job would pay more to start and would offer the possibility of a share in the ownership if the company survived the competition of the larger firms.

Imagine that you are advising Mr. A. Listed below are several probabilities or odds of the new company's proving financially sound. Please decide the *lowest* probability that you would consider acceptable to make it worthwhile for Mr. A to take the new job.

    a. The chances are 1 in 10 that the company will prove financially sound.

    b. The chances are 3 in 10 that the company will prove financially sound.

    c. The chances are 5 in 10 that the company will prove financially sound.

---

* The following items are from Appendix E, from *Risk Taking: A Study in Cognition and Personality*, by Nathan Kogan and Michael A. Wallach. Copyright © 1964 by Holt, Rinehart and Winston, Inc. Adapted and reprinted by permission of Holt, Rinehart and Winston, Inc.

d. The chances are 7 in 10 that the company will prove financially sound.

e. The chances are 9 in 10 that the company will prove financially sound.

f. Mr. A should not take the new job no matter what the probabilities.

2. Mr. B, a 45-year-old accountant, has recently been informed by his physician that he has developed a severe heart ailment. The disease is sufficiently serious to force Mr. B. to change many of his strongest life habits—reducting his work load, drastically changing his diet, giving up favorite leisure-time pursuits. The physician suggests that a delicate medical operation could be attempted which, if successful, would completely relieve the heart condition. But its success could not be assured, and in fact, the operation might prove fatal.

Imagine that you are advising Mr. B. Listed below are several probabilities or odds that the operation will prove successful. Please decide the *lowest* probability that you would consider acceptable for the operation to be performed.

a. Mr. B should not have the operation no matter what the probabilities.

b. The chances are 9 in 10 that the operation will be a success.

c. The chances are 7 in 10 that the operation will be a success.

d. The chances are 5 in 10 that the operation will be a success.

e. The chances are 3 in 10 that the operation will be a success.

f. The chances are 1 in 10 that the operation will be a success.

3. Mr. C. is the quarterback of College X's football team. College X is playing its traditional rival, College Y, in the final game of the season. The game is in its final seconds, and Mr. C's team, College X, is behind in the score. College X has time to run one more play. Mr. C, the quarterback, must decide whether it would be best to settle for a tie score with a play that would be almost certain to work or, on the other hand, to try a more complicated and risky play that could bring victory if it succeeded, but defeat if not.

Imagine that you are advising Mr. C. Listed below are several probabilities or odds that the risky play will work. Please decide the *lowest* probability that you would consider acceptable for the risky play to be attempted.

a. Mr. C should not attempt the risky play no matter what the probabilities.

b. The chances are 9 in 10 that the risky play will work.

c. The chances are 7 in 10 that the risky play will work.

d. The chances are 5 in 10 that the risky play will work.

e. The chances are 3 in 10 that the risky play will work.

f. The chances are 1 in 10 that the risky play will work.

4. Mr. D is currently a college senior who is very eager to pursue graduate study in chemistry leading to the doctor of philosophy degree. He has been accepted by both University X and University Y. University X has a world-

wide reputation for excellence in chemistry. While a degree from University X would signify outstanding training in this field, the standards are so very rigorous that only a fraction of the degree candidates actually receive the degree. University Y, on the other hand, has much less of a reputation in chemistry, but almost everyone admitted is awarded the doctor of philosophy degree, although the degree has much less prestige than the corresponding degree from University X.

Imagine that you are advising Mr. D. Listed below are several probabilities or odds that Mr. D would be awarded a degree at University X, the one with the greater prestige. Please decide the *lowest* probability that you would consider acceptable to make it worthwhile for Mr. D to enroll in University X rather than University Y.

a. Mr. D should not enroll in University X no matter what the probabilities.

b. The chances are 9 in 10 that Mr. D would receive a degree from University X.

c. The chances are 7 in 10 that Mr. D would receive a degree from University X.

d. The chances are 5 in 10 that Mr. D would receive a degree from University X.

e. The chances are 3 in 10 that Mr. D would receive a degree from University X.

f. The chances are 1 in 10 that Mr. D would receive a degree from University X.

5. Mr. E is an American captured by the enemy in World War II and placed in a prisoner-of-war camp. Conditions in the camp are quite bad, with long hours of hard physical labor and a barely sufficient diet. After spending several months in this camp, Mr. E notes the possibility of escape by concealing himself in a supply truck that shuttles in and out of the camp. Of course, there is no guarantee that the escape would prove successful. Recapture by the enemy could well mean execution.

Imagine that you are advising Mr. E. Listed below are several probabilities or odds of a successful escape from the prisoner-of-war camp. Please decide the *lowest* probability that you would consider acceptable for an escape to be attempted.

a. The chances are 1 in 10 that the escape would succeed.

b. The chances are 3 in 10 that the escape would succeed.

c. The chances are 5 in 10 that the escape would succeed.

d. The chances are 7 in 10 that the escape would succeed.

e. The chances are 9 in 10 that the escape would succeed.

f. Mr. E should not try to escape no matter what the probabilities.

First Group Meeting

The first meeting of each discussion group is to deal with the Stoerpenberg Camp case. In particular, students are to try to decide what action they would recommend for dealing with the apparent theft of food described in this case.

Second Group Meeting

The second meeting of each group is to focus upon the five dilemmas described above. Participants are to discuss their recommendations for risk-taking in each case. At the end of this meeting each student is to fill out Worksheet 8b.

Third Group Meeting

The third meeting of the group is to discuss this topic: "The Future of the Democratic Party." At the end of this meeting each student is to fill out Worksheet 8c.

Instructions for additional meetings or activities of these groups may be given by the instructor.

PROJECT 8

Worksheet 8a

Discussion Groups

Name or Initials:_____

Class and Group:_____

Date:_____

This sheet is to be turned in *before* the first group meeting. Please indicate your answer for each of the questions posed by the five dilemmas by drawing a circle around the letter of your answer.

1. Mr. A, the electrical engineer, and his job dilemma.
   a b c d e f

2. Mr. B, the heart patient, and his dilemma regarding surgery.
   a b c d e f

3. Mr. C, the football quarterback, and his dilemma in calling a play.
   a b c d e f

4. Mr. D, the chemistry student, and his dilemma about graduate study.
   a b c d e f

5. Mr. E, the prisoner of war, and his dilemma regarding escape.
   a b c d e f

Also answer the following two questions by checking one of the five choices for each.

A. Which of the two main political parties of the United States do you prefer? (Check one.)

   _____My preference is definitely in favor of the Democratic Party.

   _____My preference is slightly toward favoring the Democratic Party.

   _____I have absolutely no preference between the two parties.

   _____My preference is slightly toward favoring the Republican Party.

   _____My preference is definitely in favor of the Republican Party.

B. How valuable do you think your discussion-group meetings will be? (Check one.)

   _____Extremely valuable and worthwhile.

   _____Of considerable value.

   _____Slightly valuable.

   _____Rather useless.

   _____Utterly worthless.

PROJECT 8

Worksheet 8b

Discussion Groups

Name or Initials:_____

Class and Group:_____

Date:_____

This sheet is to be filled out at the end of the second group meeting.

Please indicate your answer for each of the questions posed by the "Five Dilemmas" by drawing a circle around the letter of your answer. Note that you are to give *your own answer*, not a summary of the views of your group.

1. Mr. A, the electrical engineer, and his job dilemma.
   a b c d e f

2. Mr. B, the heart patient, and his dilemma regarding surgery.
   a b c d e f

3. Mr. C, the quarterback, and his dilemma in calling a play.
   a b c d e f

4. Mr. D, the chemistry student, and his dilemma about graduate study.
   a b c d e f

5. Mr. E, the prisoner of war, and his dilemma regarding escape.
   a b c d e f

PROJECT 8

Worksheet 8c

Discussion Groups

Name or Initials:_____

Class and Group:_____

Date:_____

This sheet is to be filled out at the end of the third group meeting.

Considering the various members of your group *other than yourself,* decide who best fits each of the following three criteria. Identify each individual by the same nickname or initials that others answering this questionnaire would use. Note that it is possible that the same person may be named for more than one of these questions.

1. Who has had the best ideas in these discussions? _____

2. Who has done the most talking? _____

3. All in all, which person do you like best? _____

Also answer the following question by giving an estimate of percentage somewhere between zero and 100 percent.

What do you believe are the chances that the next President elected by the United States will be the candidate nominated by the Democratic party?

Your answer: _____

PROJECT 9
Personality Profiles

Fifteen Needs

Following are fifteen variables.* These represent different psychological needs that individuals have in varying degrees. On the left is a label for the need, and to the right are identifying features of this need.

Aba   To blame oneself for problems
To feel inferior to others
To be depressed by inadequacies in oneself

Ach   To accomplish things
To be successful
To do a good job

Aff   To do things with friends
To be a good friend
To have many good friends

Agg   To tell other people off
To get revenge for hurts
To make fun of others

Aut   To act independently
To be free to plan one's own actions
To say what one thinks

Chg   To do new and different things
To avoid the same old routine
To go to new places and see new faces

Def   To accept the leadership of others
To receive ideas from others
To let others make important decisions

Dom   To be a leader
To have one's authority recognized
To persuade and influence others

End   To complete any job undertaken
To work hard on a problem until it is solved
To avoid interruptions

Exh   To attract attention
To have others notice
To talk about oneself

---

*These variables are based upon Allen L. Edwards (1953). Originally most of these variables were suggested by Henry A. Murray (1938).

Het   To be with members of the opposite sex
       To talk about sex
       To feel erotic

Int   To analyze motives and feelings
       To understand one's own feelings
       To understand the motives of others

Nur   To help persons in trouble
       To show sympathy to others
       To give encouragement

Ord   To have things well organized
       To make careful plans
       To keep things neat and orderly

Suc   To receive help from others
       To get encouragement
       To receive sympathy

Which of the psychic needs above do you think especially characterize your own personality? Think of yourself in relationship to most other people, and consider which of the needs above are especially strong in yourself, and which are weaker than in most people.

Now fill out the first column of Worksheet 9a by making a rank order of these fifteen variables. Rank them in the order in which you consider them characteristic of yourself as a person—at least as compared to most persons. List as number one whatever need you think is most strongly characteristic of your personality. Rank-order all needs—even if it may be very difficult in some cases to decide between two or three that seem about equally strong.

Comparing Notes

After ranking these needs for your own personality, find a friend who will also give his impression of you. Select someone who knows you fairly well, a person with whom you can frankly discuss each other's personality characteristics. Without giving this friend any information about your own ranking of the need variables, have him (or her) give a rank order of these fifteen needs in regard to the degree to which he considers them characteristic of himself. Have him do this by using the first column of Worksheet 9b. He should do this without talking to you about the way he is ordering the fifteen variables.

Before obtaining any results of your friend's judgment of himself, you and he should proceed to rate each other (using the second columns of Worksheets 9a and 9b respectively). Do this without indicating the results to each other until both of you are finished. Again, each is to give a rank order for the fifteen needs, but this time each gives the rank order for which he perceives the psychological needs are characteristic of the other.

After this it will be interesting to compare notes. Feel free to do so. The data obtained should now include four different arrangements of the above list of psychological needs:

(1) The rank order as you perceive them in yourself (Worksheet 9a, Column 1)

(2) The rank order as your friend perceives them in himself (Worksheet 9b, Column 1)

(3) The rank order as you perceive them in your friend (Worksheet 9a, Column 2)

(4) The rank order as your friend perceives them in you (Worksheet 9b, Column 2).

How closely does your view of yourself correspond to your friend's view of you? It is possible to measure this by means of a coefficient of rank-order correlation. A technique for measuring such correlation (*rho*) is described in the appendix of this book.

After studying the section of the appendix on correlation, you should be ready to compute coefficients of rank correlation for each of the following comparisons:

(1) Your own ranking of psychic needs, as compared to your friend's ranking of needs for you;

(2) Your friend's ranking of his own needs, as compared to your ranking for him;

(3) Your ranking of your own needs, as compared to your friend's ranking of his own needs.

Report these coefficients on Worksheet 9c. Which of these three correlations is highest? Which is lowest? What do the first two correlations say about the accuracy of perception of your friend and yourself?

Remember that correlations of near zero show an absence of association, that positive correlations show direct association, and that negative correlations show an inverse relationship. Your instructor may ask the class to report a distribution of coefficients of correlation for the third relationship above (your ranking of your own needs, as compared to your friend's ranking of his own needs). This may help answer the question of whether friends tend to be similar in personality patterns. Comparisons may also be made between male pairs, female pairs, and male-female pairs.

PROJECT 9

Worksheet 9a

Student's Name:_____

Personality Profiles

Class:_____

Date:_____

The following is to be filled out by the *student*.

	RANK ORDER OF VARIABLES AS CHARACTERISTIC OF SELF	RANK ORDER OF VARIABLES AS CHARACTERISTIC OF FRIEND
Aba	_____	_____
Ach	_____	_____
Aff	_____	_____
Agg	_____	_____
Aut	_____	_____
Chg	_____	_____
Def	_____	_____
Dom	_____	_____
End	_____	_____
Exh	_____	_____
Het	_____	_____
Int	_____	_____
Nur	_____	_____
Ord	_____	_____
Suc	_____	_____

PROJECT 9

Worksheet 9b

Personality Profiles

Student's Name:_____

Class:_____

Date:_____

The following is to be filled out by a *friend* of the student.

	RANK ORDER OF VARIABLES AS CHARACTERISTIC OF SELF	RANK ORDER OF VARIABLES AS CHARACTERISTIC OF STUDENT
Aba	_____	_____
Ach	_____	_____
Aff	_____	_____
Agg	_____	_____
Aut	_____	_____
Chg	_____	_____
Def	_____	_____
Dom	_____	_____
End	_____	_____
Exh	_____	_____
Het	_____	_____
Int	_____	_____
Nur	_____	_____
Ord	_____	_____
Suc	_____	_____

PROJECT 9

Worksheet 9c

Personality Profiles

Student's Name:_____

Class:_____

Date:_____

RHO COEFFICIENT
OF CORRELATION

Your own ranking of needs, as compared to your friend's ranking of needs for you (Column 1 of Worksheet 9a with Column 2 of Worksheet 9b)   _____

Your friend's ranking of his own needs, as compared to your ranking for him (Column 1 of Worksheet 9b with Column 2 of Worksheet 9a)   _____

Your ranking of your own needs, as compared to your friend's ranking of his own needs (Column 1 of Worksheet 9a with Column 1 of Worksheet 9b)   _____

Also check the following:

Sex of student: _____ male   _____ female

Sex of friend: _____ male   _____ female

PROJECT 10
Analysis of Change in the Self-Concept

In Selection 26 we were given some data to test the hypothesis that personality traits supported by a consensus of others are more stable than those traits for which a person perceives less consensus.

In a first session of this study, subjects ranked themselves on fifteen need variables (the same variables used in Project 9). Subjects were also given the Edwards *Personal Preference Schedule* (which attempts to measure the relative strength of these same needs) and another instrument of personality assessment. At this same first session they were asked to write down the names of five friends and to select the need statements that each friend would consider most characteristic of the subject.

In the second session subjects were given the "results" of their earlier personality testing in the form of a rank ordering of the fifteen needs. Actually, these "results" were the same as the subject's self-ranking given in the first session except that two needs among the highest five were each reduced eight steps downward. These two needs were selected to include one for which there appeared to be a high consensus of support by the subject's friends and one for which the consensus was low.

After being informed of these "results," subjects were given an opportunity to give a final self-ranking of the same variables. The results reported in tabular form by Backman, Secord, and Peirce indicate for each subject the movement shown for these two traits selected for manipulation. (See Table 1, Selection 26.)

How much reduced was the second self-rating of the trait given a high consensus of support by friends? How much reduced was the second self-rating of the trait given a low consensus of support? Did the difference favor the greater stability of the high-consensus trait, and, if so, how strongly? Answers to these questions, for each subject, are given by the previous table. This table (Table 1, Selection 26) shows that most subjects showed greater change in the low-consensus trait than in the high-consensus trait. This is as predicted; but is the evidence strong enough to be really convincing? This is the question to which we turn our attention in the rest of this project.

For their test of statistical significance, Backman, Secord, and Peirce chose to use the Wilcoxon signed-ranks test. Since this is a rather simple statistical technique (and one widely applicable in behavioral sciences), let us also proceed with this analysis.

The Wilcoxon signed-ranks test (see Siegel, 1956, pp. 75–83 for a fuller discussion) is applicable to situations in which measurement allows a ranking of the magnitude of difference scores. Some of the differences will be in the predicted direction, and others will not. The Wilcoxon test allows us to take into account the *magnitude* of the differences in either direction.

We can summarize the procedures of the signed-ranks test as follows:

(1) Eliminate those cases for which the difference scores of matched pairs of observations are zero (for example, subjects that show no difference between two scores).

(2) Rank the magnitude of the remaining difference scores without respect to sign, giving the least difference the rank of 1 (and giving tied difference scores the average of their combined ranks).

(3) Assign the appropriate sign (+ or −) to each rank.

(4) Compute the sum of ranks having the less frequent of the two signs. Call this value T, and compare it with N, the number of differences that are not zero.

(5) Evaluate the significance of T by means of the following formula:

$$z = \frac{T - \left(\frac{N(N+1)}{4} \right)}{\sqrt{\frac{N(N+1)(2N+1)}{24}}}$$

The final step is a translation of T into a well-defined normal distribution of z scores for which tables may be found in practically any statistics book. Where N is less than 25, the evaluation of statistical significance can be simplified by use of a table from which T can be evaluated directly; but for larger samples a translation into z scores is necessary. In evaluating z scores for testing hypotheses about differences (for which most differences are in the hypothesized direction), the following z scores offer especially useful bench marks for evaluating significance:

$z \geq 1.65$ has a probability of less than .05
$z \geq 2.33$ has a probability of less than .01
$z \geq 3.11$ has a probability of less than .001

Let us now apply the signed-ranks test to the data of Backman, Secord, and Peirce. Use the difference scores as given in the last column of their table (Table 1, Chapter 26), and record the analysis on Worksheet 10.

Since the difference scores of subjects 27 and 28 are zero, we eliminate these cases, leaving an N of 38. We next proceed to rank these 38 cases without respect to sign. Since there are 5 difference scores of 1 (+ or −), each one will receive the average rank of 3. The 9 difference scores of 2 will each be given the average for ranks of 6 through 14, or 10. The 7 scores of 3 will each have an average rank of 18. And so forth till the difference score of 10 is given the rank of 38.

The next step is to assign signs to these ranks and then obtain the value of T. Since there are fewer negative than positive scores (as predicted), our T will be the sum of all negative ranks. What is this value of T?

After T is obtained, it should be translated into a z score by means of the formula given above. What value of z is obtained? Is this result sufficiently extreme that it would be unlikely to occur by chance (e.g., would it have a probability of less than 5 times out of 100)?

Is this convincing evidence that personality characteristics which are supported by high consensus among significant others are more likely to resist change than those not supported by such consensus?

PROJECT 10

Worksheet 10

Analysis of Change in Self-Concept

Student's Name:_____

Class:_____

Date:_____

SUBJECT	DIFFERENCE SCORE	RANK OF DIFFERENCE (SIGN DISREGARDED)	SIGNED RANK
1	10	_____	_____
2	8	_____	_____
3	7	_____	_____
4	7	_____	_____
5	7	_____	_____
6	7	_____	_____
7	7	_____	_____
8	5	_____	_____
9	5	_____	_____
10	5	_____	_____
11	5	_____	_____
12	4	_____	_____
13	3	_____	_____
14	3	_____	_____
15	3	_____	_____
16	3	_____	_____
17	3	_____	_____
18	3	_____	_____
19	2	_____	_____
20	2	_____	_____
21	2	_____	_____
22	2	_____	_____
23	2	_____	_____
24	2	_____	_____
25	1	_____	_____
26	1	_____	_____
27 (omitted)			
28 (omitted)			
29	−1	_____	_____
30	−1	_____	_____
31	−1	_____	_____
32	−2	_____	_____
33	−2	_____	_____
34	−2	_____	_____
35	−3	_____	_____
36	−4	_____	_____
37	−4	_____	_____
38	−7	_____	_____
39	−7	_____	_____
40	−8	_____	_____

T (sum of ranks having the less frequent sign) = _____.

$$Z = \frac{T - \left[\dfrac{N(N+1)}{4}\right]}{\sqrt{\dfrac{N(N+1)(2N+1)}{24}}}$$

$$= \frac{T - \left[\dfrac{(38)(39)}{4}\right]}{\sqrt{\dfrac{(38)(39)(77)}{24}}}$$

$$= \frac{T - 370.5}{68.95} = \underline{\hspace{2cm}}.$$

Evaluation of probability of z (check one):

_____ $p > .05$
_____ $p < .05$
_____ $p < .01$
_____ $p < .001$

Appendix: Selected Statistical Techniques

There are three main applications of mathematics to the social sciences:

(1) To help describe phenomena with precision
(2) To help make inferences concerning hypothetical probabilities
(3) To help analyze the logical implications of theoretical propositions

These three general applications may be labeled respectively as *descriptive statistics, statistical inference,* and *mathematical logic.* In the following discussion we will not be concerned with mathematical logic; we will limit our attention to some simple applications of descriptive statistics and statistical inference.

Measurement

The use of statistics presupposes some kind of measurement. Sometimes only a rough form of measurement is possible; at other times a very precise form of measurement is possible. We can divide forms of measurement into the following categories:

(1) Frequency measurement, in which measurement is limited to counting the number of cases in different categories
(2) Ordinal measurement, in which cases may be described in terms of an ordered ranking
(3) Interval measurement, in which cases may be described in terms of a scale of units

Let us illustrate briefly in terms of height. A group of persons might be divided into those who are tall or not tall on the basis of some arbitrary dividing point. Thus everybody at least as tall as Joe might be said to be "tall," and everyone shorter than Joe could be called "not tall." We could then compare everyone to Joe and count the respective frequencies of "tall" and "not tall" persons. Each person could be placed into one or the other of these two categories.

A somewhat more precise measure of tallness could be obtained by comparing the heights of everyone in the group and then placing them into a rank order. A person's height could then be measured by saying that he was the third (or seventh, or whatever) tallest person in the group.

If we have a fixed unit of measurement (for example, inches or centimeters), we can do a more precise job of measuring height. Thus we can say how tall each member of a group is in terms of inches.

From this example it should be clear that interval measurement gives more information than ordinal measurement, and that ordinal measurement gives more information than frequency measurement. We might therefore be tempted to conclude that social psychologists should always use interval measurement. But this is not necessarily the case. Interval measurement requires a precise unit of measure, and usually there is no obvious unit (such as inches) for social psychologists to use. Often social psychologists will develop a scale to provide units of measurement (for example, ratings of behavior made by an observer, or a scale to measure a particular attitude by questionnaire responses); but even with such apparent precision, the reliability may be little better than a more simple rank ordering. Often the precision of interval measurement in social psychology is more apparent than real.

Another feature of the relationship of these three kinds of measurement may also be pointed out: interval measurement may always be reduced to ordinal measurement, and ordinal measurement may always be reduced to frequency measurement. In other words, the more rigorous forms of measurement can always be translated into cruder forms (although the reverse is not the case). Since statistical manipulation of the simpler forms of measurement tends to be easier than that of more refined measures, this reduction to a simpler form may be especially useful for a beginning social psychologist. In the remainder of this appendix we will explain some of the simpler statistical techniques usable with frequency or ordinal data. These techniques will be adequate for the projects in this book.

Descriptive Statistics: Central Tendency and Dispersion

Among the simplest uses of statistics is to summarize a set of data. Two common ways of summarizing a set of data are by indicating measures of central tendency and of dispersion.

With frequency data, central tendency can be indicated by identifying the most frequent category. Dispersion can be indicated by describing the number or proportion of cases in each of the other categories.

With ordinal data, central tendency can be indicated by the *median* (the case with the same number ranked above it as are ranked below it, thus the midpoint of a ranked distribution). Dispersion can be indicated by describing extreme cases or by pointing to particular locations on the continuum of ranks (such as quartiles, deciles, or percentiles).

With interval data, central tendency is most commonly measured by the arithmetic *mean* (the common average, found by adding the values of all the cases and dividing by the number of cases). The most common measure of dispersion is that of the *standard deviation* (which is a way of measuring average differences from the mean).

To illustrate these measures of central tendency and dispersion, let us consider the case of twenty-two college men who lived in the same house just off the campus of a midwestern university. Since these men did all their own housekeeping and meal preparations (one of the authors was among them), it might not be far off to refer to this setting as the "Pig Pad." Anyway, the twenty-two men of Pig Pad filled out an inventory designed to measure various areas of personal values (the Allport-Vernon-Lindzey *Study of Values*), and the following is a list of their scores on the religious area of values:

PERSON	RELIGIOUS VALUES SCORE
BL	58
CM	60
DR	61
DW	57
EH	57
GR	60
HE	59
JB	54
JS	48
LC	40
MA	53
NF	27
NH	28
PD	42
PL	34
RB	42
RS	44
SC	15
SD	39
TD	54
TG	27
WE	41

For a reduction of these scores to frequency data, we may note that the editors of the values instrument suggest that any religious scores below 33 be considered low and any scores above 47 be considered high (based on general norms).* Using these categories, we can say that more of the men of Pig Pad were high on religious values (11) than were either moderate (7) or low (4). The authors of the test furthermore identified religious scores below 25 as outstandingly low and those above 55 as outstandingly high. Using these extreme categories, we can say that the range of scores for religious values varied from one person who was outstandingly low to a goodly number (7) who were outstandingly high.

This data may also be expressed in ordinal form. For this we would rank the men as follows (from highest to lowest emphasis on religious values); DR, CM and GR (tie), HE, BL, DW, and EH, JB and TD, MA, JS, RS, PD and RB, WE, LC, SD, PL, NH, NF and TG, SC. The midpoint could be identified as being between JS (rank 11) and RS (rank 12). The extremes could be identified by the cases of DR (very high) and SC (very low). If we compare these men to the general norms presented by the authors of the *Study of Values*, we can say that the top 11 men (including JS) were all in the top quartile of the general population, while only 4 men (NF, NH, SC, and TG) were in the lowest quartile.

Using interval measurement as given for this study, we can compute the mean and standard deviation for this list of scores on religious values. Since

* Gordon W. Allport, Philip E. Vernon, and Gardner Lindzey, *Study of Values*, 3rd rev. ed. Boston: Houghton Mifflin, 1951.

the sum of scores is 1,000 and the number of scores is 22, dividing 1,000 by 22 gives a mean score of 45.45. To find the standard deviation we can apply the following formula:

$$SD = \sqrt{\frac{N\Sigma X^2 - (\Sigma X)^2}{N(N-1)}}$$
$$= \sqrt{\frac{(22)(49,098) - 1,000^2}{(22)(21)}}$$
$$= \sqrt{\frac{1,080,156 - 1,000,000}{462}}$$
$$= \sqrt{\frac{80,156}{462}}$$
$$= \sqrt{173.50} = 13.2$$

In this formula, N stands for the number of scores and X represents the particular scores. Sigma (Σ) means "sum of." Thus ΣX^2 means the sum (49,098) of the squares of the individual scores and $(\Sigma X)^2$ means the square of the sum (1,000) of the individual scores.

Descriptive Statistics: Correlation

A somewhat more complex use of statistics is to describe the relationship between two sets of data. For instance, suppose we have measures on two different variables for each member of a group. We may then ask if these two sets of measures show similar patterns of variation from person to person. The degree of such similarity (or dissimilarity) could be indicated by a *coefficient of correlation.*

Most correlation coefficients vary from 1.00 (for perfect positive correlation between two variables) to −1.00 (for perfect negative, or inverse, correlation). A correlation coefficient close to .00 usually indicates an absence of systematic association between the variables. For example, if height and weight are positively correlated, most tall men would be heavy and short men would be light; with negative correlation, tall men would be light and short men heavy. An absence of correlation would apply if about as many tall men (or short men) were light in weight as were heavy.

The most commonly used measure of correlation is the *product moment correlation coefficient* (usually symbolized by r). This applies only to interval data, and it measures the extent to which the relations between variables fall into a straight-line pattern (that is, the variables show proportionate increases or decreases with each other when going from case to case).

Other measures of correlation are applicable with frequency data or with ordinal data. In the following discussion we present one example, Spearman's coefficient of rank correlation (*rho*).

A coefficient of rank correlation measures the degree of correspondence between two sets of ranks. Let us follow further with the example of Pig Pad (first mentioned in the previous section. We have popularity ratings as well as religious values scores available for each member of this group. The popularity ratings indicate how many other members of the group named the given individual on one or more of several sociometric questions. We can present these two sets of scores as follows:

PERSON	RELIGIOUS VALUES SCORE	POPULARITY INDEX
BL	58	12
CM	60	1
DR	61	1
DW	57	9
EH	57	9
GR	60	4
HE	59	1
JB	54	1
JS	48	3
LC	40	3
MA	53	0
NF	27	1
NH	28	3
PD	42	1
PL	34	14
RB	42	2
RS	44	2
SC	15	0
SD	39	1
TD	54	7
TG	27	0
WE	41	0

We might be interested in the question whether religious values tend to be associated with popularity in this apparently rather religious group. The degree of association between emphasis on religious values and popularity in the group may be measured by Spearman's coefficient of rank correlation (*rho*).

The first step in obtaining *rho* is to provide a ranking for each of the two variables. This can be done as follows for the two variables in our Pig Pad example:

PERSON	RANK IN RELIGIOUS VALUES	RANK IN POPULARITY
BL	5.0	2.0
CM	2.5	15.0
DR	1.0	15.0
DW	6.5	3.5
EH	6.5	3.5
GR	2.5	6.0
HE	4.0	15.0
JB	8.5	15.0
JS	11.0	8.0
LC	16.0	8.0
MA	10.0	20.5
NF	20.5	15.0
NH	19.0	8.0
PD	13.5	15.0
PL	18.0	1.0
RB	13.5	10.5
RS	12.0	10.5
SC	22.0	20.5
SD	17.0	15.0
TD	8.5	5.0
TG	20.5	20.5
WE	15.0	20.5

Note that in these rankings ties are given the average rank of all scores involved.

Rho measures the extent to which two rank orders are similar. Once two variables are both expressed in rank-order form, the next step is to find the difference in ranks for corresponding cases. Then the following formula may be applied:

$$rho = 1 - \frac{6\Sigma d^2}{N^3 - N}$$

In applying this formula, N represents the number of cases (22) in each variable (the religious rating and the popularity rating), and d represents the difference in ranks between the two ratings for each person.

We may present differences in ranks as follows:

PERSON	d	d^2
BL	3.0	9.00
CM	12.5	156.25
DR	14.0	196.00
DW	3.0	9.00
EH	3.0	9.00
GR	3.5	12.25
HE	11.0	121.00
JB	6.5	42.25
JS	3.0	9.00
LC	8.0	64.00
MA	10.5	110.25
NF	5.5	30.25
NH	11.0	121.00
PD	1.5	2.25
PL	17.0	289.00
RB	3.0	9.00
RS	1.5	2.25
SC	1.5	2.25
SD	2.0	4.00
TD	3.5	12.25
TG	0.0	0.00
WE	5.5	30.25
		$\Sigma = 1{,}240.50$

Adding the third column above, we get a total of 1,240.50 for Σd^2. Since we also know that we have 22 cases of each variable, we are now ready to solve our equation to find *rho*.

$$rho = 1 - \frac{6\Sigma d^2}{N^3 - N}$$

$$= 1 - \frac{6\,(1,240.5)}{22^3 - 22}$$

$$= 1 - \frac{7,443}{10,648 - 22}$$

$$= 1 - \frac{7,443}{10,626}$$

$$= 1 - .70045$$

$$= \quad .2995$$

So we find a rank-order correlation coefficient of .2995, or .30, describing the association between these two variables. This is a positive but fairly weak correlation. Is it statistically significant? While this question takes us into the subject of the next section, we can here say that this would not meet ordinary standards of statistical significance (with $N = 22$, a correlation coefficient of about .36 would be necessary to be significant at the 5 percent level).

When a great number of tied ranks are present, *rho* should be obtained by the following formula:

$$rho = \frac{\Sigma x^2 + \Sigma y^2 - \Sigma d^2}{2\sqrt{\Sigma x^2\, \Sigma y^2}}$$

The values for this formula of Σx^2 and Σy^2 are obtained as follows:

$$\Sigma x^2 = \frac{N^3 - N}{12} - \Sigma T_x$$

$$\Sigma y^2 = \frac{N^3 - N}{12} - \Sigma T_y$$

The values of T (for either variable, designated above as x and y) may in turn be found as follows:

$$T = \frac{t^3 - t}{12}$$

In this formula, t is the number of observations tied at a given rank.

Let us now apply this formula, which corrects for ties, to our Pig Pad example. Let us consider religious values to be our x variable and popularity to be our y variable. In the x (religious) variable, we find ties at the following ranks: 2.5, 6.5, 8.5, 13.5, and 20.5. Each of these represents a tie between 2 persons. Thus:

$$T = \frac{t^3 - t}{12} = \frac{2^3 - 2}{12} = \frac{8 - 2}{12} = \frac{1}{2}$$

With each T equal to $\frac{1}{2}$, the sum of all five Ts would equal $\frac{1}{2} + \frac{1}{2} + \frac{1}{2} + \frac{1}{2} + \frac{1}{2} = 2\frac{1}{2}$. Thus $\Sigma T_x = 2\frac{1}{2}$, and

$$\Sigma x^2 = \frac{N^3 - N}{12} - \Sigma T_x = \frac{22^3 - 22}{12} - 2\frac{1}{2}$$

$$= \frac{10,626}{12} - 2\frac{1}{2}$$

$$= 885.5 - 2.5 = 883$$

So we obtain a value of 883 for Σx^2.

Before we can use our general formula, we must also find the value of Σy^2. In the y (popularity) variable we find ties at the following ranks: 3.5 (2 cases), 8 (3 cases), 10.5 (2 cases), 15 (7 cases), and 20.5 (4 cases). We thus find the following respective values of T:

$$T=\frac{2^3-2}{12}=\frac{8-2}{12}=\frac{1}{2}$$

$$T=\frac{3^3-3}{12}=\frac{27-3}{12}=2$$

$$T=\frac{2^3-2}{12}=\frac{8-2}{12}=\frac{1}{2}$$

$$T=\frac{7^3-7}{12}=\frac{343-7}{12}=28$$

$$T=\frac{4^3-4}{12}=\frac{64-4}{12}=5$$

Summing these values of T, we get a total of 36. Thus
$$\Sigma T_y=36$$

$$\Sigma y^2=\frac{N^3-N}{12}-\Sigma T_y$$

$$=\frac{22^3-22}{12}-36$$

$$=\frac{10,626}{12}-36$$

$$=885.5-36=849.5$$

So we obtain a value of 849.5 for Σy^2.

We now have values for Σx^2 and Σy^2. Earlier (when we did the problem without the special formula for ties) we obtained the value of Σd^2. Therefore we are now ready to solve the general formula for finding *rho* with ties:

$$rho=\frac{\Sigma x^2+\Sigma y^2-\Sigma d^2}{2\sqrt{(\Sigma x^2)(\Sigma y^2)}}$$

$$=\frac{883+849.5-1,240.5}{2\sqrt{(883)(849.5)}}$$

$$=\frac{1,732.5-1,240.5}{2\sqrt{750,108.5}}$$

$$=\frac{492}{2(866.1)}$$

$$=\frac{492}{1,732.2}$$

$$=.284$$

Thus with the special formula for ties, we find a value of *rho* of .284, just a little reduced from the value of .30 obtained from the simpler formula.

Statistical Inference: Chi Square

In statistical inference we ask a question about data and use statistics to help us decide on the answer. Most commonly the question is in the form of a hypothesis. Statistics may often be used to evaluate evidence for the hypothesis.

Let us take the example of the Pig Pad, previously introduced. We might formulate the hypothesis that persons high on religious values would be more popular than persons low on religious values. This in turn would be based on the theory that the persons who tend to be most popular in a group will be those who best exhibit the values that are dominant in that population. In our particular Pig Pad group we found religious values unusually high; therefore, it may be reasonable to expect religious values to be associated with popularity in this particular group.

In scientific investigations, it is important to formulate our questions in ways that can be contradicted by data. Unless we do this, we can never really test a hypothesis. To help make our hypothesis sensitive to negative evidence, it may be reformulated to predict what one would expect if the theory is *not* true. This new reverse hypothesis, called the *null hypothesis,* helps us see clearly what evidence would contradict our original hypothesis. In the Pig Pad case, the null hypothesis is that the variables of religious values and popularity show only a random relationship.

How can the competing hypothesis of a random or chance distribution be rejected? By showing that a particular pattern of data is outside the bounds of usual random variation. But any distribution could *sometimes* occur by chance. Therefore what we need is a means of assessing the *relative improbability* of a given distribution. This is given by a measure of statistical significance. Statistical significance indicates how improbable a given pattern of results would be if derived from a random distribution of cases.

There are many different tests of statistical significance, each applicable to slightly different classes of problems. For example, in the preceeding section we made brief mention of a test of significance applicable to rank-order data. In the present section we will discuss a technique applicable to frequency data, the *chi-square test.* This is one of the simplest statistical techniques and, since interval or ordinal data can always be converted into frequency data, one of the most widely usable. The chi-square (χ^2) test measures the extent to which a given pattern of frequencies departs from a random distribution.

We will follow up with our example of religious values and popularity among the residents of Pig Pad. We can divide the residents in half based on their religious value scores; 11 had scores of over 45 (given by the authors of the questionnaire as the beginning point for high scores) and 11 had scores of under 45. We can also divide the popularity ratings in half by distinguishing between those named by two or more others on sociometric questionnaires and those named by one or none. There are 11 cases in each of these 2 categories.*

---

* The chi-square test does not require that variables be divided exactly in half, but it is convenient to use dividing lines near the midpoint when the data is divided into two groups. Also, effective use of the chi-square test requires expected frequencies of 5 or more in each final category, which (with a total number of cases of 22, divided 4 ways) is possible in our example only with a division very close to the midpoint for each variable.

Combining the two variables, we can obtain the following table of frequencies (this kind of table is known as a two-by-two contingency table):

	PERSONS CHOSEN BY 2 OR MORE OTHERS	PERSONS CHOSEN BY FEWER THAN 2 OTHERS
PERSONS WITH HIGH RELIGIOUS VALUES	6	5
PERSONS WITH MEDIUM OR LOW RELIGIOUS VALUES	5	6

In other words, of the 11 more popular persons, 6 have high religious values and 5 have medium or low religious values; of the 11 less popular men, 5 have high religious values and 6 have medium or low religious values. The total number of cases is, of course, 22, the total number in our study.

Does this pattern of frequencies differ significantly from what would be expected by chance? To answer this question, we are now ready to apply the chi-square test, which gives a measure of the extent to which a given distribution departs from what would be expected in a random distribution.

The general formula for chi square is the following:

$$\chi^2 = \sum \frac{(o-e)^2}{e}$$

In this formula, e represents the frequency of a given outcome expected by chance and o represents the corresponding frequency actually obtained.

To apply this formula, we must first determine what the average chance frequencies would be. Let us take the data from the Pig Pad problem. There are 22 persons in all, distributed into 4 divisions, or "cells," of the table. We can find the expected frequency of any one cell by multiplying the total frequency times the proportion of this frequency in the row of this cell times the proportion of this frequency in its column. For example, with the following matrix

$a=6$	$b=5$	$a+b=11$
$c=5$	$d=6$	$c+d=11$
$a+c=11$	$b+d=11$	$N=22$

the expected frequency of the upper left cell would be given by:

$$(a+b+c+d) \left(\frac{a+b}{a+b+c+d} \right) \left(\frac{a+c}{a+b+c+d} \right)$$

or in this particular case:

$$22\left(\frac{11}{22}\right)\left(\frac{11}{22}\right) = 5.5$$

The expected frequency of the cell indicated by a (upper left) would thus be 5.5. The expected frequencies of cells b, c, and d could likewise be determined to be 5.5 each.

We could now use the general formula given above $\left[x^2 = \Sigma \frac{(o-e)^2}{e} \right]$

to find the value of chi square. However, for the special case of a two-by-two table, the following formula (which does not require the direct computation of expected frequencies) is preferred:

$$x^2 = \frac{N\left(|ad-bc| - \frac{N}{2}\right)^2}{(a+b)\,(c+d)\,(a+c)\,(b+d)}$$

where a, b, c, and d stand for the frequencies of the 4 cells (as previously labeled) and N stands for the total number of cases.* In our particular example:

$$x^2 = \frac{22\left(36 - 25 - \frac{22}{2}\right)^2}{(11)(11)(11)(11)}$$

$$= \frac{22\,(11-11)^2}{14{,}641}$$

$$= \frac{(22)\,(0)}{14{,}641} = 0$$

Here the chi-square value is zero $(x^2 = 0)$. This is obviously not large enough to be statistically significant. We can therefore conclude that our distribution of cases is not significantly different from what would be expected by chance. Therefore our evidence is in favor of the null hypothesis of random variation and against the original hypothesis that persons high in religious values would be more popular in this group than those low in religious values.

Let us take another example for a chi-square test. Let us assume the following distribution is obtained for two variables (with one variable divided three ways, as represented by the three rows, and the other variable divided two ways, as represented by two columns);

---

* The expression $|ad-bd|$ means that the difference between a times d and b times d is to be taken, regardless of the sign of this difference. That is, the absolute difference between ad and bd is to be used and treated as a positive number.

$a=8$	$b=4$	$a+b=12$
$c=7$	$d=4$	$c+d=11$
$e=3$	$f=10$	$e+f=13$

$a+c+e=18$ $b+d+f=18$ $N=36$

Is this distribution of frequencies significantly different from a random distribution?

To answer this question, we need to know what frequencies would be expected by chance for each cell. For cell a we can obtain the expected value as follows:

$$N\left(\frac{a+b}{N}\right)\left(\frac{a+c+e}{N}\right)$$

$$=36\left(\frac{12}{36}\right)\left(\frac{18}{36}\right)=6$$

For cell c we can obtain the expected value as follows:

$$N\left(\frac{c+d}{N}\right)\left(\frac{a+c+e}{N}\right)$$

$$=36\left(\frac{11}{36}\right)\left(\frac{18}{36}\right)=5.5$$

Knowing these two expected frequencies, we can derive the others by subtraction from the marginal totals. The resulting expected frequencies are as follows:

6	6
5.5	5.5
6.5	6.5

We are now ready to apply the chi-square formula. This time we will use a more general formula than was used before (the previous formula was applicable only to a two-by-two table, while in the present case we have a three-by-two table). We shall use this formula:

$$\chi^2=\sum\frac{(o-e)^2}{e}$$

In this formula, *e* represents the frequency of a given outcome expected by chance and *o* represents the corresponding frequency actually obtained. For computation it is convenient to use the following form:

Cell	e	$o-e$	$(o-e)^2$	$\dfrac{(o-e)^2}{e}$
a	6	2	4	.67
b	6	−2	4	.67
c	5.5	1.5	2.25	.41
d	5.5	−1.5	2,25	.41
f	6.5	−3.5	12.25	1.88
e	6.5	3.5	12.25	1.88
				$\Sigma = 5.92$

Here the value of χ^2 is equal to 5.92. Is this within the range of random variation as indicated by a table of chi-square values? Let us look at some excerpts from such a table before we decide.

df	PROBABILITY THAT A VALUE OF χ^2 AS LARGE OR LARGER THAN THAT IN THE TABLE MIGHT BE OBTAINED BY CHANCE		
	.05	*.01*	*.001*
1	3.84	6.64	10.83
2	5.99	9.21	13.82
3	7.82	11.34	16.27

To read a chi-square table, we need to know the number of degrees of freedom (*df*) at which to enter the table. This can be determined for simple arrangements of frequency data as 1 less than the number of rows times 1 less than the number of columns. In the present example,

$$(3-1)(2-1) = 2 \times 1 = 2df$$

Entering the chi-square table at 2*df*, we learn that a χ^2 value of greater than 5.99 would happen by chance less than 5 times out of 100. This 5 percent level is often used in social psychology as a conventional standard for deciding whether or not to accept a result as being within the range of random variation. However, in our present example, we find our value of χ^2 to be 5.92, which is just short of what would be required for statistical significance at the .05 (or 5 percent) level. We therefore do not have a good basis for rejecting the hypothesis of random variation.

On the earlier problem of the association between religious values and popularity in our Pig Pad group, we can see now what value of χ^2 would have been necessary for statistical significance (at the 5 percent level). Entering the above table for 1 *df* (a two-by-two contingency table will always have only one degree of freedom), we see that a χ^2 value of 3.84 or larger would be necessary for significance. Any lower value of χ^2 would be within conventional expectations for random variation.

Bibliography

Adorno, T. W., Frenkel-Brunswik, E., Levinson, D. J., and Sanford, R. N. *The authoritarian personality*. New York: Harper, 1950.

Allport, G. W. *The nature of prejudice*. Cambridge, Mass.: Addison-Wesley Press, 1954.

Angyal, A. *Foundations for a science of personality*. New York: Commonwealth Fund, 1941.

Aronson, E., and Mills, J. The effects of severity of initiation on liking for a group. *J. abnorm. soc. Psychol.*, 1959, 59, 177–181.

Bach, G. R. Father fantasies and father-typing in father-separated children. *Child Develpm.*, 1946, 18, 63–79.

Backman, C. W., and Secord, P. F. Liking, selective interaction, and misperception in congruent interpersonal relations, *Sociometry*, 1962, 25, 321–335.

———, and Peirce, J. R. Resistance to change in the self-concept as a function of consensus among significant others. *Sociometry*, 1963, 26, 102–111.

Baldwin, A. L. Socialization and the parent-child relationship. *Child Develpm.*, 1948, 19, 127–136.

———, Kalhorn, J., and Breese, F. H. The Appraisal of Parent Behavior. *Psychol. Monogr.*, 1945, 58, 268.

Bales, R. F. *Interaction process analysis*. Cambridge, Mass.: Addison-Wesley Press, 1951

Bandura, A., and Walters, R. H. *Adolescent aggression*. New York: Ronald Press, 1959.

Barber, B. Participation and mass apathy in associations. In A. W. Gouldner (Ed.), *Studies in leadership*. New York: Harper and Brothers, 1950. Pp. 477–504.

Barnard, C. I. *The functions of the executive*. Cambridge, Mass.: Harvard University Press, 1938.

Bateson, N. Familiarization, group discussion, and risk taking. *J. exper. soc. Psychol.*, 1966, 2, 119–129.

Becker, W. C. Consequences of different kinds of parental discipline. In M. L. Hoffman and L. W. Hoffman (Eds.), *Review of child development research*. Vol. 1. New York: Russell Sage Foundation, 1964. Pp. 169–208.

Bem, D. J., Wallach, M. A., and Kogan, N. Group decision making under risk of aversive consequences. *J. pers. soc. Psychol.*, 1965, 1, 453–46.

Berlyne, D. E. *Conflict, arousal and curiosity*. New York: McGraw-Hill, 1960.

Blau, P. M. *The dynamics of bureaucracy*. Chicago: University of Chicago Press, 1955.

Brehm, J. Post-decision changes in desirability of alternatives. *J. abnorm. soc. Psychol.*, 1956, 52, 384–389.

———. Increasing cognitive dissonance by fait accompli. *J. abnorm. soc. Psychol.*, 1959, 58, 379–382.

———. Attitudinal consequences of commitment to unpleasant behavior. *J. abnorm. soc. Psychol.*, 1960, 60, 379–383.

Bronfenbrenner, U. Socialization and social class through time and space. In E. Maccoby, T. Newcomb, and E. L. Hartley (Eds.), *Readings in social psychology* (3rd ed.). New York: Holt, 1958. Pp. 400–425.

————. Some Freudian theories of identification and their derivatives. *Child Developm.*, 1960, *31*, 15–40.

————. Some familial antecedents of responsibility and leadership in adolescents. In L. Petrullo, and B. M. Bass, *Leadership and interpersonal behavior.* New York: Holt, Rinehart and Winston, 1961a, Pp. 239–271.

————. The changing American child—a speculative analysis. *J. Soc. Issues,* 1961b, *17*, 6–18.

Bronson, W. C., Katten, E. S., and Livson, N. Patterns of authority and affection in two generations. *J. abnorm. soc. Psychol.*, 1959, *58*, 143–152.

Brookover, W. B., LePere, J. M., Hamachek, D. E., Thomas, S., and Erickson, E. L. *Self-concept of ability and school achievement.* Vol. 2. East Lansing, Mich.: Bureau of Educational Research Services, 1965.

Brookover, W. B., Thomas, S., and Paterson, A. Self-concept of ability and school achievement. *Sociol. Educ.*, 1964, *37*, 271–278.

Brown, R. Social psychology. New York: Free Press, 1964.

Burdick, H. A., and Burnes, A. J. A test of "strain toward symmetry" theories. *J. abnorm. soc. Psychol.*, 1958, *57*, 367–369.

Carlson, E. R. Attitude change and attitude structure. *J. abrnorm, soc. Psychol.*, 1956, *52*, 256–261.

Cartwright, D. Some principles of mass persuasion. *Hum. Relat.*, 1949, *2*, 253–267.

————, and Harary, F. Structural balance: a generalization of Heider's theory. *Psychol. Rev.*, 1956, *63*, 277–293.

Chein, I. Behavior theory and the behavior of attitudes. *Psychol. Rev.* 1948, *55*, 175–88.

Clausen, G. S. Risk taking in small groups. Unpublished Ph.D. dissertation, University of Michigan, 1965.

Cohen, A. R. Attitudinal consequences of induced discrepancies between cognitions and behavior. *Publ. Opin. Quart.* 1960, *24*, 297–318.

Cooley, C. H. *Human nature and the social order.* New York: Scribner, 1922.

Couch, C. J. Self-attitudes and degree of agreement with immediate others. *Amer. J. Sociol.*, 1958, *63*, 490–496.

————, and Murray, J. S. Significant others and evaluation. *Sociometry*, 1963, *27*, 502–509.

Crane, S. *The red badge of courage.* New York: D. Appleton, 1925.

Dewey, J. *How we think.* New York: Macmillan, 1910.

Edwards, A. L. *Edwards personal preference schedule.* New York: Psychological Corporation, 1953.

Ehrlich, D., Guttman, I., Schonback, P., and Mills, J. Post-decision exposure to relevant information. *J. abnorm. soc. Psychol.*, 1957, *54*, 98–102.

Ellison, R. *Invisible man.* New York: Random House, 1952.

Fenichel, O. *The psychoanalytic theory of neurosis.* New York: Norton, 1945.

Festinger, L. *A theory of cognitive dissonance.* Evanston, Ill.: Row, Peterson, 1957.

————, Back, K., Schachter, S., Kelley, H. H., and Thibaut, J. (Eds.), *Theory and experiment in social communication.* Ann Arbor: Research Center for Group Dynamics, University of Michigan, 1950.

————, and Carlsmith, J. M. Cognitive consequences of forced compliance. *J. abnorm. soc. Psychol.*, 1959, *58*, 203–210.

————, Riecken, H., and Schachter, S. *When prophecy fails*. Minneapolis: University of Minnesota Press, 1956.

————, Schachter, S., and Back, K. *Social pressures in informal groups*. New York: Harper, 1950.

Flanders, J. P., and Thistlethwaite, D. L. Effects of familiarization and group discussion upon risk taking. *J. pers. soc. Psychol.*, 1967, 5, 91–97.

Franke, R. Gang and character. *Beihefte, zeitschrift fur angewandte psychologie*, 1931, 58.

Freud, A. *The ego and the mechanisms of defense*. (Trans. by C. Baines). New York: International Universities Press, 1946.

Freud, S. The interpretation of dreams. In A. A. Brill (Trans. and Ed.), *The Basic Writings of Sigmund Freud*. Modern Library Series. New York: Random House, 1938.

————. *Inhibitions, symptoms, and anxiety*. London: Hogarth, 1949.

————. *A general introduction to psychoanalysis*. New York: Washington Square Press, 1958.

Gerard, H. B. The anchorage of opinions in face-to-face groups. *Hum. Relat.*, 1954, 7, 313–325.

Goffman, E. *The presentation of self in everyday life*. Garden City, New Jersey: Doubleday, 1959.

————. The moral career of the mental patient. *Psychiatry*, 1959, 22, 123–142.

————. *Encounters*. Indianapolis, Ind.: Bobbs-Merrill, 1961.

Gold, M., and Slater, C. Office, factory, store—and family: a study of integration setting. *Amer. Sociol. Rev.*, 1958, 23, 64–74.

Gross, N., Mason, W. S., and McEachern, A. W. *Explorations in role analysis*. New York: Wiley, 1958.

Haggard, E. A. Socialization, personality, and academic achievement in gifted children. *The School Review*, 1957, 65, 388–414.

Hall, O. *The informal organization of medical practice*. Unpublished Ph.D. dissertation, University of Chicago, 1944.

Harlow, H. F. The nature of love. *Amer. Psychol.*, 1958, 13, 673–685.

Hebb, D. O. *The organization of behavior*. New York: Wiley, 1949.

Heider, F. Attitudes and cognitive organization. *J. Psychol.*, 1946, 21, 107–112.

Heinicke, C., and Bales, R. F. Developmental trends in the structure of small groups. *Sociometry*, 1953, 16, 7–38.

Herzog, H. What do we really know about daytime serial listeners? In P. F. Lazarsfeld and F. N. Stanton (Eds.), *Radio research 1942–1943*. New York: Duell, Sloan and Pearce, 1944, Pp. 3–33.

Hilgard, E. R. Human motives and the concept of the self. *Amer. Psychol.*, 1949, 4, 374–382.

Himmelstrand, U. Verbal attitudes and behavior: a paradigm for the study of message transmission and transformation. *Pub. Opin. Quart.*, 1960, 24, 224–250.

Hinds, W. C. Individual and group decisions in gambling situations. Unpublished master's thesis, Massachusetts Institute of Technology, 1962.

Hoebel, E. A. *The Cheyennes: Indians of the Great Plains*. New York: Holt, Rinehart and Winston, 1960.

Homans, G. C. Social behavior as exchange. *Amer. J. Sociol.*, 1958, 62, 597–606.

————. *Social behavior: its elementary forms.* New York: Harcourt, Brace & World, 1961.

Hovland, C. I., Janis, I. L., and Kelley, H. H. *Communication and persuasion: psychological studies of opinion change.* New Haven, Conn.: Yale University Press, 1953.

Hughes, E. C. Dilemmas and contradictions of status. *Amer. J. Sociol.,* 1945, *50,* 353–359.

Hull, C. L. *Principles of behavior.* New York: Appleton-Century, 1943.

Hunt, R. G. Role and role conflict. In E. P. Hollander and R. G. Hunt (Eds.), *Current perspectives in social psychology.* New York: Oxford University Press, 1967. Pp. 259–265.

Inkeles, A., Hanfmann, E., and Beier, H. Modal personality and adjustment to Soviet political system. *Human Relations,* 1958, *11,* 3–22.

Jennings, H. H. *Leadership and isolation.* New York: Longmans, Green, 1950.

Jones, E. E., and Kohler, R. The effects of plausibility on the learning of controversial statements. *J. abnorm. soc. Psychol.,* 1958, *57,* 315–320.

Jordan, N. Behavioral forces that are a function of attitudes and cognitive organization. *Hum. Relat.,* 1953, *6,* 273–287.

Kahn, R. L., Wolfe, D. M., Quinn, R. P., Snock, J. D., and Rosenthal, R. A. *Organizational stress.* New York: Wiley, 1964.

Kardiner, A. *The psychological frontiers of society.* New York: Columbia University Press, 1945.

————, and Linton, R. *The individual and his society.* New York: Columbia University Press, 1939.

Katz, D. The functional approach to the study of attitudes. *Pub. Opin. Quart.,* 1960, *24,* 163–204.

————, and Stotland, E. A preliminary statement to a theory of attitude structure and change. In S. Koch, (Ed.), *Psychology: a study of science.* Vol. 3. New York: McGraw-Hill, 1959. Pp. 423–475.

Katz, E., and Lazarsfeld, P. F. *Personal influence.* Glencoe, Ill.: Free Press, 1955.

Kelley, G. A. *The psychology of personal constructs.* New York: Norton, 1955. 2 vols.

Kelman, H. C., and Hovland, C. I. "Reinstatement" of the communicator in delayed measurement of opinion change. *J. abnorm. soc. Psychol.,* 1953, *48,* 327–335.

Kinch, J. W. A formalized theory of the self-concept. *Amer. J. Sociol.,* 1963, *68,* 481–486.

Kogan, N., and Wallach, M. A. *Risk taking: a study in cognition.* New York: Holt, Rinehart and Winston, 1964.

————. Group risk taking as a function of members' anxiety and defensiveness levels. Paper presented at the annual convention of The Eastern Psychological Association, New York City, April, 1966.

————. Risk taking as a function of the situation, the person, and the group. In *New directions in psychology.* Vol. 3. New York: Holt, Rinehart and Winston, 1967.

Kohn, M. L. Social class and parental values. *Amer. J. Sociol.,* 1959, *44,* 337–351.

————, and Clausen, J. A. Parental authority behavior and schizophrenia, *Am. J. Orthopsychiatry,* 1956, *26,* 297–313.

Krech, D., and Crutchfield, R. S. *Theory and problems of social psychology.* New York: McGraw-Hill, 1959.

Kuhn, M. H. Self-attitudes by age, sex, and professional training. *Sociol. Quart.*, 1960, *1*, 39–55.

————, and McPartland, T. S. An empirical investigation of self-attitudes. *Amer. Sociol. Rev.*, 1954, *19*, 68–76.

Lazarsfeld, P. F., Berelson, B. R., and Gaudet, H. *The people's choice.* New York: Columbia University Press, 1948.

Lecky, P. *Self-consistency: a theory of personality.* New York: Island Press, 1945.

Levinson, D. J. Idea systems in the individual and society. Mimeographed. Boston: Center for Socio-psychological Research, Massachusetts Mental Health Center, 1954.

————. Role, personality, and social structure in the organizational setting. *J. abnorm. soc. Psychol.*, 1959, *58*, 170–180.

Lewis, O. *Five families.* New York: Basic Books, 1959.

Linton, R. *The study of man.* New York: Appleton-Century-Crofts, 1936.

————. *The cultural background of personality.* New York: Appleton-Century-Crofts, 1945.

Lippmann, W. *Public opinion.* New York: Macmillan, 1922.

Lynn, D. B., and Sawrey, W. L. The effects of father-absence on Norwegian boys and girls. *J. abnorm. soc. Psychol.*, 1959, *59*, 258–262.

Madaras, G. R., and Bem, D. J. Risk and conservatism in group decision-making. *J. exper. Soc. Psychol.*, 1968, *4*, 350–364.

Maehr, M. L., Mensing, J., and Nafzgu, S. Concept of self and the reaction of others. *Sociometry*, 1962, *25*, 353–357.

Maine, H. *Ancient law.* London: J. Murray, 1861.

Marquis, D. G. Individual responsibility and group decision involving risk. *Indstr. Mgemnt. Rev.*, 1962, *3*, 8–23.

Marshall, T. H. A note on status. In K. M. Kapadia (Ed.), *Professor Ghurye felicitation volume.* Bombay: Popular Book Depot.

McNemar, Q. *Psychological statistics* (3rd ed.). New York: Wiley, 1962.

McPartland, T. S., Cuming, J., and Garretson, W. S. Self-conception and ward behavior. *Sociometry*, 1961, *24*, 111–124.

Mead, G. H. The genesis of the self and social control. *Int. J. Ethics*, 1925, *35*, 251–277.

————. *Mind, self, and society.* Chicago: University of Chicago Press, 1934.

Merton, R. K. The role-set: problems in sociological theory. *Br. J. Sociol.*, 1957, 8.

Miller, D. R., and Swanson, G. E. *The changing American parent.* New York: Wiley, 1958.

————. *Inner conflict and defense.* New York: Holt, Rinehart and Winston, 1960.

Miller, N. E., and Dollard, J. *Social learning and imitation.* New Haven, Conn.: Yale University Press, 1941.

Mills, J., Aronson, E., and Robinson, H. Selectivity in exposure to information. *J. abnorm. soc. Psychol.*, 1959, *59*, 250–253.

Miyamoto, S. F., and Dornbash, S. M. A test of interactionist hypotheses of self-conception. *Amer. J. Sociol.*, 1956, *61*, 339–403.

Moore, H. T. The comparative influence of majority and expert opinions. *Amer. J. Psychol.*, 1921, *32*, 16–20.

Morrissette, J. O. An experimental study of the theory of structural balance. *Hum. Relat.*, 1958, *11*, 239–254.

Mowrer, O. H. *Learning theory and behavior.* New York: Wiley, 1960.

Murray, H. A. *Explorations in personality.* New York: Oxford University Press, 1938.

Mussen, P., and Distler, L. Masculinity, identification, and father-son relationships. *J. abnorm. soc. Psychol.*, 1959, *59*, 350–356.

Newcomb, T. M. An approach to the study of communicative acts. *Psychol. Rev.*, 1953, *60*, 393–404.

————. The prediction of interpersonal attraction. *Amer. Psychol.*, 1956, *2*, 575–586.

————. *The acquaintance process.* New York: Holt, Rinehart and Winston, 1961.

Nørdhoy, F. Group interaction in decision making under risk. (Unpublished master's thesis, Massachusetts Institute of Technology, 1962.)

Orlansky, H. Infant care and personality. *Psychol. Bull.*, 1949, *46*, 1–48.

Osgood, C. E., Suci, G. J., and Tannenbaum, P. H. *The measurement of meaning.* Urbana: University of Illinois Press, 1949.

Osgood, C. E., and Tannenbaum, P. H. The principle of congruity in the prediction of attitude change. *Psychol. Rev.*, 1955, *62*, 42–55.

Papanek, M. *Authority and interpersonal relations in the family.* Unpublished Ph.D. dissertation on file at the Radcliffe College Library, 1957.

Peak, H. Attitude and motivation. In Jones, M. (Ed.), *Nebraska symposium on motivation.* Lincoln: University of Nebraska Press, 1955, Pp. 149–188.

————.The effects of aroused motivation on attitudes. Technical report to the Office of Naval Research, 1959.

Piaget, J. *The origins of intelligence in children* (Trans. Margaret Cook). New York: International Universities Press, 1952.

Rabow, J., Fowler, F. J., Bradford, D. L., Hofeller, M., and Shibuya, Y. The role of social norms and leadership in risk taking. *Sociometry*, 1966, *29*, 16–27.

Reeder, L. G., Donohue, G. A., and Biblarz, A. Conception of self and others. *Amer. J. Sociol.*, 1960, *66*, 153–159.

Riecken, H. W., and Homans, G. C. Psychological aspects of social structure. In G. Lindzey (Ed.), *Handbook of social psychology.* Vol. 2. Cambridge, Mass.: Addison-Wesley Press, 2, 1954, 786–832.

Rim, Y. Risk taking and need for achievement. *Acta Psychol.*, 1963, *21*, 108–115.

————. Personality and group decisions involving risk. *Psychol. Rec.*, 1964a, *14*, 37–45.

————. Social attitudes and risk taking. *Hum. Relat.*, 1964b, *17*, 259–265.

Rogers, C. R. *Client-centered therapy.* Boston: Houghton-Mifflin, 1951.

————, and Dymond, R. (Eds.), *Psychotherapy and personality change.* Chicago: University of Chicago Press, 1954.

Rogler, L. H., and Hollingshead, A. B. *Trapped: families and schizophrenia.* New York: Wiley, 1965.

Rosen, B. L. and D'Andrade, R. The psychosocial origins of achievement motivation. *Sociometry*, 1959, *22*, 185-217.

Rosenberg, M. J. Cognitive structure and attitudinal affect. *J. abnorm. Soc. Psychol.*, 1956, *53*, 367–372.

————. A structural theory of attitude dynamics. *Pub. Opin. Quart.*, 1960, *24*, 319–340.

————. Parental interest and children's self-conception. *Sociometry*, 1963, *26*, 35–49.

Rosenthal, R., and Jacobson, L. *Pygmalion in the classroom.* New York: Holt, Rinehart and Winston, 1968.

Sansom, W. *A contest of ladies.* London: Hogarth, 1956.

Sarbin, T. R. Role theory. In G. Lindzey (Ed.), *Handbook of social psychology.* Vol. 1. Cambridge, Mass.: Addison-Wesley, *I*, 1954, 223–258.

Sarnoff, I. Psychoanalytic theory and social attitudes. *Pub. Opin. Quart.*, 1960, *24*, 251–279.

Schachter, S. Deviation, rejection, and communication. *J. abnorm. soc. Psychol.*, 1951, *46*, 190–207.

————. *The psychology of affiliation.* Stanford, Cal.: Stanford University Press, 1959.

Sears, R. R., Maccoby, E., and Levin, H. *Patterns of child rearing.* Evanston, Ill.: Row, Peterson, 1957.

Sears, R. R., Pintler, M. H., and Sears, P. S. Effects of father-separation on preschool children's doll play aggression. *Child Develpm.*, 1946, *17*, 219–243.

Secord, P. F., and Backman, C. W. Personality theory and the problem of stability and change in individual behavior: an interpersonal approach. *Psychol. Rev.*, 1961, *68*, 21–32.

————.Interpersonal congruency, perceived similarity, and friendship. *Sociometry*, 1964, *27*, 115–127.

Shaw, M. E. A comparison of individuals and small groups in the rational solution of complex problems. *Amer. J. Psychol.*, 1932, *44*, 491–504.

Sherif, M. An experimental study of stereotypes. *J. abnorm. soc. Psychol.*, 1935, *29*, 371–375.

Sherwood, J. J. Self-identity and referent others. *Sociometry*, 1965, *28*, 66–81.

Siegel, S. *Nonparametric statistics for the behavioral sciences.* New York: McGraw-Hill, 1956.

Skinner, B. F. *Science and human behavior.* New York: Macmillan, 1953.

Slater, P. E. Role differentiation in small groups. *Amer. Sociol. Rev.*, 1955, *20*, 300–310.

Smith, B. The personal setting of public opinions: a study of attitudes toward Russia. *Pub. Opin. Quart.*, 1947, *11*, 507–523.

Stephens, W. N. *The family in cross-cultural perspective.* New York: Holt, Rinehart and Winston, 1963.

Stoner, J. A. F. A comparison of individual and group decisions involving risk. Unpublished master's thesis, Massachusetts Institute of Technology, 1961.

Strodtbeck, F. L. Family interaction, values, and achievement. In D. C. McClelland, A. L. Baldwin, U. Bronfenbrenner, and F. L. Strodtbeck, *Talent and society.* Princeton, N.J.: *Van Nostrand*, 1958. Pp. 135–194.

Stryker, S. Conditions of accurate role-taking: a test of Mead's theory. In Arnold Rose (Ed.), *Human behavior and social process.* Boston: Houghton-Mifflin, 1962. Pp. 41–62.

Tannenbaum, P. H. Initial attitude toward source and concept as factors in attitude change through communication. *Pub. Opin. Quart.*, 1956, 20, 413–425.

Teger, A. I., and Pruitt, D. G. Components of group risk taking. *J. exper. soc. Psychol.*, 1967, *3*, 189–205.

Thibaut, J., and Kelley, H. H. *The social psychology of groups.* New York: Wiley, 1959.

Thomas, S., Brookover, W. B., LePere, J. M., Hamachek, D. E., and Erickson, E. L., *Modifying self-concept and school performance*. Unpublished monograph.

Thorndike, R. L. The effect of discussion upon the correctness of group decisions when the factor of majority influence is allowed for. *J. soc. Psychol.*, 1938, *9*, 343–362.

Tiller, P. O. Father-absence and personality development of children in sailor families. *Nordisk psykologis monograph series*. 1958, 9.

Tolman, E. C. A psychological model. In T. Parsons and E. A. Shils (Eds.), *Toward a general theory of action*. Cambridge, Mass.: Harvard University Press, 1951, Pp. 279–359.

Videbeck, R. Self-concept and reaction to others. *Sociometry*, 1960, 23, 351–360.

Wallach, M. A., and Kogan, N. The roles of information, discussion, and consensus in group risk taking. *J. exper. soc. Psychol.*, 1965, *1*, 1–19.

————, and Bem, D. J. Group influence on individual risk taking. *J. abnorm. soc. Psychol.*, 1962, *65*, 75–86.

————, and Bem, D. J. Diffusion of responsibility and level of risk taking in groups. *J. abnorm. soc. Psychol.* 1964, 68, 263–274.

————, and Burt, R. B. Can group members recognize the effects of group discussion upon risk taking? *J. exper. soc. Psychol.*, 1965, 1, 379–395.

Wallach, M. A., and Wing, C. Is risk taking a value? Unpublished manuscript, 1967.

White, R. W. Motivation reconsidered: the concept of competence. *Psychol. Rev.*, 1959, 66, 297–333.

Whiting, J. W. M., and Child, I. L. *Child training and personality*. New Haven, Conn.: Yale University Press, 1953.

Whyte, W. H., Jr. *The organization man*. New York: Simon and Schuster, 1956.

Winterbottom, M. R. The relation of need achievement to learning experiences in independence and mastery. In J. W. Alkinson (Ed.), *Motives in fantasy, action, and society*. Princeton, N.J.: Van Nostrand, 1958. Pp. 453–494.

Wylie, R. L. *The self concept*. Lincoln: University of Nebraska Press, 1961.

Zajonc, R. The concepts of balance, congruity, and dissonance. *Pub. Opin. Quart.*, 1960, *24*, 280–296.

Author Index

Subject Index